BRAVER CANADA

McGill-Queen's/Brian Mulroney Institute of Government Studies in Leadership, Public Policy, and Governance

SERIES EDITOR: DONALD E. ABELSON

Titles in this series address critical issues facing Canada at home and abroad and the efforts policymakers at all levels of government have made to address a host of complex and multifaceted policy concerns. Books in this series receive financial support from the Brian Mulroney Institute of Government at St Francis Xavier University; in keeping with the institute's mandate, these studies explore how leaders involved in key policy initiatives arrived at their decisions and what lessons can be learned. Combining rigorous academic analysis with thoughtful recommendations, this series compels readers to think more critically about how and why elected officials make certain policy choices, and how, in concert with other stakeholders, they can better navigate an increasingly complicated and crowded marketplace of ideas.

1   Braver Canada
    Shaping Our Destiny in a Precarious World
    Derek H. Burney and Fen Osler Hampson

BRAVER CANADA

Shaping Our Destiny in a Precarious World

Derek H. Burney
and Fen Osler Hampson

McGill-Queen's University Press
Montreal & Kingston • London • Chicago

© McGill-Queen's University Press 2020

ISBN 978-0-2280-0092-1 (cloth)
ISBN 978-0-2280-0218-5 (ePDF)
ISBN 978-0-2280-0219-2 (ePUB)

Legal deposit first quarter 2020
Bibliothèque nationale du Québec

Printed in Canada on acid-free paper that is 100% ancient forest free (100% post-consumer recycled), processed chlorine free

We acknowledge the support of the Canada Council for the Arts.
Nous remercions le Conseil des arts du Canada de son soutien.

Library and Archives Canada Cataloguing in Publication

Title: Braver Canada : shaping our destiny in a precarious world / Derek H. Burney and Fen Osler Hampson.
Names: Burney, Derek H. (Derek Hudson), 1939– author. | Hampson, Fen Osler, author.
Description: Series statement: McGill-Queen's/Brian Mulroney Institute of Government Studies in Leadership, Public Policy, and Governance ; 1 | Includes bibliographical references and index.
Identifiers: Canadiana (print) 20190234342 | Canadiana (ebook) 20190234431 | ISBN 9780228000921 (cloth) | ISBN 9780228002185 (ePDF) | ISBN 9780228002192 (ePUB)
Subjects: LCSH: Canada—Foreign relations—Forecasting. | LCSH: Canada—Foreign economic relations—Forecasting. | LCSH: Canada—Economic policy—21st century—Forecasting. | LCSH: Canada—Social policy—Forecasting.
Classification: LCC FC242 .B867 2020 | DDC 327.71009/05—dc23

This book was typeset in 11/14 Sabon.

Contents

Preface and Acknowledgments vii

1 The Triple Perils of Protectionism, Populism, and Authoritarianism 3

2 No Longer a "Special" or Privileged Partnership 23

3 Regaining a Competitive Advantage 34

4 Dancing with the Chinese Dragon and the Indian Elephant 48

5 Energy Development and Environmental Protection: The Elusive Search for "Balance" 73

6 Democratic Alliances versus Authoritarians: Russia's and NATO's Future 98

7 In Search of a Middle East Policy 118

8 Finding Moorings in a Brewing Cyber Storm 137

9 Immigration and Refugees 159

10 Shaping Our Destiny 180

Notes 191
Index 231

Preface and Acknowledgments

"America First" Trumpism, the rise of China, populism, and authoritarianism are creating a less interdependent world, requiring a significant shift in Canada's global approach in an era of profound change. So too is the erosion of international institutions and conventions that have held the West together for seven decades – a trend that will persist after President Donald Trump leaves office. As former Canadian prime minister Stephen Harper has observed, "it is a polarized world," and regardless of whether Trump succeeds, Trump's "America First" motto will likely survive his presidency.[1]

As a new tide of protectionist populism sweeps across the United States, Europe, and other corners of the globe, the open economic trading and investment regime that was crafted after the Second World War is under siege. Beggar-thy-neighbour policies are redefining NAFTA's future and relations between Canada, the United States, and major trading partners in the Pacific and Europe. Europe is struggling with its own internal problems as populist pressures manifest themselves in Brexit and public disenchantment with the dominance of Brussels and Berlin in the European Union.

The centre of economic and political gravity in the world is also rapidly shifting toward the Indo-Pacific as China and India become global powers and other countries in the region, like Indonesia, Vietnam, and the Philippines, experience rapid growth. Canada has no coherent policy to deal with these rising powers, especially with China. It needs to consider a more rules-based economic partnership and to adopt a clearer position on the burgeoning military and cyber threat posed by China in the region, if not globally.

For the past three decades, the bedrock of Canada's foreign policy and international engagements has been a strong economic and political relationship with the United States and a commitment to maintaining and strengthening the international institutions of the postwar liberal international order – the United Nations, the Bretton Woods institutions, the World Trade Organization, and NATO. That bedrock is now crumbling as the United States unilaterally erects new barriers to trade and investment, transatlantic security ties weaken, and international institutions are assaulted by the twin forces of populism and authoritarianism, which are emerging not just among the West's adversaries but also within the West itself.

As Canada looks for new economic partnerships, its first task is on the home front, where it must reverse the decline in its competitiveness in North America and establish genuine free trade within Canada. A strong global performance depends on constructive policies at home. Responsible development of Canada's energy resources, which contribute roughly 10 per cent of its GDP, is also needed. So too are realistic and balanced commitments on climate change. Canada's security, economic prosperity, and democratic institutions are increasingly compromised by the threat from cyber space, as the *New York Times*' Washington bureau chief, David Sanger, underscores in his book *The Perfect Weapon*.[2] Canada is ill-prepared and poorly served by a basket of mediocrity at the bureaucratic and political levels. It is overly reliant on the United States, as always, for its own cyber security, but there is no longer an automatic guarantee that the United States regards Canada's interests, infrastructure, and so on as identical to those of the United States, especially as Canada contributes so little of its own resources, including on intelligence. Canada's contribution to cyber security is considered to be "somewhere between mediocre and risible."[3] Canada is content being a fast follower, but can it be sure that the United States will continue to share technology on things like quantum computing in a more narrowly drawn competitive world?

When Canada got into a very public spat with Saudi Arabia over that nation's treatment of jailed human rights activists, Canada found that it could not count on the support of two of its closest allies: the United States and the United Kingdom. The episode serves as a stark reminder of how much the world has changed during the past several years. A new generation of despotic leaders around the world – from Southeast Asia to Sub-Saharan Africa to the Middle East – whose nations have traditionally sought to curry favour with the West, now brazenly thumb their noses at the West and Western values. (Canada is no exception; Sweden and Germany have also experienced Saudi wrath.) Democracy worldwide is in decline. The West is more confused and divided, not least because of the political and diplomatic discord sowed by US president Donald Trump and the antics of Russian president Vladimir Putin, who is manipulating Western disunity to his own advantage in Ukraine, eastern Europe, the Middle East, and China. The NATO Alliance, which has been the bedrock of global security since the early days of the Cold War, is also fracturing because of volatile and unpredictable US behaviour and because of alliance partners, notably Germany, who are reluctant to carry their proper share of the defence burden.

Confronted with the greatest refugee crisis since the Second World War, governments throughout Europe are closing borders to stem the human tide from Syria, North Africa, and points beyond. Xenophobia is also manifesting itself in the rise of extreme right-wing populist parties. The refugee-asylum-immigration nexus has to be handled in a way that meets legitimate concerns about abuse of procedural loopholes and bureaucratic incompetence and in a way that fosters constructive actions that remedy a mounting backlash against immigration generally.

Canada requires a new global strategy that reduces the country's economic reliance on the United States, opens new gateways to the markets of the Indo-Pacific region, and establishes new political and security partnerships that go beyond the framework of Canada's traditional alliances and commitments to international institutions. To date, Canada has struggled unsuccessfully to define a new economic partnership with Asia's economic powerhouses: India and China. Its relations with key countries in the Middle East have soured as it struggles to promote a progressive agenda on human rights and democratic values. Its profile and presence in Africa and Asia have been diminished due to the unforced errors of omission and commission made by successive Conservative and Liberal governments. Canada also needs a new strategy to deal with key emerging global challenges in the realm of cyber security, big data, e-commerce, a mounting global refugee and migration crisis, and the adverse consequences of climate change, where existing policies and approaches have either failed or proven counterproductive.

This book explores the major challenges that Canada confronts in a world that is becoming more protectionist, more dangerous, and less predictable, one where populism and authoritarianism pose major threats to democratic values and the prevailing norms and rules of the international economic and security order crafted after the Second World War. Reviewing the foreign policy challenges, achievements, and missteps of Prime Minister Justin Trudeau's government, the book discusses why the country's leadership must craft a new approach to global affairs that is based on a solid grasp of current and emerging global political and economic realities. It expands on the ideas and policy recommendations in our previous book, *Brave New Canada*,[4] which called for a diversification of Canada's economic ties away from the United States. But it also explains how the global and regional environment has changed dramatically since *Brave New Canada* was published in 2014, while advancing new ideas about how Canada can best promote its values and interests.

In the course of writing this book, we have benefited from the generous assistance and input of many friends and colleagues. In particular, we thank the following individuals who either were interviewed during the course of writing the book or commented on individual chapters or the manuscript in its entirety: Jim Balsillie, Bruce Carson, Joan Burney, David Runnalls, Bob Fay, Paul Heinbecker, Philip Hampson, Melissa Hathaway, Cara O'Blenis, Marshall Palmer, Allan Rock, and Andrew Thompson. We also thank the three anonymous reviewers of the manuscript for McGill-Queen's University Press, who offered thoughtful comments and suggestions for revision prior to publication. We also thank Jeff Burney for his cover design, which brilliantly captures the core message of this book, and Philip Cercone at McGill-Queen's University Press and his able editorial and production team for their fine work and support.

BRAVER CANADA

1

The Triple Perils of Protectionism, Populism, and Authoritarianism

In *Brave New Canada*, published in 2014, we presented ideas on how Canada could diversify economic ties in order to end excessive dependence on the United States and how it could chart a more confident and more competitive course in world affairs.[1] The election of President Donald Trump in the United States and the global surge of protectionism, populism, and authoritarianism have intensified the need for a realignment of domestic and foreign politics in an even more precarious world. What was once desirable is now imperative.

Trump's tumultuous presidency turned much conventional wisdom about global affairs on its head. American-led global institutions and alliances that have ensured seven decades of peace and prosperity are being buffeted by "America First" prescriptions that, in the view of authors like Robert Kagan, risk letting "the jungle grow back and engulf us all."[2]

In his book *Fear: Trump in the White House*, Bob Woodward depicts an administration in the midst of a "nervous breakdown" as it tries to manage affairs at home and abroad with a president who has a wilful disregard for facts, institutional linkages, and experience.[3] The fact that Trump's most affectionate global relationships seem to be with Chairman Kim Jong-un of North Korea and President Vladimir Putin of Russia is one symptom of the disruption underway. His approach to global affairs is sending shock waves everywhere, most particularly for allies like Canada that had grown accustomed to and benefited from a more balanced, if not benign, leadership role for the United States. Despite contributing vitally to Canada's security and economic well-being, this dependence also inspired a mood of complacency.

Fear is what Trump's approach to governance conveys most, both to those within his administration and to others, including non-Americans. The fact that few in Washington know from one day to the next what will command his attention or be the topic of his Twitter posts has created a prevailing atmosphere of uncertainty. He claims to prefer bilateral rather than multilateral engagement, but he operates almost entirely on unilateral impulses.

America under Trump is flaunting its economic and military muscle with the singular purpose of advancing exclusively American interests and doing so with less regard for fundamental values, long-standing alliance commitments, and multilateral institutions. Bashing or insulting friends while warmly cultivating what were formerly perceived foes of the United States, like Russia and North Korea, has become customary. Trump's blunt use of tariffs ostensibly to eradicate trade deficits that he regards as "ripping off"[4] the United States are shaking the foundation for stability on global trade and giving rise to fears of a 1930s-style, worldwide, tit-for-tat trade war that would pit particularly the United States against China but also engulf others, including Canada.

These changes are occurring despite a general consensus among economists that trade deficits are actually advantageous to American consumers and producers. Warnings that aggressive tariffs may retard the strong, economic growth in America have been vigorously rejected by the administration, especially those like Peter Navarro, Robert Lighthizer, and Wilbur Ross who are steeped in neo-mercantilist visions of trade policy and share the president's view that American interests have not been served by trade liberalization agreements. Support from Trump's hard-core base thrives as he persistently targets the flaws of the "elitist globalists."

Trump openly mocks the "failures" of globalist presidents who preceded him in the White House, seemingly oblivious to the damage his criticism is causing to the bedrock structures of the Western alliance and to positive attributes that distinguish the Western democratic model of governance. Rabid polarization of political debate in America and the all too persistent dysfunction of government in Washington are tarnishing the attraction of the American model throughout Asia, Africa, and Latin America. China, not the United States, is now seen in a more compelling light. As support for alliances and international institutions erodes, corrosive trade practices rise to the surface, with "to each his own" becoming the beacon for survival.

"RIPPING OFF" AMERICA?

The United States is intent on using its economic leverage to rectify what Trump and his key advisors believe has been decades of being short-changed by trade partners. The assault on NAFTA – deemed by Trump to be "the worst trade deal ever made"[5] – is a symptom of a broader, aggressively bilateral approach by the United States. By preserving key elements of NAFTA as well as some modernization elements of the Trans-Pacific Partnership (TPP), an agreement that Trump had spurned in his first days in office, Canada and Mexico were able to conclude the semblance of a rules-based framework for continental trade, which, if ratified, gives their investors and exporters some degree of certainty. In the circumstances, a deal, warts and all, was deemed better than no deal. But American demands for concessions by Mexico and Canada were not matched in the negotiation by any reciprocal concessions by the United States.

The Trump administration's capricious use of section 232 of the US trade law to impose tariffs on steel and aluminum against Canada (and Mexico) on dubious grounds of "national security" and the threat of more of the same undermine the potential value of any agreement signed by the United States. As the successor to NAFTA, the United States–Mexico–Canada Agreement (USMCA) was less than a "win-win-win" victory but a respectable salvage in the circumstances. Saving the binding dispute settlement mechanism was a worthy achievement by Canada. But the results are tilted heavily in America's favour, crudely reflecting the success of the twin American tactics of "divide and conquer" and "might is right." Both Mexico and Canada made concessions in the negotiations: Canada gave on dairy and on pharmaceutical patents, and Mexico gave on autos. The only "concession" by the United States was a last-minute retreat from some of its more egregious, initial demands.

The lesson from the rancorous renegotiation of NAFTA and the mini-tariff war spawned during those negotiations is that diversification of Canada's economic interests must now be mandatory. There is no reason why Canada should be confident that the terms of the new agreement will prevent flagrant abuse by the United States. When tariffs were imposed on imports of Canadian steel and aluminum, the Trump administration was oblivious to the fact that these industries are highly integrated in North America and that damage to one inevitably damages the other. Canadian steel and aluminum are essential components for US fighter planes and naval vessels. Protecting and expanding access to the US market will always be the priority for Canada, but recent experience has demonstrated that access cannot be taken for granted and needs to be complemented by a systematic approach to diversification.

On matters of trade, Donald Trump pays little heed to any concept of mutual benefit. The negotiating well was poisoned from the outset by his persistent claim that the United States has been "ripped off" by its partners in virtually all trade agreements.[6] Factual contradictions to this theory and the wisdom of most economists about the benefits of liberalized trade carry no weight with a president whose elasticity on truth is setting standards never before seen in Washington.

The problem is that, when America goes rogue on alliances and multilateral institutions it was instrumental in creating, the stability of global security and prosperity is the real loser. When narrow definitions of American self-interest become paramount, others like Canada are left more to fend for themselves and attempt to consolidate cohesive strength with the remnants of alliances and multilateral agreements that have anchored trade and security since 1945. It was one thing to suffer from benign neglect from the West's superpower; it is quite another when the disposition becomes self-serving, if not malign.

Trump operates essentially on instinct or impulse rather than strategy in a style befitting the producer of reality television shows. It is a popular tactic on the home front, and some of his instinctual actions have generated dividends. His tax cuts and regulatory reforms have prompted a surge in the US economy. Increases in defence expenditures and quick responses in defence of Americans held hostage and American interests abroad have inspired respect, if not fear, of America elsewhere.

It remains to be seen whether the "off the wall" flirtation with North Korea will produce the desired outcome of a denuclearized Korean Peninsula or whether scrapping the Iran nuclear deal engenders greater stability in the Middle East. Trump is battling on many fronts simultaneously, in sharp contrast to the more nuanced "globalism" of previous US administrations, notably that of his predecessor, Barack Obama. Overt expressions of nationalism and populism wrapped in a cloak of patriotism are what Stephen Harper describes as a triumph of the "somewheres" over the "anywheres."[7] Trump is the symptom, not the cause, of hard divisions in America, which is why, as Harper also contends, the visceral, populist sentiments being stoked by Trump will most certainly persist in America long after he leaves office.

THE DANGERS OF POPULISM AND IDENTITY POLITICS

In his book *Identity: The Demand for Dignity and the Politics of Resentment*, Francis Fukuyama describes a world that is experiencing waves of right-wing and left-wing populism, which is sapping support for liberal democracy and resulting in a turn more to authoritarianism and "identity politics."[8] He observes that the global surge toward democracy that began in the mid-1970s has gone into recession, fuelled in large part by a fragmentation into politics defined more by identity, such as who people are in terms of race, ethnicity, and economic status and where they are from – urban versus rural, bedrock "Middle America" versus trendy Americans on the East and West Coasts.[9] He cites a study by Larry Diamond that shows the number of democratic countries had risen from 35 in 1970 to 120 by the early 2000s but has eroded sharply ever since.[10]

However, the political trend is influenced heavily by economics. On the plus side, the world's output of goods and services quadrupled from 1970 to 2008 and spread to virtually all regions of the world. The number of people living in extreme poverty dropped from 42 per cent in 1993 to 27 per cent in 2011.[11] But income inequality also increased sharply in democracies as growth flowed primarily to segments defined essentially by higher levels of education. "Them that's got shall get."[12] The huge dislocation of wealth coincided with the financial debacle and recession spawned in the United States in 2008, which, in turn, rattled confidence in democratic governance. Wall Street bankers were bailed out by taxpayers, but those who paid the price in "Middle America" were not. Between 2000 and 2016,

51 per cent of Americans saw no gain in real income. The proportion of national output going to the top 1 per cent went from 9 per cent of GDP in 1974 to 24 per cent in 2008.[13]

Along with the threat to the European Union posed by Greek insolvency, these events in the United States damaged the reputation of liberal democracy everywhere, culminating in the Brexit vote in the United Kingdom, the Trump election in America, and the rise of authoritarian populism in places like Turkey, Poland, Hungary, and the Philippines where leaders are subverting democratic norms.[14]

With an argument directly relevant to Canada as well, Fukuyama asserts that the United States "cannot build its national identity around diversity." Rather, national identity has to be related to substantive ideas: "constitutionalism, rule of law, and human equality." Diversity, he says, is critical to resilience but is not an unalloyed good. An inclusive sense of national identity remains critical for the mainstream of a successful, modern political order. Diversity can and does contribute to the dynamism and enrichment of society, but it is not in itself an intrinsic value of society unless it is embedded in something more unifying.[15] Canada should understand that multiculturalism is a description of its pluralist society, not a core value, because, taken to the extreme, identity politics subsumes or overwhelms the basic unifying values of Canadians, which are anchored in their history and political institutions.[16]

Opposing economic views can often split the difference and find genuine workable compromises, whereas identity issues are harder to reconcile: "Either you recognize (or respect) me or you do not." It may have been hoped that the advent of social media would reinforce liberal democratic values through more exchanges of opinion. Instead, social media have accelerated the fragmentation of liberal societies and played into the hands of particular identity groups that connect the like-minded with one another in "filter bubbles" while stifling genuine debate. Anonymity removes restraint, and these media outlets fuel the circulation of bad information ("fake news") and the blatant smearing of reputations.

Donald Trump is the "perfect practitioner of the ethics of authenticity that defines our age: he may be mendacious, malicious, bigoted, and unpresidential, but at least he says what he thinks."[17] Real answers will not come from theory or exhortation but from inspired political leadership in a post-Trump America.

Contemporary politics is driven by the quest for equal recognition by groups that have been marginalized by their societies: the "deplorables."[18] Yet individuals are so obviously varied in their talents and capacities that we need to understand in what sense we are willing to recognize individuals with different attributes and capabilities as being equal for political purposes. That was to be the genius of democracies. However, the less that liberal democracies demand from their citizenry, the more that they dilute the meaning, value, and history of their national identity. In turn, the responsibility of their citizenry for that identity is also diminished. Social and economic disorientation and marginalization are what stimulate much of the twenty-first century's populist fervour. Anti-establishment and anti-globalist sentiments have been further stoked by emotional, nationalist reactions to the heavy influx of refugees into western Europe and by the chronic challenges posed by more than 11 million illegal or undocumented entrants into the United States.

Traditional political parties have had trouble responding to the tides of resentment. Among democracies everywhere, except Canada, parties advocating customary social democracy are on the wane, largely because social democratic partners, notably in Europe, have focused more on societal identity issues than on the bread and butter concerns of the working class. Feeling left behind and dismissed as bigots or racists, many have turned to more extreme politicians on the right and the left.

Anxieties about change and the implications of the massive changes generated by automation and technology are also pervasive. The soaring rate of opiate deaths in America – almost 80,000 in 2017 – is more than double the combined total from guns and traffic deaths.[19] It is a graphic demonstration of anxieties about the speed of change. Many Americans feel abandoned or threatened by change that affects their daily lives. Despair and a sense of hopelessness spark rage, hatred, and occasionally, irrational bouts of violence. They also believe that globalization has enfeebled America and reduced benefits principally to "Middle America."

Donald Trump turned those fears into electoral support. His positions on trade and immigration are wrapped in a patriotic "America First" platform branded with the prominent "Make America Great Again" logo. He wants America to be respected, if not feared, in the rest of the world and invokes pride from his supporters as he delivers with actions that correspond to his unilateralist, nonglobalist approach. When he says that "the era of economic surrender is over," he means it.[20]

Anne Applebaum – historian, London School of Economics professor, and journalist – probes deeper into the prevailing mood. She worries that the West is losing not only a sense of unity and purpose but also a belief in those things that define the West: democracy, the rule of law, and pluralism. "Younger people," she contends, "are far less likely than their parents are, to say that living in a democracy is essential."[21] A quarter of American youth view democracy with alarmingly detached interest. (Radically, among Americans, notions of socialism now have more attraction. Fewer today have any memories of the horrors of communism.)

Applebaum defines populism as anti-pluralism. Extreme political advocates have always been around but are increasingly gaining traction and political power in Hungary, Poland, and other parts of Europe. She sees the disastrous Iraq War and the 2008 financial crisis as major contributors. A protracted, inconclusive war in Afghanistan has not helped. But the real culprit in her view may be "information overload in a globalized world." People have the sense "that their politicians no longer control events," and as a result, "the voters' most powerful implement, their ballot, simply doesn't work in this era."[22]

The anti-pluralist (populist) parties promise to do something about societal angst, to reduce immigration, to abandon free trade, and to bring jobs back – notions that counter perceptions about a loss of control. Traditional institutions – media, religious, and governmental – are being rendered obsolete as social media echo chambers dominate discourse. Applebaum observes that "people are seeking new identities and new affiliations online." Meanwhile, traditional political parties that used to be based on real-life institutions – labour unions and the church being two examples – are now being "whittled away across the West" by internal and external forces.[23] As confirmed by the report of US Special Counsel Robert Mueller, social media are being weaponized, notably by Russia, to hack and disrupt Western election campaigns.[24]

Applebaum contends that the West is going to have to get more serious about regulating the Internet. She also recommends that NATO

– "or some analogous Western institution" – should "make cybersecurity and cyberwarfare" its "central role."[25] Party loyalties are not as reliable as they once were. As indicated by the election of Justin Trudeau, Emmanuel Macron, and Donald Trump, personality is a more powerful determinant of political success than policy or ideology. But popular support can be transitory unless real change is delivered.

The West suffers from a vacuum of strong political leadership. Donald Trump is focused on what is good for his vision of America. The United Kingdom's Theresa May fell due to her confused machinations over Brexit and was replaced by a leader who sowed more confusion, Boris Johnson. Buffeted by the backlash against a massive influx of refugees, Germany's Angela Merkel has decided to leave office. French president Emmanuel Macron, of whom so much was expected, is subject to persistent protest in the streets over his inability to deliver on changes he promised. Prime Minister Shinzō Abe of Japan offers a modest island of stability but it is not one with much global resonance.

THE DEMISE OF THE LIBERAL INTERNATIONAL ORDER

It is now widely accepted that many of the developments described above have stuck a knife into the liberal international order.[26] Whether the wounds are ultimately going to prove fatal is a matter of continuing debate.[27] But it is undeniable that the core institutional elements of global cooperation that have fostered greater political and economic interdependence are now under assault on many fronts, feeding widespread uncertainty about future prospects for global prosperity and security.[28] The financial collapse of 2008 brought immense discredit to Western capitalism, notably the banking sector, requiring massive bailouts from governments, which in turn spawned skepticism and populist fervour among those, notably many Americans, who perceived themselves to be less favoured by the government. "Where is my bailout?" became the cry from "Middle America," a lament that anchored much of Trump's support.

For Chinese authorities, this financial crisis prompted a strong sense that they had little to learn from the United States and the West generally. It inspired more reason than ever for them to pursue their own state-controlled, macroeconomic policies, delivering a severe psychological jolt globally to views on political as well as economic systems. China also had largesse to spread around, notably in Africa and, through its Belt and Road Initiative, in Asia. Several Third World countries saw more advantage in emulating the tightly controlled Chinese approach to economic growth and political power rather than the free-wheeling American approach. There are lingering doubts about whether this type of financial crisis can be avoided in the future, but confidence in Western banking systems and in the global monitoring mechanisms is no longer guaranteed.

For similar reasons, the World Trade Organization (WTO) and rules governing international trade are being seriously questioned, causing Trump to threaten US withdrawal from an organization of which America was the principal architect. The United States refuses to name panelists to the WTO's dispute resolution panels, thereby stymieing the enforcement of trade rules.

Any perceived infringement on US sovereignty, whether by the WTO, NATO, or the United Nations, is now seen in negative terms by the US administration, reinforced by Trump's mantra that the United States has been used and abused as a "piggy bank" and looted systematically by others.[29] Allies are attacked openly and quite legitimately for not paying their fair share of the security burden, eliciting a curious proposal from French president Emmanuel Macron for a European army that would defend that continent against "China, Russia, and even the United States of America"[30] – a concept dismissed abruptly in a tweet by Donald Trump as "insulting" on the eve of celebrations commemorating the 100th anniversary of the end of the First World War.[31] Such is the tenor of diplomatic dialogue these days. The fact that the Trump administration is in the vanguard of efforts to downgrade, if not eliminate, the commitments to institutions that the United States helped to design and lead graphically illustrates what a topsy-turvy world we are experiencing.

Although it has become fashionable to describe the past seven decades of peace and prosperity as resulting from the liberal international order led by the United States, Graham Allison, formerly the director of Harvard University's Belfer Center for Science and International Affairs, offers a different perspective. In his view, international order emerged for the most part after the Second World War from a balance of power – a Cold War that John F. Kennedy once described as "the precarious status quo"[32] – in which the United States and the Soviet Union developed a "strategy for a form of combat never previously seen – the conduct of war by every means short of physical contact between the principal combatants."[33]

After the collapse of the Soviet Union and what Francis Fukuyama has wistfully dubbed "the end of history," the new world of unipolar order proved to be anything but.[34] The United States used military power to try to impose liberalism on countries like Libya, Iraq, and Afghanistan, with decidedly mixed results, especially since the roots of democracy and fundamental freedoms were minimal in each.

As the US share of global economic power, on the basis of purchasing power parity, has dropped by 50 per cent since the end of the Second World War to less than a quarter of global GDP today, Allison contends that we are actually witnessing a "return of history."[35] Revisionist powers like China and Russia are, as stated in the National Security Strategy of the United States issued in late 2017, "fielding military capabilities designed to deny America access in times of crisis and to contest our ability to operate freely."[36]

Allison's core thesis is that "[l]ong before Trump, the political class that brought unending, unsuccessful wars in Afghanistan, Iraq, and Libya, as well as the financial crisis and Great Recession [of 2008–09], had discredited itself."[37] In his view, these disasters shook confidence in liberal self-government more than the antics of the impetuous Donald Trump have done. The problem on the home front is whether America can reconstruct a working democracy, not one to convert the world to a new liberal order but one that will help "to sustain a world order 'safe for diversity' – liberal and illiberal alike."[38] Allison concludes somberly, "Achieving even a minimal order that can accommodate that diversity will take a surge of strategic imagination as far beyond the current conventional wisdom as the Cold War strategy that emerged over the four years after [American diplomat George] Kennan's Long Telegram was from the Washington consensus in 1946."[39] His is not a reassuring prophecy.

GLOBAL INSECURITY

During the long period from 1990 to 2017, the value of global trade increased. More than 1 billion people escaped poverty,[40] and infant mortality rates decreased by more than 50 per cent.[41] It was an environment uniquely conducive to economic growth. The United States had no real competitor, and most countries supported Washington's liberalization moves on trade and investment. Few challenged that prevailing orthodoxy.

However, by the time Donald Trump took office, there were signs of a growing strategic rivalry from rising powers like China and revisionist or nuisance powers like Russia and Iran. Basic assumptions about the framework for global economic policy also began to change. Geopolitical goals began to supersede economic ones. "If," as Walter Russell Mead observes, "the U.S. is in a serious strategic competition with China, an American president might well be willing to sacrifice some economic growth to banish China from important supply chains."[42]

By invoking a direct link between economic security and national security, the Trump administration is upsetting conventional norms on trade and using tariffs as a blunt instrument in support of national security, even against close allies like Canada. Business firms have been essentially complacent in the face of tariffs and other measures upsetting supply chains and restricting employment practices or joint venture choices. US business firms seem reluctant to risk being caught on the wrong side of patriotism or a Trump tweet. They undoubtedly see "America First" as more than a slogan. It is an unvarnished, strategic use of raw power.

Given the geopolitical changes underway, some recalibration of the US-China relationship is inevitable. Whether tariff battles will lead to a sensible modus vivendi or make matters worse remains to be seen. The havoc in financial markets is already evident as the world enters a new, complicated, and dangerous era of nationalist competition. For the next few decades, attention will focus on the manner and degree to which the United States and China can navigate through major differences on trade and security issues and avoid an abrupt clash. History offers compelling lessons of success and failure when one great power is ascending while the other is levelling off. Mutual self-interest and a degree of interdependence may be the most promising foundation for stability.

China protects its strong economic growth in its own inimitable way by ignoring at will many conventional norms of international trade and investment. Despite the pretense of a market economy, China's authoritarian government is doubling down on state control of the actions of foreign and domestic business. Theft of intellectual property is chronic. Rules on foreign investment are one-sided. Instead of becoming a responsible stakeholder in global affairs, China is using its burgeoning economic power to assert influence in its own self-interest. The tariff wars between the two leading world economies are a further symptom of the breakdown in international order, which is being driven by a depressing plunge into populist protectionism around the globe.

China's Belt and Road Initiative is a blueprint for economic and political domination of its immediate periphery. China is also using its immense wealth across Africa to tie down access to resources and to build new channels of influence. Along with the Chinese-led Asian Infrastructure Investment Bank, these efforts counter sharply the role customarily played by the World Bank and various UN agencies. The United States is on its back foot in most of Africa, giving China virtually free rein for economic penetration and political influence. Congress's Build Act, which allotted US$60 billion to development, was intended to check the spread of Chinese involvement but pales in comparison to the US$1 trillion allotted by Beijing.

What remains to be seen, however, is whether the United States under any subsequent leader can manage a stable relationship with China, whose leader, Xi Jinping, has assumed power for life in a manner not seen since the days of Mao Zedong. Instead of harnessing the combined concerns of allies in Europe, Canada, Japan, and Korea about China, America is taking a unilateral approach. Some see a clash of horrendous proportions between the two major powers as inevitable. But it is very much in the self-interest of both major powers to find ways to manage their complicated relations without recourse to a war neither would win. More likely is a decade of uncertainty and increasing self-interest – a stormy and precarious "law of the jungle" world with less institutional glue or mutual resolve to underpin peace or prosperity.

Efforts by the United States to denuclearize North Korea may be noble in principle, but there is, as yet, little assurance of tangible success and not much evidence of a coherent engagement strategy. Chinese cooperation is essential to any progress. Meanwhile, South Korea has manifested a stronger interest in a peaceful peninsula, one that could eventually bring about unification. However, there is some risk that the Trump charm offensive with Chairman Kim could have the unintended consequence of unravelling the close security ties between Seoul and Washington, driving the South Koreans closer to China across the North Korea bridge but with little denuclearization of the peninsula. Such a development would stimulate a tangible response from an increasingly apprehensive and potentially nuclear Japan, shifting the power balance and adding increased strain to Asia generally.

Russia under Putin has grandiose visions of regaining global respect and recognition similar to that once given the Soviet Union. It has enormous nuclear weaponry and a tremendous capacity for mischief in and beyond its immediate region, but its economic power (less than that of Canada) has diminished, notwithstanding Putin's grandiose view that the country "is back at the top table with history on his side" and his claim that "the liberal idea has 'outlived its purpose.'"[43] At best, Russia may seek to play its hand and its limited leverage astutely by choosing sides selectively on issues between the United States and China.

The Middle East remains a cauldron of insecurity. The brutal civil war in Syria spawned a global tide of refugees, who have moved predominantly into Europe, on a scale never before seen in history, with negative consequences for democracy in many of the receiving nations and with no consequences for Syrian president Bashar al-Assad as the initiator or for his abettors. Tension is escalating between Saudi Arabia and Iran. Iran has launched sophisticated attacks against oil tankers in the Gulf of Oman, and it shot down a US surveillance drone that it alleged had entered Iranian air space.[44] The United States under Trump has intensified commitments to Israel and to Saudi Arabia – aligning the three nations in a peculiar troika, to say the least.

Iraq is slowing coming back together, but the aspirations of Iran in the region, especially its open support for terrorism, is a chronic concern for the United States, Israel, and Saudi Arabia, among others. With American withdrawal from the Joint Comprehensive Plan of Action, there is no longer even a limited brake on Iran's nuclear ambitions. President Trump is confident that economic sanctions will bring Iran to heel, but nuance is never part of his diplomatic tool kit. The Iranians may, as former secretary of state John Kerry has observed, simply "wait Trump out"[45] or surreptitiously reignite their nuclear ambitions.

The erratic behaviour of the Saudi regime, notably the brutal murder of journalist Jamal Khashoggi, poses a powder keg of its own that could erupt into serious consequences for the region. Greater repression by autocratic regimes lays the seeds for future rebellion. Afghanistan was a failed state when it became a launch pad for the 9/11 terrorist attacks on the United States. Eighteen years later, and after billions of dollars in economic and military assistance and thousands of deaths to combatants and civilians, the "graveyard of Empires" is still a quagmire for which there is no apparent solution.[46] A Vietnam-style evacuation by the United States is likely, with little to ensure real stability for the beleaguered Afghan citizenry.

Threats from cyber space, for which there are virtually no rules nor globally sanctioned monitoring mechanisms, add a uniquely twenty-first-century challenge of incalculable proportions to global stability. Many foresee the threats from cyber space as more troubling in the decade ahead than those from terrorism or nuclear proliferation. This situation calls for the negotiation of standards and/or an agreed rule of behaviour (i.e., codes of conduct in cyber space).

PRUDENT INTERNATIONALISM

The pronounced shift to "America First" populism poses a substantial challenge for global affairs, one that obliges Canada to move away from the false comfort of conventional wisdom and time-worn nostrums and toward the contemplation of economic and security strategies that will serve distinct Canadian interests first and foremost. Canada needs to accept the simple fact that, however outrageous it may seem, Donald Trump means what he says on global affairs and intends to do what he promised to do in his presidential campaign. When he leaves office, the world will not be the same.

The world is now also in an age when authoritarian China is in the ascendancy while the United States is jostling to maintain leadership and to blunt the combined threat from China and Russia as well as from rogue states like Iran. Great powers act differently from all others on the global stage. Both the United States and China today illustrate a willingness to play by the global rules on international trade until they decide not to. That is particularly true of China today under the leadership of a counter-reformer who is quite different from many of his predecessors. When both abandon the rules simultaneously, the ramifications for the rest of the world can be disconcerting. A "law of the jungle" environment on trade offers little sanctuary to many and intensifies the risk of global instability. The saving grace is that, although each major power jockeys overtly to outdo the other, there is a significant degree of interdependence. Both, one hopes, are clever enough to realize that a major military clash must be avoided, as it would not be winnable by either side.

In a more turbulent world where benign US leadership is no longer a given and where protectionism, populism, and authoritarianism are on the rise, the consequences for Canada are serious. Relations with the United States will no longer be special or privileged. A coherent rebalancing of Canada's international policies is no longer simply desirable; it is essential. Canada is going to have to look out for its own interests and vigorously promote them bilaterally and globally but with the knowledge and public awareness that the road will be rocky. In recent years, Canada has sometimes found that it was left standing alone because its traditional allies did not have its back. Canada also runs the risk of getting caught in the downdraft of rising geopolitical tensions. The collateral damage that Canada suffered when China blocked canola and pork imports and incarcerated two Canadians in retaliation for the arrest of Huawei executive Meng Wanzhou is a case in point.

The core assumption of Canada's postwar foreign economic and security policies was that international institutions and the maintenance of a strong, liberal international order would automatically serve its best interests because they gave Canada both a voice and power in setting norms and establishing new rules. That set of operative conditions no longer fully obtains. Key international institutions have been sidelined (or gridlocked) and their rules openly ignored or violated by great powers. Rigor mortis is setting in with some, as in the case of the WTO and NATO.

Stephen Harper's Conservative government was often accused of pursuing a foreign policy that did not take international institutions, like the United Nations, seriously. Canada's ill-fated bid for a nonpermanent seat on the UN Security Council in 2010 may have been a casualty of that indifference. Harper was also accused of promoting a narrowly focused economic agenda to the exclusion of other issues. But if, as some alleged, the Harper government's "pragmatic" approach to Canada's international relations suffered from a lack of worldly ambition, his successor has not done much better with his own brand of progressive, virtue-signalling internationalism. After four years in office, the Trudeau government has also fallen well short of its own lofty 2015 election campaign ambitions to "bring Canada back." As critics noted, Trudeau was resorting to political hyperbole.

Canada had never exited from the world stage, even if Harper's critics didn't like what he was doing. As we show in later chapters in this book, despite several acts of omission, such as its reluctance to build a new pipeline to tidewater or to promote more effective trade relations with China, the Harper government did most of the heavy lifting on getting free trade agreements with Korea and the European Union, leaving its Liberal successor to consummate the latter deal, which has not yet been ratified by the European Union, and also to take much of the credit. Harper also introduced greater accountability in international institutions like the G7 and G20 by ensuring that pledges would be honoured and reviewed annually. His government also successfully secured Canada's admission to the Trans-Pacific Partnership negotiations despite strong American opposition. When an agreement was successfully concluded in 2018, Canada was the winner. Even though the Trump administration opted out, Canada now enjoys preferential access to the markets of key TPP countries, namely Japan, Malaysia, and Vietnam.

The Trudeau government is, of course, to be applauded for playing a difficult game of defence to protect many of the key elements of the NAFTA agreement, which was negotiated by Prime Minister Brian Mulroney more than twenty-five years ago.[47] Unlike Mulroney, who dealt with two American presidents who were supportive of free trade principles, Trudeau has had to deal with a capricious and volatile American leader like none before.

However, the Trudeau government's virtue signalling did not make matters easy for itself. That was especially the case when it injected its progressive agenda into Canada's economic and commercial relations. The Chinese quickly showed Trudeau the door when he insisted that any deal must include standards of human rights, labour, the environment, and gender. Taking to Twitter to deliver moral reprimands to a country like Saudi Arabia, as Foreign Minister Chrystia Freeland discovered, is a futile gesture if it fails to achieve a positive outcome for jailed human rights activists and damages bilateral relations.

In this book, we make the case for a new kind of prudent, sensible internationalism, one framed not only by a keen appreciation of what and where Canada can best contribute in a manner that serves its own unique values and interests but also by a keen appreciation of the formidable challenges and tough choices that Canada now faces in a turbulent world. In laying out the requirements for a strategy of selective internationalism, we take issue with those who believe that Canada should retreat into fortress North America and let the United States shoulder the burden when it comes to advancing Canada's interests and dealing, for example, with China or Russia. We also believe that Canada can no longer rely on a privileged or special relationship with the United States. It should be abundantly clear after more than a decade of dealing with both Democratic and Republican administrations that Canada is not always at the forefront of American concerns or interests. Canada also has to engage pragmatically with China and creatively with India. We also take issue with dewy-eyed, indiscriminate multilateralists who believe that any kind of multilateral institution or venture is automatically good for Canada. They are detached from an appreciation of vital Canadian interests or the capabilities that Canada brings to bear, not to mention the abject performance of many of these shop-worn institutions.

We believe that Canada must stand on its own two feet and not be timid or suffer from a lack of fortitude or ambition to promote its interests. However, Canadians and their leaders should also not delude themselves that the world is breathlessly waiting, in that wearisome phrase, for "more Canada."

In a world that is suffering from an excess of nationalist fervour, populism, economic protectionism, xenophobia, and resurgent great-power rivalries, Canada must stand on guard for the values and principles it cherishes but also be circumspect about the limitations of its global engagements and ambitions. Canada needs to make choices, not spread itself too thinly and not assume that it can remake the world in its own image. When Canada does engage, it should be prepared to bring the full weight of its diplomatic wits, wallets, and muscle to the game. It cannot continue to give lip-service alone to its military or to the threat from cyber space. The world is no place for amateurs, the naive, the weak, or the half-hearted.

Canada should also focus its energies on selectively strengthening those multilateral institutions that matter, especially those where other members share its interests and values and are committed to upholding them. Euphemistic aspirations about "middle power" status and nostalgic notions about the intrinsic value of any form of multilateralism offer no prescription for relevance or achievement.[48] Democratic values and institutions are under attack throughout the world. Rather than being a consummate joiner of any institution that will have it, Canada should concentrate on those that best serve its interests and reflect its basic values. Strengthening clubs of the democratically likeminded, such as NATO and the G7, should be a major foreign policy priority for all democracies, including Canada, as many scholars and practitioners argue.[49] Deepening Canada's relationships with major democracies of the Indo-Pacific, like South Korea, Australia, and India, should also be a goal in a world where the political and economic centre of gravity is shifting westward. Ensuring the effective functioning of rules-based multilateral institutions like the WTO, which are critical to global economic prosperity, is also a paramount priority.

As the UN Security Council becomes increasingly hobbled, or deadlocked, by the reassertion of great-power geostrategic rivalries, Canada must be realistic about diminished UN capacity for collective action to promote global peace and security and not see the United Nations through rose-coloured glasses. Notwithstanding the vital work of some specialized UN agencies to promote development and provide humanitarian assistance, Canada also needs to take a hard look at the large number of conferences and other bodies that have been spawned by the UN Economic and Social Council and carefully assess whether they all equally deserve its support.

As great-power tensions spike dangerously upward, Canada must also work harder to ensure that it does not become a proxy battlefield, as it has in US-China trade wars. A strategy of dislocation prevention – anticipating how its interests might be affected before conflicts erupt and taking preventive action to ensure that Canada does not get sideswiped or, at the very least, to limit the damage – is the only prudent thing to do. It is a bit like being cautious on the stairs to avoid falls or wearing a hard hat and steel-toed boots on a construction site.

Chapters 2, 3, and 4 of the book discuss, respectively, how Canada should adapt to a changing relationship with the United States, address its declining competitiveness, and establish effective relations with China and India. Chapter 5 addresses the challenges of calibrating Canada's energy and climate change policies. Chapter 6 deals with Russia and NATO. Chapter 7 assesses Canada's role in the turbulent politics and security of the Middle East. The next two chapters explore the main challenges for Canadian policy in two key areas of national policy: cyber security (chapter 8) and immigration and refugees (chapter 9). In the concluding chapter, we offer a coherent strategy on how all of these challenges can best be met. We assess the requirement for Canada as a global leader and how its leaders can best advance Canadian interests and values in a precarious world.

2

No Longer a "Special" or Privileged Partnership

The renegotiation of NAFTA was the overwhelming foreign policy priority for Canada during Donald Trump's first two years in office. Foreign Minister Chrystia Freeland had little time for much else. The prime minister, his office, and most of his Cabinet were also engaged in an intensely bruising, aggravating, and at times insulting spectacle in which Trump demonstrated vividly his antagonism toward any trade deal, including NAFTA, which he claimed was "the worst trade deal ever made."[1] Simply by ignoring the bombast and bullying tactics, the government earned plaudits from the public at large and ultimately received credit for holding much of its ground in the negotiations. It was a textbook case of how to deal with a mercurial, moody, volatile, and highly unpredictable president who took to social media to issue presidential edicts and berate enemies and putative friends alike: keep your head down, ignore the tweets, don't rise to the bait, argue with facts (although facts meant little to the president), and, at the very least, muster support in Congress and across the United States.

THE NEGOTIATIONS

The full story of what went on behind the scenes of the negotiations has yet to be told. What we do know is that the thirteen-month negotiations were bruising and contentious. The main points of disagreement revolved around dispute resolution, automotive rules of origin and regional content value, dairy market access, intellectual property, whether the agreement would contain a sunset clause, and section 232 tariffs on steel and aluminum, which the United States levied on its key trading partners, including Canada and Mexico, and which were removed only in May 2019, well after the agreement was signed.

The Trudeau government knew that Trump had NAFTA in his sights because he openly criticized the agreement during the presidential campaign, but then so did other candidates, including Democratic front runner Hillary Clinton and her main competitor for the Democratic nomination, Senator Bernie Sanders. If Trump had a bone of contention, however, it appeared to be with Mexico, which was the focus of much of his ire about job losses, especially in the automobile sector. (Mexican illegal immigration was the other big issue for Trump.) When Canada did come up, Trump talked initially about "tweaking" the agreement with Canada, not revoking or radically changing it.

All that would change in April 2016 when the American president told a group of Wisconsin farmers that Canada was "cheating" American farmers because they could not sell their filtered milk, which is used to manufacture cheese, in Canadian markets because of high Canadian tariffs. It was "very unfair" he told the farmers. Shortly afterward, to underscore his displeasure with Canada, he slapped tariffs on softwood lumber, a sector that was not covered by NAFTA but has been a perennial irritant in the bilateral relationship. "'Canada,' he said, was 'very rough' and had 'outsmarted our politicians for many years ... We don't want to be taken advantage of.'"[2]

Things went downhill from there. White House officials drafted an executive order for the president to withdraw the United States from NAFTA. Ottawa was reeling. After a series of frantic phone calls between Ottawa and White House officials, and a storm of protest from friendly Republicans and business leaders from states that traded heavily with Canada, the executive order was withdrawn. However, it was followed by official notification to the US Congress delivered on 18 May 2017 by US trade representative Robert Lighthizer that the Trump administration intended to renegotiate the terms of NAFTA. On 17 July, Lighthizer made public the US government's key objectives in the negotiations, which included raising American content in autos and modernizing intellectual property rights, regulatory practices, labour and environmental standards, and government procurement.[3] On 16 August 2017, the parties formally sat down at the table.

Canada's negotiating team was led by Foreign Minister Chrystia Freeland, but much of the heavy lifting was done by trade officials in Global Affairs Canada and by a bureaucratic team led by seasoned trade negotiator Steve Verheul. His negotiating counterpart was US trade representative John Melle. The Mexicans were led by Economy Secretary Ildefonso Guajardo Villarreal. To coordinate strategy across government and with the provinces, a special unit was set up in the Prime Minister's Office led by Brian Clow, who had previously served as Freeland's chief of staff. The prime minister's chief of staff, Katie Telford, and his principal secretary, Gerry Butts, were also heavily involved in the negotiations, especially when they entered the finishing stretch and tough decisions had to be made by the prime minister and conveyed directly to the White House.

There were seven rounds of negotiations that alternated among the three countries from August 2017 to May 2018. During these negotiations, the bureaucrats cleared much of the underbrush, reaching an agreement on the less contentious issues. But on the big, outstanding issues, there was clearly little agreement. One of the biggest was country versus North American content percentages. Washington initially proposed that the North American content of vehicles had to increase from 62.5 per cent to 85 per cent, of which 50 per cent had to be American.[4] Both Mexico and Canada refused to accept the proposed US content rules, not least because they would have eviscerated the automobile sector in both countries. In a less noticed but equally contentious provision, the Americans also demanded that tracing lists be expanded to all the components of a car. Items on the tracing list that were imported would count as non-NAFTA input when calculating rules of origin. The measure was strongly opposed by automobile manufacturers in all three countries, not least because it would have driven up production costs and made the North American industry uncompetitive.

The impasse on autos was broken when the Canadians suggested tying automobile content rules in some fashion to wage levels. Mexico is an attractive location for automobile manufacturing because of its low-wage economy. If Mexico agreed to raise wages in its automobile sector, which were roughly one-third of wages paid to workers in Canada and the United States, the 50 per cent US content rule could be relaxed. In the end, it was agreed that 45 per cent of an automobile's content had to be produced by workers who earn a minimum wage of $16 per hour.[5]

By early spring 2018, it looked as though the talks had sufficient momentum to meet House Speaker Paul Ryan's 17 May deadline to put a revised agreement to Congress before the mid-term congressional elections. But optimism was misplaced. There were major unresolved issues over dispute settlement, whether the agreement should contain a sunset clause, pharmaceutical patent protection, intellectual property, and dairy. In the case of dairy, the United States demanded that Canada remove all restrictions on unfiltered milk and all tariffs (which ran nearly as high as 300 per cent) on US dairy imports.[6]

As negotiators spun their wheels, Trump grew increasingly impatient at the lack of progress. In June he extended tariffs on steel and aluminum, which he had imposed in March on other countries, to the European Union, Mexico, and Canada. At the concluding press conference at the G7 Summit, which was hosted by Prime Minister Trudeau in Charlevoix, Quebec, Trudeau let down his guard and announced that Canada would not be "pushed around" by the Americans. Trump had already left the summit but was watching the press conference on television monitors aboard Air Force One as he winged his way toward Singapore for his first meeting with North Korean leader Kim Jong-un. Outraged by Trudeau's remarks, which he considered a major betrayal from a NATO ally just as he was about to launch major negotiations with the North Koreans to denuclearize, Trump tweeted that Trudeau had "acted so meek and mild" and was "very dishonest and weak." He also warned that Trudeau's stance "is going to cost a lot of money for the people of Canada."[7]

Matters were not helped when Chrystia Freeland accused the United States of "putting its thumb on the scale" at a *Foreign Policy* magazine tribute in Washington honouring her as "Diplomat of the Year." She promised a "dollar-for-dollar response" to President Donald Trump's tariffs and warned that American businesses and consumers would pay a price for their country's protectionism. Freeland's stern reprimand did not go unnoticed by the White House.[8]

On Canada Day, when most Canadians were roasting hot dogs and hamburgers on the barbecue and celebrating the beginning of the summer holidays, Canada retaliated with its own 25 per cent tariffs on US steel and aluminum, along with a wide range of other products, including California wine, playing cards, and felt-tipped pens.

While the Canadians were playing hard ball, the Mexicans were cozying up to the Americans. During the summer, the Mexicans quietly conducted their own bilateral negotiations without Canada at the table. Still chafing at what they saw as a double-cross – the Mexicans accused the Canadians of having presented the automobile wage-content formula to the Americans without first running it by them, a claim the Canadian delegation vigorously denied – Mexico appeared willing to throw Canada under the bus to reach its own separate agreement with Washington.

On 27 August, Mexico announced that it was prepared to strike a bilateral trade pact with the US alone. The Canadian negotiating team was clearly caught by surprise. Canada had been left with the impression that negotiations between Mexico and the United States were only about autos. But it was now clear that the Mexicans and Americans had covered the whole gamut and produced a complete draft covering many of the issues under consideration. When news broke about the impending deal, Freeland, who was headed to Europe, diverted her travel to Washington, where she spent the better part of the next month in negotiations. It was not just Ottawa that felt betrayed. Senior Mexicans were aghast too. Writing in the *Globe and Mail*, former deputy foreign minister Andres Rozental called the "reality show organized by the White House ... to announce a 'deal' between Mexico and the United States" nothing more "than a typical Donald Trump sham." He rightly pointed out that "Congress has only given President Trump authorization to submit a trilaterally approved text, not a bilateral one; Canada has its own bilateral issues with the United States that also need to be resolved and which don't involve Mexico."[9]

With the pressure on Ottawa clearly mounting, the White House upped the ante by announcing that Canada would have to meet a 30 September deadline to reach a deal or Washington would go it alone with Mexico. In his inimitable, tactless fashion, Trump chose to rake Canada over the coals at the UN General Assembly's annual gathering of world leaders in New York. "We're very unhappy with the negotiations and the negotiating style of Canada," he said, adding in a direct swipe at Freeland, "We don't like their representative very much."[10]

Freeland didn't rise to the bait. Nor did Trudeau. They doggedly soldiered on right down to the wire. On 30 September, following a marathon round of negotiations that lasted seventy-two hours, a deal was reached. The prime minister's short, six-word response to reporters said it all: "It's a good day for Canada."[11] That was the view of most Canadians. There was little cheering and more of a collective sigh of relief. An October public opinion poll that was taken a "few weeks after the Trudeau Liberals' victory lap on North American trade" showed that "[m]ore Canadians are disappointed than pleased with the U.S.-Mexico-Canada Agreement ... While it seemed like a late-September push from Foreign Minister Chrystia Freeland [and the prime minister's personal secretary, Gerry Butts] and her negotiators saved Canada from finding itself out of a two-way trade pact between Mexico and the United States, poll respondents aren't so sure the deal was better than no deal at all: the country appears evenly split three ways as to whether it was better, the same or worse for Canada than not being part of the new deal."[12] The C.D. Howe Institute has since claimed that Canada and Mexico will both lose from the agreement; in Canada's case, its GDP is expected to shrink by 0.4 per cent.[13]

Although the three countries signed the agreement on 30 November on the margins of the G20 Summit of world leaders in Argentina, both Canada and Mexico made it very clear that they would not ratify the agreement until the Americans lifted their tariffs on steel and aluminum and would not accept any kind of quota to limit exports. Although there were repeated rumours throughout the winter and early spring of 2019 that the tariffs would be lifted, Trump did not make the decision to lift tariffs until 17 May when it became clear that both the Republicans and Democrats in Congress would review the agreement only after tariffs were lifted. Again, agreement was reached first with Mexico and then with Canada. Despite the nasty presidential tweets and personal attacks on him and his team, Trudeau took the high ground: "This decision reflects what is known by true friends on both sides of the border ... Canada has been America's most steadfast ally for more than 100 years, and our long-standing partnership and closely linked economies make us more competitive around the world and improve our combined security."[14]

OUTCOME

Eventually, but certainly not smoothly or easily, a modicum of reason prevailed. If you give Trump an inch, he will celebrate a mile, but the new NAFTA, or United States–Mexico–Canada Agreement (USMCA), as Trump prefers to label it, was more of a salvage or rescue – a source more of relief than celebration – being what some Mexicans cheekily dubbed NAFTA 0.8. The saving grace was that a more negative outcome had been avoided.

Elements of success came primarily from staring down some of the most egregious US demands: removal of both the dispute settlement mechanism and Canada's supply management systems for dairy and poultry and acceptance of a one-sided "Buy America" proposition on procurement. A significant compromise by Mexico on wages for autoworkers and on North American content rates for auto production preserved a substantive element of the original agreement and was initially deemed a "win" by the United States and Canada. (Autos and auto parts represent 25 per cent of Canadian exports to the United States.) But no sooner had the ink on the signature page dried than General Motors announced that it would close five plants, four in the United States and one in Oshawa, Ontario. For a company that had been bailed out with billions of dollars of taxpayer funds from both countries less than a decade before, this decision was a bitter pill to swallow and shattered any illusion about stability or growth for the US-Canada auto sector.

Preserving the dispute settlement mechanism was a definite plus, as were safeguarding supply management, at least politically – Canada made a minor concession on imports of US dairy products and on patent protection for pharmaceuticals – and the addition of some of the modernization housekeeping issues adapted from the Trans-Pacific Partnership agreement, which Donald Trump had spurned immediately upon taking office. Left unresolved, however, were the tariffs on steel and aluminum that had been introduced on dubious "national security" grounds, prompting reciprocal retaliatory tariffs by both Canada and Mexico. The seemingly perennial tariffs on Canadian softwood lumber also remain in place.

Having triumphantly pocketed a deal with its two North American neighbours, the Trump administration shifted its strident trade and tariff tactics to China and, with less gusto, to the European Union, both of which run surpluses on trade with the United States, which Donald Trump sees as blatantly unfair.

Even with a renewed NAFTA, the Trump administration's embrace of tariffs as the weapon of choice is rattling conventional norms for liberalized trade and institutions like the World Trade Organization meant to defend those rules. History demonstrates that tariffs are not a prescription for growth. They may initially help to galvanize political attention and generate emotional support, but the effect on growth is predictably negative. Consumers and producers alike are left with higher costs.

Trump's tactics on trade and similar attacks on institutions like NATO have tarnished the tone, if not the fabric, of relations more generally with Canada and with several of the United States' staunchest allies. The question is whether Trump's "America First" manner and method are an aberration or a harbinger of more of the same approach, wherein the law of the jungle and principles of raw power and self-interest are asserted more generally. If the latter is the case, self-reliance and self-interest will become the watch words for all, including erstwhile allies like Canada.

PERSONALITIES VERSUS INTERESTS

Relations between Canada and the United States ordinarily experience ups and downs, often reflecting the leadership personalities of the moment. Fortunately, the shared network of business, social, and family linkages usually provides a bulwark against even the most outlandish stresses and strains emanating from personalities. Congress is important too. It was reported that when Trump at one luncheon gathering told Republican senators "not to get too excited" about how his administration was "handling the NAFTA matter," Senator Pat Roberts, a Republican from Kansas, who chaired the Agriculture Committee, responded, "I am excited [Mr President] ... Basically, I'm trying to point out that if you start the clock on NAFTA [withdrawal] that's going to send a very bad signal throughout the entire farm economy."[15]

But the experience with Trumpism is having a sobering effect on many Canadians – a blunt reminder that Canada's geographic proximity to the United States can be a two-edged sword that conveys benefits in economics and security most of the time but openly exposes the vulnerability of overdependence. What is inescapable is that relations with the United States will continue to be the dominant foreign policy concern for any Canadian government, whether Canada likes it or not. But it will require nimble footwork on Canada's part in the future, looking beyond the personalities of the moment and their idiosyncrasies, and finding new instruments for equilibrium in a more volatile, unpredictable environment. Despite the foreign policy axiom that relations are determined by interests more than by personalities, a quick scan of the history between Canada and the United States suggests that the tenor and substance of their relationship can be influenced by both factors.

When faced with the unknown but impulsive Donald Trump, the Trudeau government turned promptly to former prime minister Brian Mulroney for regular advice and counsel. Mulroney's close relationship with Presidents Ronald Reagan and George H.W. Bush represented a high point in bilateral and global cooperation between Canada and the United States and was symbolized most poignantly by the fact that Mulroney was invited to deliver eulogies at the funerals for both presidents (and for Nancy Reagan as well). He also knew Donald Trump and several family members. No one in the Trudeau government did. Like most Americans, Trudeau had fully expected Hillary Clinton to win in 2016, and his government had planned accordingly.

Mulroney's basic advice on a new NAFTA was that the government should be very firm in deciding what would constitute an acceptable result and what would not, adopting the bottom line position that he had followed with the initial Free Trade Agreement negotiation that "no deal is preferable to a bad deal." He added that the prime minister should avoid getting into a "Twitter war" with the president – of the kind that few have been able to win – and that the government should instead work directly with Congress and state governors throughout the negotiations, emphasizing the value and significance of trade with Canada for Americans and American jobs while recognizing too that Congress has the ultimate authority over trade policy and the responsibility for approving trade agreements.[16]

Mulroney made precisely the same points when he testified before the Senate Foreign Relations Committee in January 2018 – the first former foreign leader to appear before a US Senate committee.[17] He stressed with numbers and facts why a positive negotiating outcome was in the best interests of all three partners. He also underscored at home that there was neither a Liberal nor a Conservative way to negotiate with the Americans but a Canadian way. (He had not encountered such nonpartisan sentiment himself in Canada's Parliament during his similar negotiations with the United States, but it served a useful purpose in 2017–18, helping to rally support for Canada's beleaguered prime minister.) When the negotiations concluded, Trudeau publicly acknowledged the steadfast support his government had received from the former prime minister.[18]

Trump's abusive manner and his penchant for mistruths – such as his incorrect insistence that Canada had a huge trade surplus with the United States and that the tariffs imposed on steel and aluminum were for "national security" – left a bitter residue from the negotiations with many Canadians. The fact that other allies were treated with similar "my way or the highway" disdain amplified concern in many quarters that the United States was no longer interested in being the responsible leader of the Western alliance. Those who customarily jockeyed for position as having a "special" relationship with the United States, wanting really to be more special than others, began to search for distance or avenues for greater independence.

For Canada, the lines of interdependence with the United States outside government are stronger and more lasting than any government personalities of the moment. Equally, however, notions of establishing greater distance or independence from America have tended to be more fanciful than real. (The "Third Option" preference of Prime Minister Pierre Trudeau is just one example.)[19] Geography alone obliges Canada to be more pragmatic and prudent by taking a long-game approach and looking for new ways to strengthen its interdependence through new avenues for bilateral cooperation while reducing its vulnerability through diversification of trade wherever possible. As the smaller partner, Canada will undoubtedly have more to gain potentially than to lose if it plays its hand carefully and on the basis of rigorous analyses of mutual self-interest. At the same time, Canada's ability to exercise "independent" influence on global issues has often depended on the degree to which it is seen as an *interlocuteur valable* with the United States. Canada cannot alter its geography, and management of relations with the United States will inevitably be its predominant priority. But the notion of privilege or special status, which served it well in recent decades and was often stimulated by the personalities of the moment, can no longer be taken for granted. In a world with self-interest at the core, realistic actions to defend and advance Canada's own interests should become paramount. Canada's capacity for better influence on global affairs will hinge on its own capacities, not on any sense of privilege vis-à-vis Washington. As Anne Applebaum warns, "there will be no automatic return to the status quo ante" once Trump leaves the White House; rather, the United States is entering "a long period of disengagement."[20]

3

Regaining a Competitive Advantage

Quite apart from the importance of the recently concluded United States–Mexico–Canada (USMCA) Agreement to Canadian jobs, economic growth, and investment, there are clearly other elements of public policy that are just as important, if not more so, to Canada's prosperity and competitiveness vis-à-vis the United States. The USMCA is a useful but by no means sufficient condition for future economic growth.

Canada's top economic priority should be to revitalize its competitive edge with the United States. Since the middle of the last century, a cardinal rule on macroeconomic policy for virtually all Canadian governments has been the need to sustain a competitive edge with the United States in order to attract investment and production in Canada that will enable it to sustain funding for social programs like health, education, and pensions. By rowing in the opposite direction of the United States on taxes, regulations, and the cost of doing business, the government of Justin Trudeau has severely depleted much of Canada's competitive advantage in North America. When the administration of Donald Trump reformed corporate and income tax rates, Canada moved in the opposite direction. When the United States revamped regulations for energy development and manufacturing to bolster growth, Canada adopted regulations that increased burdens of approval in each sector and sharply diluted the appetite for investment. Whereas business investment grew by 7 per cent in the United States in 2018 – the best in many years – it dropped in Canada by 4.5 per cent. The C.D. Howe Institute estimates that $100 billion in investment was lost in the energy sector alone in the past two years due to regulatory uncertainties.[1] We are not suggesting that Canadian policymakers should mimic US policies, but they need to ensure that the spread between Canadian and US regulations and the costs of doing business are not damaging to Canadian interests.

As the Trump administration withdrew from the Paris Accord on climate change, Canada doubled down with a national carbon tax, albeit one that, at an initial level, falls well short of the intended goals. Along with the strain and uncertainty of renegotiating NAFTA, all of these differentiations on policy have sapped much of Canada's competitive edge. Productivity continues to earn a failing grade. Economic output has been propped up modestly by a surge in immigration, not by efficiency or innovation.

Where Canada has fallen in line with the United States is on generating larger deficits, but this approach is not a prescription for growth, nor does Canada share with the world's largest economy the luxury of contravening basic financial disciplines. Deficits are normally intended for rainy days or recessions such as the financial crisis of 2008. Because of its sheer size, the United States may be able to ignore basic economic norms on deficits, but it cannot ignore forever the path that it is on. In the past three years, government spending in Canada has increased by 20 per cent, whereas the GDP has grown by 1.9 per cent annually.[2] As Jack Mintz observes in the *Financial Post*, federal spending "is being sprayed onto hundreds of different programs" targeted more at potential electoral support than at sustainable growth.[3]

Even though Canada's debt metrics are better than those of the United States, that is no reason for complacency. If the debt continues to expand, it should not be for consumption but for measures that boost productivity because that would eventually help to pay off the new debt. Olivier Blanchard in a recent paper for the Peterson Institute for International Economics points out that if the growth of the economy exceeds the interest rate, debt can continue to expand on a sustainable path.[4] That may be true, but there is clearly an increased risk premium associated with rising deficits and debts, namely that they can shoot up quickly, transforming a seemingly sustainable path into one that is unsustainable.

The Tax Cuts and Job Act became law in the United States at the end of 2017.[5] At 23 per cent, corporate income tax rates in the

United States were reduced to well below the combined average of those in Canada, removing in a single stroke what had been one of Canada's compelling advantages and, in particular, a magnet for investment. Providing full and immediate expensing for most types of new equipment until 2022, with gradual reductions in the subsequent five years, made the United States even more attractive for capital-intensive investment than Canada. This was offset to some extent by an announcement in late 2018 that capital expenditures in Canada would be allowed accelerated write-offs, but they apply only to companies earning profits that enable investment. They do little for those in the oil sector, which was hit not only with collapsing world prices for oil but also with a record-high Canadian discount on exports to Canada's only market, the United States.

Reducing personal income tax rates in the United States to an average that is about 20 per cent below Canada's rate has created a serious disincentive for talent retention and recruitment by Canadian firms. An additional factor at play is the fall in the value of the Canadian dollar, which also makes Canada a less attractive place to work. Regulatory changes affecting both energy development and environmental protection as well as manufacturing put the United States in an even stronger competitive position. Some suggest that the regulatory changes introduced by the Trump administration contributed more to growth than did the tax changes. To the extent that this claim is true, there is large scope for regulatory reform at all levels of government in Canada. The World Economic Forum's *Global Competitiveness Report* (2017–18) "identifies government regulation as a relatively strong factor depressing Canada's competitiveness ... Canada ranks 38th of all countries in the sample compared to Switzerland (which is ranked 6th) and to the US (ranked 12th)."[6]

The tax and regulatory measures implemented by the Trump administration have sparked record growth in the US economy and record low unemployment numbers. In terms of exports alone, Canada is of course a beneficiary from any uptick in the American economy, but the sharp distinctions on policy are hobbling its capability to keep pace. Study after study – by the Senate, the Fraser Institute, the C.D. Howe Institute, and Canada's Business Council – has underscored the extent to which policies moving in a direction opposite that of the

United States undermine Canada's competitive position, with inevitably negative consequences for economic growth.[7]

Canada's resource base should be a source of continuous growth, but it has become stunted by excessive or unpredictable government regulation. As Conrad Black has observed, "We cannot solemnly absent ourselves from this competition because we happen to have three million square miles that are rich in base and precious metals, forest products, energy and all agriculture except tropical fruit, and that we have an educated, law-abiding population of 36 million. All countries, large and small and naturally rich and poor, are striving to better their lot, and so are we, and the worrisome fact is that we are not doing a particularly brilliant job of it, and that will not be disguised by smiling platitudes about our equable and comfortable society or our leader's self-described congeniality."[8] An obsession with climate change has led to confusion, if not outright paralysis, on responsible energy development in Canada. Whereas energy competitors like the United States and Australia have moved to exploit increasing global demand for oil and natural gas, Canada has fallen behind. What once was a major competitive strength for Canada – the abundance of its natural resource base – is now shunned or stunted by ambivalent regulatory and court rulings. The effort to strike a balance between energy development and environmental protection has left Canada in a muddle on both halves of the equation.

Far from being a plus, the heavy concentration in sectors such as banking, telecommunications, and transportation in Canada has stifled competition and constrained both productivity and creativity. Yet concerns about declining competitiveness and productivity tend to be more yawn-inducing than alarming. The most persistent drag on Canada's growth potential may well be a sense of complacency, if not apathy, prevalent both in government and in the private sector. In 2018 the World Economic Forum's Global Competitiveness Index ranked Canada twelfth, whereas the United States was ranked first. The gap between Canada and a country receiving 75 per cent of its exports underscores the serious problem for the Canadian economy.[9] The same study placed Canada a distant thirty-fourth on the adoption of information and communications technology and a dismal fifty-third on innovation, suggesting a similar lag by Canadian business.[10] Canada's economic growth has generally been superior to that of several G7 countries (other than the United States), but much of the growth has been in the housing market and, to a lesser extent, consumption, both of which have been fuelled by easy monetary policy. The downside is that this growth has resulted in a large run-up in household debt, which is now a major vulnerability in Canada.

Because of its inconsistent, if not incoherent, approach to critical policy issues and its reliance primarily on deficit spending to stimulate growth, Canada has obliged investors and talented individuals to look elsewhere. Investment in Canada has essentially collapsed, and Canadian companies are increasingly investing in other countries. Foreign investment has dropped by 55 per cent in the past five years, whereas Canadian investment in foreign countries has risen by 74 per cent during the same period. A total of $70 billion more in investment left Canada in 2017 than came in.[11]

Deficit spending is not a prescription for sustained growth either; however, it has been the most prominent policy lever for three years running. Government spending has risen higher than at any time other than during a war or a recession. Unfortunately, as a result, the cupboard will be bare if and when the economy turns sour. As the Fraser Institute warns, "Many of the factors that contributed to the deficits of the mid-1960s to the mid-1990s, such as the risk of actual revenue being below budgeted projections, actual program spending exceeding budget, and higher than expected interest costs are all risks present today," and they are further exacerbated by declining labour-force participation as Canada's population ages.[12]

Despite a period of strong recovery in the United States and the global economy, merchandise export volumes have increased by less than 1 per cent over the past three years for the simple reason that Canada has lost market share to China in capital goods and to Mexico in auto parts. Canada ran a current account deficit of $60 billion in 2017, equal to 3 per cent of GDP. That trend continued in 2018.

The competitiveness challenge is certainly not one for governments alone. Canada needs a more robust culture of innovation and risk taking in the private sector. There should be more indications that firms are seizing the advantage of the preferential market access they will have as a result of the Comprehensive Economic and Trade Agreement with the European Union, the Canada-Korea Free Trade Agreement, and the Comprehensive and Progressive

Agreement for Trans-Pacific Partnership (CPTPP), or "mini TPP." Evidence to date suggests that Canada's agricultural sector is ahead of all others in capturing these openings. For example, exports of Canadian beef to Japan grew by 72.9 per cent and exports of pork expanded by 7 per cent.[13]

FISCAL POLICY

Top-down dictates via tax credits and subsidies are not necessarily the right answer. Creating a more competitive climate for business, especially start-up businesses, may be. Some suggest that a poor business culture or sunny acceptance of the status quo is the problem or that managerial expertise and competence are deficient. In either case, stimulating a more competitive business environment would be salutary, as would a sharper focus on recruitment of highly educated immigrants.

Canada's tax structure is a significant inhibitor. On the "effect of taxation on incentives to invest," the World Economic Forum ranked Canada forty-ninth, the United States eighteenth, and Switzerland sixth. One more example is that "Canada's top marginal tax rate on capital gains is above the average of all developed countries in the OECD."[14] The regulatory burden in Canada is especially oppressive to small and medium-sized firms. Excessive regulations stifle both competition and innovative start-ups. For too many bureaucrats, additional regulations justify their employment. Canada needs to put some brakes on measures that tax or regulate whatever moves in its economy. As Ronald Reagan once riffed, "The nine most terrifying words in the English language are: I'm from the Government, and I'm here to help."[15]

Manitoba offers just one example of what should be done. When Premier Brian Pallister found that his province was burdened by almost 950,000 regulations in more than 12,000 statutes, his government decided to shrink the total and prevent further regulation creep by law with a one-for-one rule: for every new requirement to be added, one had to be removed. Through active consultation on ways to reduce red tape, Manitoba shed more than 24,000 regulations in two years, adopting where practical national as opposed to provincial standards. Pallister is convinced that these changes helped to spur both investment and employment in his province. It is a model that other provinces should emulate, along with the federal government.[16] A 2019 Chamber of Commerce study, for example, gave the government poor grades for its own efforts to trim the roughly 130,000 regulations on business, which sap Canadian competitiveness and investment.[17]

As rising interest rates collide with high levels of indebtedness, the combination poses a serious risk to countries like Canada where household debt alone stands at record levels. That is why some, like Citigroup, see Canada as particularly vulnerable: "Canada's current debt-service ratio suggests risk of financial crisis within three years."[18] What is needed most to bring its fiscal position more in line is firm political leadership complemented by enlightened policy prescriptions based on studies already on record.

Most noticeably absent during the Trudeau years has been a clear fiscal policy framework that includes careful scrutiny of the manner in which hundreds of billions of tax dollars are being spent and whether they are delivering measurable results. Describing the discrepancy between current fiscal and monetary policy, Kevin Page and Randall Bartlett of the Institute of Fiscal Studies and Democracy state that it is "as if the Governor of the Bank of Canada is doing his best to remove the punch bowl from the party while the Finance Minister chooses to keep the bar open."[19] They urge that budgetary deficits be reined in and offer four suggestions for a fiscal policy framework: (1) a medium-term path to budgetary balance or modest surplus; (2) bringing fiscal policy in line with monetary policy through a set of annual targets for spending and deficit reduction; (3) enhanced transparency for direct program spending; and (4) a plan for multiyear spending commitments on things like national defence and infrastructure. Similarly, the International Monetary Fund (IMF) has called for a fiscal framework that explicitly incorporates clear fiscal rules: "The federal fiscal rule could include both a debt rule to anchor the course of medium-term fiscal policy, with the aim of reducing net federal debt to less than 30 percent of GDP as envisaged in the Budget 2018 forecast, and operational rules to guide annual budget decisions. Provincial fiscal rules should consider the sources of budget deficits and strike the right balance between stabilizing debt levels and protecting public investment."[20]

Manufacturing inefficiencies related to tax and regulatory policy and poor productivity stemming from weak investment and innovation seldom arouse strong political demands for change. Yet, without a healthy growing economy, Canada will not be able to sustain, let alone increase, funding of its health, education, and pension systems. Healthcare and pension costs already capture more than half of provincial budgets, putting pressure on the federal government for increased transfer payments.

The notion that the government's objective has been to improve the well-being of the middle class is shattered by the Fraser Institute's finding that "81 per cent of middle-income Canadians pay more tax than three years ago, about $840 per family. The average Canadian family pays 43.2 per cent of its income on taxes, more than on housing, food, and shelter combined." And that excludes the carbon tax. Seven of Canada's ten provinces "now have a combined federal-provincial income tax rate of over 50 per cent."[21] Further, as Bob Fay points out, "Canada's tax and benefit system ... is not equipped for looming demographic challenges; and it is not ready for the changing nature of work brought on by the 'fourth industrial revolution' and artificial intelligence."[22] At a minimum, governments should keep a tighter lid on spending so that taxes can be directed to public and social services that are effectively administered, but the situation may have to get worse before concrete reform to boost Canada's competitiveness takes root.

Canada's easy access to its most vital market is no longer certain. Tariffs on steel, aluminum, and softwood lumber took their toll on exports to the United States and inhibited investments in many sectors. There is always the risk with Trump that they might be reimposed. Any notion that trade diversification would provide the means to help reduce excessive dependence on the US market has been sharply constrained by indifference, if not hostility, toward Canada on the part of the two most promising global markets: China and India. For distinctly different reasons, neither is showing much inclination for a broad-gauged negotiation with Canada (see chapter 4).

Canada should start right at home. The perennial theme at all First Ministers' Meetings is a clarion call to reduce interprovincial trade barriers. Inevitably, little happens beyond fine words in a communique, leaving Canada to absorb an annual hit on its economy of $50 billion to $130 billion from existing barriers. As the IMF reports, "there are significant opportunities for productivity gains from reducing domestic barriers to inter-provincial trade," which are "impeding Canadian businesses from competing on a level playing field and scaling-up." The IMF estimates that "the potential gains" from removing such barriers "are sizable and could increase real GDP by almost 4 percent – a much larger gain than expected from recently-signed international trade agreements."[23] This is clearly not an arcane issue to be left to the backroom or to homilies delivered at First Ministers' Meetings but is foremost a matter for political leadership at the federal and provincial levels.

A major overhaul of tax, regulatory, environmental, and industrial support policies with the public interest in mind is called for, one that will provide a more positive platform for investment and economic growth and give priority both to Canada's customary strengths – natural resources, agriculture, transportation, and telecommunications – and to a sharper focus on knowledge industries of the future, such as artificial intelligence and cyber security. At the same time, instead of broad-brush social engineering programs, Canada needs carefully targeted policies that will deliver growth, including, for example, programs that help jobseekers to get back to work and programs that allow Canada's youth to secure an education that provides them with the right skillsets for a rapidly evolving, technology-driven labour force.[24] That is Canada's path to competition with its southern neighbour and its other global competitors.

INNOVATION

On the strength of Canadian resources, businesses in Canada have customarily rung up healthy profits despite subpar innovation by international standards. Productivity growth ultimately depends on innovation. Because Canadian companies invest less in facilities, equipment, and innovation, Canadian workers chronically generate 25 per cent less GDP than their American counterparts. Market realities may compel better, smarter innovation, but increased government spending is demonstrably not sufficient. The 2019 Fraser Institute report *Innovation in Canada* concludes that, relative to leading developed countries, Canada's innovation performance has deteriorated in recent years and that this phenomenon has contributed to the weaker international competitiveness of the Canadian economy. Much of this deterioration is attributed "not so much to weak business start-up activity, but rather to a seeming lack of success of incumbent companies to be innovative leaders."[25] The study concludes that there is no simple prescription for success but argues that Canada must "increase competition in domestic industries, specifically by eliminating regulations that limit or discourage foreign-owned companies from competing in Canada. This is particularly relevant in the case of industries that provide critical infrastructure, such as telecommunications and transportation, as well as those providing financial capital, notably commercial banking."[26]

Peter Nicholson, a former senior advisor to Canada's finance minister, writes that Canada has, for decades, "been able to exploit its competitive advantage in natural resources to, in effect, trade commodities for technology. We have been good at employing those technologies ... but much less good at creating technologies or innovative business models ... This explains why Canada ranks so low on innovation metrics such as business R&D and knowledge-intensive exports."[27]

Most effective, suggests Nicholson, would be policy measures that directly affect the bottom line, such as greater public procurement of innovative products from Canadian suppliers, regulatory approaches that encourage rather than inhibit innovation, and trade and competitive policies that create powerful incentives for Canadian companies to "innovate to survive and grow." He laments the "siloed organization of the public sector," which lacks coherence.[28] The "ABC" syndrome – purchasing Anything but Canadian – is deeply and perversely embedded in the Canadian bureaucracy. The fact that there are at least thirty-five innovation programs at the federal level plus similar efforts at the provincial and even municipal levels has prompted William Watson to note that "if government innovation programs were a solution, Canada's innovative problems would have been solved long ago."[29]

One reason why Canadian firms seem to be complacent or risk averse is that they are actually prevented from growing by some government policies and programs that are designed to keep companies small rather than incentivize them to grow; that is, they suffer from "welfare walls" in the form of preferential tax treatment, which stunt growth.

Another problem is financing, especially for small and medium-sized enterprises (SMEs). Politicians like to characterize these firms as the real engine for growth and employment in Canada, but when it comes to access to capital by these firms, Canada ranks near the very bottom. The TSX SmallCap and the TSX Venture Composite are two of the worst-performing indices in the world. Both have minus records over spans of one, two, and five years. Too many Canadian SMEs are not eligible for a traditional credit relationship and are obliged to rely on equity capital that is expensive and in short supply. Furthermore, available capital is concentrated in too few hands, namely the six major banks, which are, by nature, risk averse. The government has stressed the need for innovation, but SMEs have high hurdles to surmount. Most of the funding in government programs goes to clusters of large and, in many cases, foreign companies (e.g., in the telecommunications sector). The credit terms offered by government agencies like the Business Development Bank of Canada are rarely better than those available from commercial banks. Shortcomings on innovation and financing inevitably act as a drag on productivity.

What national business columnist Kevin Carmichael calls the "slow march to open banking" underscores another kind of challenge in the financial services sector. Open banking is an approach that allows banks to share their clients' information with other service providers. Although there are legitimate privacy and security issues when it comes to sharing data, these concerns should not be an excuse for legacy banking institutions to protect their monopoly position and resist innovation. As Carmichael points out, "the tech scenes in Montreal, Toronto and Vancouver are incubating some potential world beaters in digital finance." It is a field in which Canada could excel, notably in the area of commercializing technology that facilitates contactless payments. The National Bank of Canada, which is the smallest of the so-called "Big Six," sees market opportunity and has begun to share its customers' data.[30]

THE "INTANGIBLES" ECONOMY

When it comes to promoting Canada as an innovator in the intangibles of "big data" and artificial intelligence (AI), there are other major challenges. The high degree of global market concentration in the technology sector allows major foreign-owned firms to manipulate prices, control market access, scoop up data (what some refer to as the "oil" of the data-driven economy), and corner direct marketing to consumers.[31] Big tech firms also have the financial resources to buy up nascent competitors and to create so-called "kill zones" around them in order to absorb and stifle competition. Existing policies to promote Canadian activity through subsidies for research and development, innovation grants, tax incentives, and so on end up subsidizing foreign multinationals, with transitory benefit to Canada. In addition, firms like Microsoft and Apple are also large venture capitalists and use their treasure trove of cash to buy out Canadian firms, both private and public.

There are essentially three approaches to dealing with this problem. One is to simply stop allocating government funds to the high-tech sector because Canada is simply, in the end, funding foreign firms. The other is to direct the funding to human capital development through educational institutions and think-tanks, but even then both ideas and human capital will leave Canada because of predatory behaviour by tech multinationals inclined to buy up ideas and/or people. A third approach is to create barriers to exit through smart regulation, as argued by Research in Motion co-founder Jim Balsillie. As he contends, "if Canada is to thrive in the tech economy, it needs to do way more to control the ideas – inventions, discoveries, data, etc. – that represent the natural resources of the future." He "points out that upwards of 90 per cent of the trillions in wealth represented by the S&P 500 companies is built on 'intangibles,' like patents." Furthermore, "[i]f Canadians don't own their intellectual property, he warns that others will fill that void, condemning us to the 21st-century version of the old gripe about Canada as a branch-plant economy." Balsillie notes that "compared to other OECD countries, Canada is falling behind in the number of AI patents it registers. Universities let foreign companies exploit the inventions created in government-funded labs. And multinationals soak up more than half of federal innovation grants." He points out that "countries like Israel, Switzerland, Germany, and Korea" generally tend to do a much better job of securing domestic intellectual property and that Canada could learn from them.[32]

Shopify, which is one of Canada's most successful purveyors of online services and offers retailers a "platform to sell products to anyone, anywhere – online," is an example of a firm that is vulnerable in this regard. More than 600,000 merchants worldwide use its e-commerce platform, but, according to its 2017 annual report, it holds "no issued patents and thus would not be entitled to exclude or prevent its competitors from using [its] proprietary technology."[33]

Similarly, a Public Policy Forum report by Robert Asselin and Sean Speer also raises "red flags about the loss of intellectual property to foreign players and outlines the potential hit to the nation's competitiveness in a world increasingly driven by data and other types of 'intangible assets.'" They also conclude that "the government should do more to keep IP [intellectual property] and data in Canada" through a combination of targeted subsidies and regulations that "encourage the development of Canadian-based technologies and protect them from foreign takeovers." Their prescriptions include "stemming the use of public funds for research by foreign tech companies, using public procurement to buy technology from domestic firms and toughening criteria for foreign acquisitions that have negative impacts on the 'broader innovation ecosystem.'"[34] Asselin and Speer argue, "This is the difference between being a landlord nation and a tenant nation in the new intangibles economy."[35]

The Trudeau government's approach to artificial intelligence, big data, and the innovation economy has been to try to focus grants and subsidies for research and development on innovation clusters,[36] as well as to make a more concerted effort to get Canadian companies to protect and patent their intellectual property.[37] The hypothesis behind this approach is that, by taking the funds deployed through various mechanisms and concentrating them on innovation clusters to achieve the desired effect, as opposed to sprinkling monies around the country, as has historically been the case, the government will achieve success versus historical failure. However, the end result is that the government may simply be making it easier for foreign firms to engage in predatory behaviour because, much like a farmer who puts a fence around a herd of sheep, it is easier for the wolf to grab its prey through a hole in the fence when the farmer is not watching.

For companies in the more traditional sectors, such as poorly performing auto manufacturers like General Motors and aerospace firms like Bombardier, this too has been the fate of massive government subsidies. The beneficial effects have been transitory. Subsidies have kept jobs for a while, but then as economic conditions change, companies reallocate their investment capital and production capacity.

Political necessity too often overrules market sense, if not the laws of gravity. The customary rationale is that, because Canada's competitors are indulged in similar fashion, such as in the aerospace sector, Canada really has no choice but to mimic what other countries are doing. Whereas government support for research and development ranks proportionately at the top of the OECD rankings, private-sector investment ranks near the bottom.[38] This problem is symptomatic of a larger issue, namely that the country is not getting value from the monies it has spent on research and development because businesses are unable or unwilling to commercialize the benefits and because there is a distinct lack of symmetry between academic research and commercial needs. The problem is not dissimilar to the massive public subsidies that municipalities have provided to sports franchises. All of the evidence suggests that there are limited economic returns and instead that taxpayers are simply putting more money into the pocketbooks of billionaire franchise owners and their teams.[39]

4

Dancing with the Chinese Dragon and the Indian Elephant

Although the US market will always be the dominant priority for Canada, the need for more diversification on trade is an essential corollary, especially in a more fractious, less certain global environment. Asian markets should be front and centre. Yet, in what many increasingly see as "Asia's century," Canada has experienced major setbacks over the past two years, notably with the two major powers – China and India – that are principally driving economic change. Efforts to promote a substantive economic dialogue and broad-gauged negotiations with each suffered from abrupt self-inflicted errors of tactics and substance. Canada initially stumbled out of the gate as well in concluding the Comprehensive and Progressive Agreement for Trans-Pacific Partnership (CPTPP), or "mini TPP," with other Asia-Pacific partners but eventually got back on side, establishing a basis for preferential access to promising markets like Japan, Malaysia, and Vietnam, among others. Along with the Canada-Korea Free Trade Agreement, the CPTPP should facilitate some degree of diversification, but openings with the two Asian giants will need a significant recalibration of strategy and nimble diplomatic manoeuvring in the years ahead.

Asia is not a monolith. It is a decidedly mixed region that spans different levels of development and has several civilizations with proud histories of their own and the confidence that they can excel by modifying, not adopting, Western methods of growth and governance. Several Asian countries are using their economic power to leverage influence throughout the world. Many are building on the success of others and often with direct help from China. As Parag

Khanna has observed, "The Asian way of doing things is spreading. Governments are taking a stronger hand in steering economic priorities. Democratic impulses are being balanced with technocratic guidance."[1] Few see the American model of governance or growth as worth emulating. Asia's changing economic fortunes underscore this trend. In 2000 Asia accounted for just under one-third of global GDP. It is now on track to reach 50 per cent by 2040.[2]

Whether the transformation will be dynamic yet benign or confrontational and violent depends heavily on how China and the United States manage their complex relationship. The fallout, good or bad, will have implications not just for Asia but also for the rest of the world, including Canada.

AUSTRALIA'S CHINA SYNDROME

The opportunity for Canada with China is not without risk. There are hard lessons to be learned from Australia's experience, particularly as the free trade negotiation with Australia was a key element of a broader Chinese strategy. Clive Hamilton's book *Silent Invasion* delivers a withering expose of the extent to which China has sought to attain comprehensive influence over his country, Australia, "economically, politically, culturally, in all ways."[3]

For many years, the Chinese systematically co-opted to their cause members of the Chinese diaspora residing in Australia, numbered at 1 million, along with senior politicians, university administrators, academics, businesspeople, and media personalities. Not only did individual, often prominent, Australians nurture and abet direct Chinese ownership of Australian infrastructure, from ports to airports and energy and mining projects, but they were also called on to help stifle expressions of concern about China's dismal human rights record and its territorial ambitions in the South and East China Seas.

Those officials in Australia labelled "panda huggers" by Hamilton,[4] like former prime ministers Paul Keating and Kevin Rudd, together with key ministers such as "Beijing Bob" Carr and Andrew Robb, the latter of whom piloted the free trade negotiation, are singled out for facilitating China's economic aspirations in Australia while muting criticism of Chinese behaviour, specifically on issues like the Dalai Lama, Tibet, Taiwan, and Falun Dong as well as on China's territorial squabbles with others in the region.[5] It is a disturbing account of the degree to which greed – "economics *über alles*" – can subvert the intrinsic value of fundamental democratic rights and freedoms.

Corruption is endemic in China and may well be the Achilles' heel of its future prosperity and unity – the latter being a chronic political concern for the Communist rulers. But corruption also helps to finance overseas influence. Hamilton contends that Chinese billionaires readily seek bolt holes for their ill-gotten gains in countries like Australia, New Zealand, Canada, and the United States in order to protect their fortunes and their family members with investments, real estate purchases, and passports.[6]

Unquestionably, China's Belt and Road Initiative is predicated on building and owning infrastructure, ports, roads, energy, and telecom networks and facilities within its overall Asian periphery. It is aimed both at securing supplies needed to sustain economic growth and at extending Chinese influence in neighbouring regions. Given its monolithic, one-party state structure, China is able to mobilize all instruments of power – political, economic, military, and cultural – together with the global Chinese diaspora (some 50 million in total) to support these primary objectives.

Confucius Institutes have systematically funnelled money from the Chinese Communist Party through the Ministry of Education to top universities in Australia, often with conditions that Hamilton claims are in blatant conflict with basic academic principles of free expression.[7] Whereas Australia has generally welcomed this financial support, the United States and Canada have been more restrained. A senior official with the Canadian Security Intelligence Service (CSIS) describes the Confucius Institutes as "forms of spy agencies used by the Chinese government."[8]

The research grants feed directly into China's unquenchable appetite for access to high-tech fields, offering significant military as well as economic potential. What they do not fund, Hamilton claims, they are likely to steal. Theft of intellectual property by China is a perennial concern for all Western nations doing business in China, estimated to cost the US economy alone upward of US$600 billion per year.[9] If only President Donald Trump could see merit in a multilateral approach, the best remedy would be a collective Western response to rein China in.

Self-censorship among academics in Australia is rife. Critics of the "kowtowing" by Australian academics are accused of being racist, xenophobic, or worse. Especially with Trump in the White House, Australia's reliance on its alliance with the United States is openly mocked by academics. Calls for a closer embrace of China are characterized as evidence of a more independent foreign policy – a soothing aphrodisiac for many aspiring "middle" powers.

China's reach extends well beyond the Australian continent. In addition to an all-out effort in Africa, where President Xi Jinping promised US$60 billion in financial support at the 2018 Forum on China-Africa Cooperation,[10] China is spending more than any other country on scientific research in Antarctica, mostly in the area overseen by Australia, and it openly intends to "better understand, protect and *exploit* the Antarctic."[11]

Hamilton is less rigorous with prescriptions for how Australia can best resist falling deeper under Chinese dominance. Diversifying trade and building a more balanced partnership with the United States are noble sentiments to be sure, as are efforts to form a closer alliance of Asian democracies and their more like-minded friends – Japan, Korea, Singapore, Indonesia, and the Philippines, along with Australia and New Zealand – to counter China's systematic undermining of the sovereignty and/or territory of each country. More somberly, he sees the potential for conflict in the South or East China Sea as real and advocates strengthening the quadrilateral dialogue between the United States, Australia, New Zealand, and Japan on security as the best defence. But in what he characterizes as a contest of "boy scouts up against Don Corleone," Hamilton offers little reason for optimism.[12] The openness of Western democracies is the advantage that monolithic authoritarian states like China can readily exploit, almost at will. Vladimir Lenin once said that the capitalists would purchase the rope that he would use to hang them. The Chinese now in power are, if nothing else, ardent students of Lenin.

Although Western democracies consistently proclaim the advantages of their openness and their tolerance for diversity of expression, neither has taken root in China. In fact, the Australian experience described by Clive Hamilton demonstrates graphically how, in some ways, both values can be turned against one's own national interests.

Because of Canada's distance from China and its proximity to the United States, it has not yet been the target of determined efforts on the scale being directed by China at Australia and New Zealand. Yet vestiges are apparent, as evidenced by reports that China was cultivating research projects at Canadian universities intended to bolster military innovation.[13] The Chinese diaspora in Canada is more divided than that in Australia. Taiwan cultivated members of Parliament long before China got in on the act, and many Canadians remain supportive of Taiwan.

Nonetheless, Richard Fadden, who headed CSIS and was the national security advisor under the governments of Stephen Harper and Justin Trudeau, has openly expressed concern about the extent to which China was mobilizing political support at the municipal and provincial levels by aiding in the election of representatives from the Chinese Canadian community. Since retiring from government service, Fadden has been even more deliberate in warning Canadians about the risks of closer economic engagement, warning that ambivalence may diminish Canada's credibility within the Five Eyes intelligence alliance – Australia, Canada, New Zealand, the United Kingdom, and the United States – in which he served.[14]

More to the point, when Chemi Lhamo, a Canadian citizen of Tibetan extraction, was elected president of the student union at the University of Toronto's Scarborough campus in 2019, she was attacked harshly in social media by Chinese students with complaints that her longstanding advocacy of Tibetan independence was "irrational" and made her "ineligible" to represent the student body.[15] Many saw these attacks, some of which included obscenities, as having been orchestrated by Chinese authorities. Among the University of Toronto's 91,000 students, 12,000 are from China. At about the same time, protestors assembled at McMaster University to denounce a talk about well-documented abuses against China's Uyghur minority. The protest claimed that the presentation promoted "hatred" against China and urged the university to "ensure that the dignity of Chinese students is not infringed."[16]

As evidenced by the student uproar at these universities, if Canada allows its openness and its freedom as a democracy to become a source of weakness for others to exploit at random, it will sacrifice the essence of its national purpose and its national interest.

THE CHINA-AUSTRALIA FREE TRADE AGREEMENT

The dramatic increase in Australian exports to China following negotiation of the China-Australia Free Trade Agreement is a compelling illustration of the attraction of a closer economic embrace. But the experience of Canada's Commonwealth cousin resulting from its negotiation with China also offers an object lesson on the difficulties that closer economic ties can bring. For one thing, Australia is in many ways Canada's natural competitor in the Chinese market.

For China, the priorities in the ten-year negotiation with Australia were investment and labour mobility more than trade per se. China has been given a relatively free hand to support its major project investments in Australia with labour imported from the mainland, an activity that has prompted opposition notably from union representatives. In the first year of the Australia-China Free Trade Agreement, investment proposals from China more than doubled, targeting particularly energy, mining, and utilities. Agricultural land purchases were not far behind.

In the decade since 2007, Australia has ranked second only to the United States as the destination for Chinese investment, taking in US$90 billion, a sum proportionately much more substantial than the US$100 billion that China has invested in the United States. The trade statistics reveal a compelling pattern of growth far in excess of that recorded by Canada. In 2008 Australia's exports to China were A$37 billion,[17] whereas Canada's exports to China were Cnd$10.5 billion.[18] By 2017 Australia's exports had increased to A$116 billion (more than tripling),[19] whereas Canada's had risen to Cnd$23.6 billion (slightly more than doubling).[20]

In 2017 there were 131,000 Chinese students enrolled at Australian universities, proportionately five times the number enrolled in the United States. (The downside, which Clive Hamilton explicitly emphasizes, is that Australian universities have "substantially withdrawn their capacity for sustained, genuinely independent analysis of contemporary China or of Chinese history.")[21] Tuition fees from Chinese students and hefty research grants from Chinese companies often come at the price of academic freedom.

"HUNDRED YEAR MARATHON"

Michael Pillsbury's book *The Hundred-Year Marathon* reads like Clive Hamilton on steroids.[22] A long-time China scholar, intelligence and Pentagon official, and advisor to congressional committees, Pillsbury spells out how China plans to become the sole superpower by 2049 (100 years following Mao Zedong's successful revolution), expunging the previous century of humiliation and abuse by Western powers.[23]

Pillsbury contends that through a combination of stealth-like deception, the flouting of international norms on trade and security, and misguided pampering by the World Bank, by several US administrations, and by all-too-willing abettors in the private sector, like Goldman Sachs, Morgan Stanley, and Boeing, among others, China is soon to become the number-one global economic power. Any notion that economic expansion would yield political freedom is "wishful thinking."[24] Following the demonstration in Tiananmen Square and the collapse of the Soviet Union, the hypernationalist hawks, personified by "President for Life" Xi Jinping, are in full charge and more determined than ever that strategies derived from their own lengthy history augur strongly and ultimately in their favour.

China has successfully violated commitments it made to the World Trade Organization (WTO) using currency manipulation, subsidies to state-owned enterprises, widespread theft of intellectual property, and support for counterfeiting industries to sustain record growth. By breaking all the rules, China rapidly became dominant in steel, auto parts, glass making, and paper production – industries where it otherwise had no comparative advantage. More troubling is China's virtual monopoly on rare earth production, materials essential to many industries, including several in the defence sector. The Chinese, says Pillsbury, "invented mercantilism" in part because their "leaders have an almost paranoid fear of a coming crisis leading to regional or global resource scarcity."[25] He does not regard their predatory trade practices as a passing phase.

China has also consistently flouted nonproliferation agreements by giving subsidized support to Pakistan, North Korea, and Iran, among others. US intelligence officials allege that 90 per cent of global cyber espionage stems from China. As it becomes economically dominant,

China will also be able to surpass America in military spending but not before the timing is right for the Chinese. Thus far, they have carefully avoided a direct challenge on military supremacy.

On the major environmental challenge of our time – climate change – China is a flagrant outlier. Between 1990 and 2050, China's cumulative carbon emissions from energy production will be 500 billion tonnes[26] – roughly the amount generated by the whole world from the beginning of the Industrial Revolution up to 1970. China's emissions were close to 10,000 tonnes in 2017, which was 270 per cent higher than in 1992 – in large part because of steadily increasing and heavily subsidized coal production.[27]

The hawks in Beijing have skilfully "persuaded the Chinese leadership to view America as a dangerous hegemon that it must replace."[28] According to Pillsbury, this is the real meaning behind Xi's public speeches about the "China Dream."[29]

The "Great Firewall of China" restricts Internet access, with American companies like Apple and Facebook meekly complying in order not to jeopardize burgeoning sales. "The total number of people employed to monitor opinion and censor content on the internet … was estimated at 2 million in 2013."[30]

China's deliberate strategy is to target perceived American weaknesses and to neutralize American strengths without overt confrontations. Nonetheless, the biggest risk may come from a miscalculation or misunderstanding that will accidentally lead to war. For China, the most important foreign policy challenge in the next decade is "how to manage the decline of the United States."[31] For too long, Western elites and opinion makers have provided their public with rose-coloured glasses to examine China in accordance with attitudes projected by the Chinses authorities. Canadians are no exception. Only recently are prominent Canadian diplomats who have served in China recognizing that they were duped into believing what China was saying and did not understand what the Chinese were doing.

Pillsbury quotes Lee Kuan Yew, who says, "It is China's intention to be the greatest power in the world – and to be accepted as China, not as an honorary member of the West." Lee adds, "If you believe that there is going to be a revolution of some sort in China for democracy, you are wrong. The Chinese people want a revived China. Their great advantage is not in military influence but in their economic influence," which "can only grow and grow beyond the capabilities of America."[32]

Pillsbury's counsel of realism includes many prescriptions, beginning with a hard-headed recognition that China is a competitor, not a welfare case, and that its anti-competitive behaviour needs to be checked frontally not by the United States alone but preferably in concert with its allies, notably those near China. He also recommends more overt support of dissidents and putative reformers along with firmer action to compel Chinese adherence to commitments made to the WTO, the nonproliferation agreement, and the like.[33] In short, he calls for more cohesive measures from democracies that have been too gullible for too long.

GEOPOLITICAL REALITIES

Any approach to a major power like China would have to take account of the geopolitical considerations at play while being mindful, too, that others like the European Union, Japan, and Korea are exploring the prospects for closer economic ties with China, if only to offset the negative fallout from "America First" actions by their erstwhile ally, the United States. China's global ambitions are driven by history. For millennia, the Middle Kingdom governed under the belief that "everything under the heavens" belonged to China.[34] In the twenty-first century, China's goal is to displace the American "barbarians" and to correct historic humiliations imposed by those who dethroned China and usurped its rightful position at the centre of the world.[35]

The most blatant manifestation of China's ambitions is the unilateral claim being made by China for much of the South China Sea despite a 500-page arbitration decision by a UN Law of the Sea tribunal rejecting that claim. China ignored the ruling, reckoning that its growing naval power and nuclear submarine capability – "might is right" – underscores an uneven power contest. Oil rigs are being established in contested waters, and artificial islands are being created to serve as unsinkable aircraft carriers in the region.[36] These activities have generated skirmishes with US and other naval forces and have raised concerns about a major military clash.

As Graham Allison observes, "the defining question about global order is whether China and the US can escape Thucydides's Trap."[37] He cites the example of Sparta and Athens as well as the example of Germany in the twentieth century, both of which ended badly. The United Kingdom adjusted to the rise of the United States in a calmer fashion. Allison contends that China thinks in much longer timeframes and "with a greater sense of hierarchy" than does the United States. "As Confucius said," Allison observes, "just as 'there are not two suns in the sky, there cannot be two emperors on earth.'"[38]

The US-China tariff war is a symptom of a more fundamental rivalry – a new cold war – and, as Robert Kaplan contends in *Foreign Policy*, "the geopolitical challenge of the first half of the 21st century is stark: how to prevent the U.S.-China cold war from going hot."[39] China is the "pacing threat" against which the US military now measures itself. At issue is a battle more of advanced technologies than of military might – a war of integration in which "China can intrude into U.S. military and business networks just as the United States can intrude into theirs."[40] What kept the old Cold War from getting hot was the fear of hydrogen bombs. But policymakers are less fearful now, as weapons have become smaller in size and increasingly tactical. The scope for non-nuclear warfare has broadened considerably.

Kaplan believes that what we really need to fear may not be a rising China but a declining one. He suggests that the more authoritarian China gets, the more it may be prone to crack up. Echoing Samuel Huntington, he suggests, "as states develop large middle classes, the greater the possibility is for political unrest."[41] That is the predominant concern of the ruling Communist Party, accentuated by President Xi Jinping's oversight of a budding personality cult that is attempting to intensify thought control by digital means. Kaplan advocates intensified diplomacy – military and civilian – as the base tactic to prevent a hot war.

CANADA-CHINA PROSPECTS

Canada's approach to a broader economic relationship with China has been spasmodic and less than strategic for more than a decade. Despite the model set by his Australian, Conservative soulmate, John Howard, and persistent prodding from the Canadian business community,

Stephen Harper was very wary of a strategic move on trade with China. While he was prime minister, the mandate for Harper's first minister of international trade stipulated as a priority cultivation of closer economic ties with "the democracies of Asia," excluding China explicitly.[42] The terminology was consistent with the Conservative Party's 2006 campaign platform and the views of Stephen Harper. Only in the final year of his time in power did Harper show a mildly more open attitude. China's totalitarian Communist system was anathema to Harper personally.

That may have also been one of the reasons why Harper refused to join the Chinese-sponsored Asian Infrastructure Investment Bank, although Harper was also influenced by US president Barack Obama's entreaties to US allies that support for the bank would undermine Bretton Woods institutions like the World Bank. The Trudeau government nonetheless changed course and signed on soon after being elected in 2015, but to date there have been few economic dividends. Furthermore, Harper's opposition to a strategic link with China has intensified since he left office. His successor as Conservative Party leader, Andrew Scheer, had pledged that, if elected, he would abrogate Canada's commitment to the bank. Also, like Harper, he prefers closer ties with the "democracies of Asia."

The scope and complementarity of the Chinese market cannot be ignored by Canada even as Chinese growth rates take a major hit as a result of the China-US trade war.[43] Nor can the risks associated with deeper engagement, particularly the acute sensitivities of its North American neighbour, which negotiated a clause in the United States–Mexico–Canada Agreement (USMCA) that would enable it to influence, if not veto, any aspirations by Canada or Mexico regarding China. With China, the raw power imbalance and distinct differences on basic values pose serious challenges for any broader partnership. Efforts by Canada to strengthen the economic fabric of its relations in order to bolster its standard of living cannot be sacrificed by diluting values essential to its well-being, but Canada cannot ignore the opportunity for increased trade, as it has much of what China needs. Striking the right balance will require nimble diplomatic footwork steeped in a hard-headed realistic assessment of the increasingly uncompromising authoritarian stance of the Chinese regime.

For Canada, the optimistic view of China, imbued by tales of Norman Bethune and the notion that economic growth will spawn political liberties in China, are no longer compelling. With superior economic growth has come brash self-confidence bordering on arrogance. Chinese attempts to infiltrate and influence opinion in Canada have flourished in recent years thanks to an oblivious, if not gullible, public, largely under the direction of the Chinese embassy and consulates, whose total staff of 211 is exceeded only by that of the United States, with 276, and more than five times that of the United Kingdom, with 38. As Jonathan Manthorpe writes in *Claws of the Panda*, it is time for Canadian politicians to "assume a much tougher and more self-assured attitude towards Beijing."[44] Manthorpe's analysis complements in spades the dire warnings posed by Clive Hamilton about China's approach to countries with large numbers of the Chinese diaspora in their population.

The motivating factors for closer economic ties between Canada and China are essentially the complementary nature of existing trade patterns and the dramatic potential for growth in what may soon be the world's largest economy. But Canada needs to manoeuvre sensitively to extract advantage from China's burgeoning economic power with a clear-eyed focus on the risks as well as the rewards. China needs much of what Canada has in abundance: agriculture products and fertilizers, energy and mining resources, along with selective high-tech and services expertise. For Canada, China has an abundance of consumer goods and increasingly sophisticated technologies to boost manufacturing and service or supply chain efficiencies.

The obstacles posed by any negotiation with China are daunting. Efforts to launch trade negotiations in December 2017 were stillborn. At that time, Prime Minister Trudeau led a major delegation to Beijing ostensibly to kick-start free trade negotiations that had been delayed sporadically for more than ten years. It was not an auspicious start. Reportedly, because of a last-minute request by Canada to include a key element of its progressive trade agenda, namely labour relations, the Chinese balked, and the prime minister left Beijing empty-handed. China's premier, Li Kequiang, had more than thirty bilateral meetings in the weeks before the Trudeau visit. He was not willing to countenance in any trade agreement vocabulary that could lead to inclusion, collective bargaining rights, or four months of maternity leave in any trade negotiation. The Canadian team should have known that beforehand.

So what went wrong? No one could really explain what happened to an objective that should have been "cooked," or agreed upon, in advance of the visit. There were grumbles about a breakdown between bureaucrats and political aides, more often than not the scapegoat for foreign policy glitches, but because Trudeau was the first Canadian prime minister to visit China in back to back years, the hiccup on trade was even more inexplicable. Canada miscalculated badly in Beijing and overplayed a weak hand.

Under strict authoritarian discipline, all economic transactions and arrangements with China come with a pronounced political overlay. Despite all the rhetorical promises from Beijing, adherence to the basic principles of a rules-based market economy are not assured. Sauce for the goose is not necessarily sauce for the gander. The raw power tactics being manifested on trade by the Trump administration could have similar, if not worse, effects if they are adopted by a monolithic regime where the line between politics and economics is opaque.

The notion that China would become a more "responsible stakeholder" in world affairs through membership in the WTO and other multilateral institutions remains aspirational, if not illusory. Similarly, the view that the benefits of a much stronger economy and recognized international status would spawn more political freedom in China has not been validated. China insists instead that moving 600 million citizens out of poverty is a more powerful advancement of human rights than the adoption of Western, democratic values.

President Xi Jinping is a more entrenched and authoritarian leader than anyone since Mao Zedong in a monolithic hard-versus-soft authoritarian system of governance that shows no interest in real political reform. He is a counter-reformer determined to consolidate government and party control over the economy. The Chinese were already wary of the advantages of political liberalization given what happened to the Soviet Union in 1991–92. The financial debacle of 2008 only accentuated their apprehension about adapting macroeconomic policies and financial systems from Western democracies to their model. The faster their economy grows, the more confident the Chinese are that they have little to learn about economics or politics from the Western world.

That is why there is serious doubt that any negotiations on trade and investment with a country like China could produce a framework of enforceable rules and mutually beneficial dividends. Although many studies underscore the complementarity of the Chinese and Canadian economies, few believe that the rules agreed to in a negotiation could ensure not only a genuine spirit of reciprocal or balanced benefit but, more importantly, also a more certain and transparent environment for rules governing trade and investment.

Critics of China point to the chronic theft of intellectual property, the forced divestitures of foreign technologies, currency manipulation, and numerous nontariff barriers like discriminatory regulatory scrutiny and customs delays that impede or distort efficient business practices by foreign companies operating in China. A concerted effort by the United States and Western democracies more generally would be the best way to address these concerns.

Jonathan Manthorpe insists that the Chinese Communist Party "is never going to allow Canadian business to have significant access to its market, whatever the agreement may say," adding that, "[f]or well over a decade, the Canadian Security Intelligence Service has been doing its best to warn successive Ottawa governments and the public about the infiltration of Canadian institutions by the political agenda of the Chinese Communist Party (CCP) and the party's quest to influence public life."[45] In Manthorpe's view, there was never the slightest chance that "an authoritarian, one-party state that does not believe in the rule of law – and which considers liberal democracy a fanciful, outdated notion – was going to buy" Trudeau's "'progressive trade agenda,' which demands common respect for issues like gender equality, employment standards and the environment."[46]

Others highlight China's flagrant abuse of human rights, particularly vis-à-vis Tibetans and Uyghurs, and the strict limits on individual freedoms within China itself as reasons why Canada should refrain from closer economic ties. Still others highlight the aggressive manner in which China weaponizes economic entities to damage the interests of countries whose noncommercial actions annoy or antagonize Beijing. When the Lotte Corporation of South Korea provided land for a US anti-ballistic missile defence system, its retail outlets in China were boycotted, often violently with protests that ultimately prompted Lotte to withdraw altogether from retail sales in China.

Similarly, after Japan arrested a Chinese trawler captain for ramming one of its Coast Guard ships, China cut off sales of rare earth oxides essential to segments of Japanese manufacturing. Japan meekly relented. In the same vein, China has also sharply reduced tourist flows abroad and the number of students at foreign universities to signal Chinese displeasure when other nations bruise its sensitivities on human rights and geopolitical issues.

In late 2018 the Public Policy Forum made a compelling case for engagement with China but was cautious in its recommendations. Perhaps overly influenced by the clause in the USMCA requiring advance notice of any "free trade" initiatives – an addition the forum criticized as "an unprecedented ceding of sovereignty" – it nonetheless advocated a sectoral approach on trade focused on agricultural and natural resources as a more prudent option and one less likely to trigger opposition in Washington.[47] But that would put the cart before the horse. What the Public Policy Forum report failed to acknowledge is that sectoral approaches work only when you can demonstrate balance or mutual benefit within a given sector. The Canada-US Auto Pact is one such example, but when efforts were made by Canada to extend the sectoral concept used with the United States to other industries like agricultural equipment and urban transit facilities, the analyses revealed sharp imbalances and proved the concept to be unworkable.[48]

The examples of agriculture and natural resources proposed by the Public Policy Forum for negotiations with China would likely suffer a similar fate because they serve distinct Canadian as opposed to Chinese objectives. Besides, a sectoral approach would run afoul of WTO restrictions on agreements that limit tariff reductions only to specific sectors. That is precisely why Australia went the free trade route, which would meet the "substantially all trade" standard required for approval by the WTO.

Although Canada's exports to China have grown, its actual market share of trade with China has fallen by about 25 per cent since 1995. US exports to China were 8.4 per cent in 2017, double the proportion of Canadian exports. If through pragmatic efforts Canada were able to replicate the US proportion, the amount would generate gains greater than current levels of sales to Japan, India, and South Korea combined. That is the scale of the opportunity and why China is worthy of attention but not necessarily negotiation.

Certainly, more clarity and consistency are needed on investment, which is closely linked to whatever can be achieved on trade. There are gaps or question marks on both sides. Canada has genuine concerns about limitations to majority stakeholders imposed by China and about theft of intellectual property and forced technology transfers. China presumably has questions about the opaque manner in which "national security" considerations have been invoked to block recent investments in Canada. Even in retirement, Richard Fadden and his former intelligence colleague Ward Elcock sought overtly and successfully, on national security grounds, to block the acquisition of Aecon, a construction firm in Canada, by a Chinese state-owned enterprise.[49] That rejection came in the wake of approvals of takeovers by other Chinese firms of two high-tech telecom manufacturers in Canada, Norsat in Vancouver and ITF Technologies in Quebec, on which their similar advice had been rejected. Taken together, these decisions reflect the somewhat schizophrenic attitude of the Trudeau government on economic relations with China.

Canada would have to decide which sectors it needed to protect and why, whereas China would need to determine to what degree it would liberate Canadian investments in China. Above all, more transparency would be needed as a basis for greater certainty in mutual investment flows along with clear intellectual property protection rights for investments. Again, a concerted effort by Western democracies would be better able to establish and preserve a more open network of rules than a solo effort at negotiation by a country like Canada.

By virtually any measure, the opportunities in the burgeoning Chinese market are unprecedented and cannot be ignored. Many suggest that, within a decade, the Chinese economy will surpass that of the United States in size alone. This growth and a corresponding increase in the middle class of the Middle Kingdom will stimulate demand for commodities and skills that constitute Canadian strengths: agricultural products like canola oil, pork, and wheat as well as energy resources like liquefied natural gas, oil, and uranium. According to the International Monetary Fund, China accounted for 33 per cent of global growth in 2017 (up from only 4 per cent in 2000), outstripping the rest of Asia (28.8 per cent), Europe (15.2 per cent), and the Western Hemisphere, including the United States (12.8 per cent).[50]

Although China is Canada's second largest export market, half of the G20 countries sell more in absolute terms to China than does Canada, including South Africa, Brazil, Saudi Arabia, and Indonesia. This situation illustrates what is being missed. China is already the second largest source of tourism to Canada, and Chinese students comprise more than 30 per cent of all international students studying at Canadian postsecondary institutions. These links involving people should in themselves add helpful texture and stability to the bilateral relationship, and although they, too, are not without risks, all such links are reasons why there is certainly scope for growth.

THE HUAWEI CONUNDRUM: CAUGHT BETWEEN A ROCK AND A HARD PLACE

Relations with China took a more dramatic turn for the worse when Canada agreed to a US request to extradite the chief financial officer (and daughter of the founder) of Huawei, Meng Wanzhou. By meeting its legal obligation under the Extradition Treaty, Canada was caught between a rock and a hard place, incurring immediate scorn from Beijing. Chinese authorities responded in a thuggish manner, apprehending two Canadians, including one former diplomat, for dubious national security reasons. They have been subjected to daily rigorous interrogation, which is a breach of basic diplomatic conventions, and formally charged with espionage. Two other already convicted Canadian drug dealers had their sentences hastily raised from fifteen years to death after little more than one hour of judicial deliberation. Canada was hectored publicly and crudely for being an American lackey.[51]

Initially, President Trump threatened to use the extradition as a lever in US trade negotiations with China. He later backed off a tactic that might have politicized, and hence sullied, the legal underpinnings of the extradition process. If that were not bad enough, Canada's ambassador to China, former immigration minister John McCallum, ventured to Chinese journalists in Toronto political views on the Meng case that were eventually deemed to be undiplomatic in the circumstances. After acknowledging that he had "misspoken" in his forty-minute commentary, McCallum added even more political flavour to the situation with similarly imprudent comments later the same week in Vancouver.[52] He was promptly fired by the prime minister, a decision that displeased Beijing even more but helped the United States given that McCallum's political commentary – namely that Meng has a "strong case" to avoid extradition[53] – had undoubtedly raised eyebrows in Washington since it could conceivably have impaired the extradition process.

The net result was a profound embarrassment for the Canadian government, adding further impetus to the notion that Canada's foreign policy has been conducted by amateurs in the Prime Minister's Office rather than by professional diplomats. Meanwhile, relations have deteriorated sharply. Canadians are being held hostage with little prospect of having their basic rights protected.

After the extradition manoeuvre, Canada rapidly became the target of authoritarian punishment by China. To make certain that Canada amended its ways, China began to turn the economic screws, banning all imports of Canadian canola due to spurious and undocumented concerns.[54] Similar dubious tactics targeted Canadian meat exports. Ottawa seemed awkwardly powerless to respond. Plaintive appeals to Western allies, notably the United States, for help were received politely, but the United States was focused exclusively on its own trade negotiations, and the enfeebled Europeans in France and Germany were concentrating on extracting economic benefits from China for themselves. It will be some time before any sense of normalcy returns in Sino-Canadian relations. Lessons born of naiveté should not be forgotten.

The incident with the Huawei executive sheds new light on Huawei's commercial activities in Canada. Whereas the other members of the Five Eyes intelligence alliance, except for the United Kingdom, have foresworn using any Huawei equipment in their 5G telecom infrastructure, Canada has stalled for time, in part because two major Canadian telecom companies, Bell and Telus, already use much Huawei equipment in their networks. If the Canadian government continues to drag its feet on the ban imposed by the United States and others in the intelligence alliance, it risks jeopardizing the credibility of its participation in this partnership.

As the United States increases pressure tactics to extinguish telecom links between Huawei and American allies, Canada is again caught between competing concerns. For companies like Bell and Telus to switch gears now would be costly. They are urging the government to adopt a pragmatic approach, one that accepts the need for a tightening of security concerns but falls short of a full ban. Officials in the United Kingdom share that attitude. Other Europeans are also flexible, putting commercial considerations at least on par with security concerns. All undoubtedly hope that some rapprochement between China and the United States on trade and investment will ease the pressure on security. Nonetheless, as we contend in chapter 8, China poses the most serious challenge in the area of cyber security, necessitating a much bolder and coordinated Western response.

LOOKING FORWARD

Far from the early "sunny day" expectations of the Trudeau government about relations with China, the atmosphere became downright chilly in early 2019. An early thaw or a significant breakthrough on trade is more elusive than ever.

Beyond the Huawei conundrum, the government has to be mindful, too, of potential geopolitical downsides to an enhanced trade and investment relationship with China. Canada cannot concede to China's territorial claims in the South and East China Seas, especially in light of judgments by international tribunals that categorically dispute these claims. Its position should continue to be supportive in principle of those adopted by others in the region, namely Japan, Korea, and the Philippines.

A greater focus on China must be achieved without compromising respect for Canada's support of fundamental values regarding freedom and human rights. Engagement with China should not be the outcome of a binary choice between trade or human rights but should seek to strike a balance that reflects the basic differences in the political systems and democratic values involved as well as the economic complementarity of the two economies. Although these political differences should be asserted in an appropriately diplomatic manner, there should be no ambiguity from Canada on any of them nor any sense that success on trade will require concessions on unrelated topics.

No country has the right to dictate to another how to manage its domestic affairs, including labour relations. Basic human rights are universal, sanctioned by the United Nations' Universal Declaration of Human Rights (written in large part by a Canadian, John Peters Humphrey). Canada can accept the reality of different political systems operating in places like China without endorsing the premise for that difference. There should also be a specific focus on threats from cyber space since the Chinese are regarded as the number-one villain in hacking to gain an edge on new technologies. Better to address these concerns overtly than through shadowboxing.

The sheer power imbalance Canada faces with China is magnified by the one-party, authoritarian political system in Beijing. Canada should have no illusions on this score. But that does not suggest Canada should ignore what makes practical sense in terms of ways to extract mutual benefits. After all, it has a long history of negotiating successfully with a neighbour ten times its size. That should help. There is even talk of inviting China to join the CPTPP as a way to finesse sensitivities, but that would likely pose a red flag for the Americans. Alternatively, Canada and others might consider joining China, India, and Japan in the less ambitious Regional Economic Partnership. Canada should be open to various options aimed pragmatically at drawing value from the dynamic changes underway in the global economy, provided the approach is collective, not bilateral.

Any prospect of a serious negotiation with China in the short term is hampered by the overwhelming attention being given to a major tariff war between the United States and China and the attendant fracas over the Huawei executive whom the United States wants extradited. The latest human rights concerns about China's authoritarian regime have risen to the surface and, especially in an election year, effectively nullified any aspirations for trade negotiation. It would be more prudent and pragmatic for Canada to seek to emulate as much as possible a position on trade with China that mirrors the terms of any deal concluded with the United States, using the USMCA clause directed at nonmarket economies like China to its advantage.

Although it may be easy to be mesmerized by the burgeoning growth of the Chinese economy and its rapid ascent into prominence in the high-tech fields of robotics, artificial intelligence, and 5G telecommunications, Martin Wolf of the *Financial Times* offers a refreshing reality check to counter all the optimistic forecasts.[55] Wolf contends that, in many ways, predictions that the Chinese economy will sustain rapid growth indefinitely are as flawed as those suggesting in the 1980s that Japan would soon become number one in the world – and for some of the same reasons. Essentially, as was the case in Japan, the policies of ultra-high investment and extensive debt accumulation that kept China growing after the 2008 financial crisis "make it vulnerable to a sharp deceleration."[56]

More fundamentally and perhaps wistfully, Wolf suggests that the benefits of centralized direction are exaggerated when compared to those of political and economic competition. Authoritarianism by its nature tends to become rigid and brittle, whereas the competitive forces in democracies are more likely to display flexibility and renewal. One can only hope.

For the past two decades, China has benefited from economic reforms introduced by former premier Zhu Rongji, but there have been no comparable recent reforms. Today, credit is still being preferentially allocated to state businesses, and state influence over large private enterprises is growing, not receding. "The triumph of despotism," in Wolf's view, "is still far from inevitable. Autocracies can fail, just as democracies can thrive" if they "learn from their mistakes and focus on renewing their politics and policies."[57]

In an age of growing populism, Wolf's analysis may have some Pollyanna elements, especially at a time when the weaknesses of democratic rule are more evident than the strengths. But the intrinsic power of competition – political and economic – may prevail and is one reason why Wolf sees brighter long-term prospects for India than for China.

A reboot of Canada's foreign policy priorities is definitely needed, one that moves away from virtue signalling for the domestic audience and adapts a pragmatic approach in order to reconcile and repair relations with China in a manner that serves Canada's tangible interests and respects its fundamental values regarding freedom and human rights. For the time being, the focus should be on repairing the serious political and economic rupture before more damage is done. It is time for a strategic rethinking of the bilateral relationship based on finding a balanced accommodation of mutual economic interests, without compromising fundamental differences on values or genuine security concerns. This is not a task for Canada alone but requires a more cohesive collective response from the Western democracies as they adjust to a world where, at least in economic terms, China is the other great power.

THE INDIAN ELEPHANT

Although most attention is concentrated on China's economic rise to superpower status, India's similarly prominent growth often plays under the radar. For Canada, whatever opportunity it commands, the prospects have been squandered. In February 2018 Prime Minister Trudeau embarked on an extensive eight-day visit to India intended once again to initiate a broadening of economic relations. The trip began with a slight: the prime minister was greeted by India's agriculture minister of state, Gajendra Singh Shekhawat, rather than by India's prime minister, Narendra Modi, who had personally greeted leaders in previous weeks from the United States, the United Arab Emirates, and Israel. Bizarrely, too, Canada's agriculture minister was not part of the Canadian delegation despite the fact that agriculture is one of Canada's major exports to India. Instead, four Sikh Canadian ministers were on the delegation, along with several members of Parliament of Indian heritage – a mix of Sikhs, Hindus, and Muslims. This created the impression that the visit had more to do with domestic Canadian politics than with bilateral relations.

Not long after the Canadian delegation arrived in New Delhi, events got worse. Inexplicably invited to a reception at the residence of High Commissioner Jaspal Atwal by the delegation was a Sikh extremist who had previously been convicted of attempting to assassinate an Indian minister. He had been added to the reception list by British Columbia's Liberal member of Parliament, Randeep Sarai, but no one seems to have vetted the list.

This episode served to reinforce concerns in India that Canada is "soft" on terrorism. Atwal had also been charged but acquitted in a 1985 assault case brought against him by Ujjal Dosanjh, who later became a federal Cabinet minister. After the ill-fated visit, Canada's national security advisor, Daniel Jean, was thrust forward to explain somewhat awkwardly to a parliamentary committee what had caused the invitation mishap. His explanation was more diplomatic than persuasive. Conservative leader Andrew Scheer denounced the faux pas as "dangerously irresponsible."[58]

To add to the embarrassment, and with a script attuned more to Bollywood than to government, Prime Minister Trudeau conspicuously wore various traditional Indian costumes throughout the trip. His attempts at local colour were denounced by some resident Indians as "fake and annoying."[59] As photos circulated around the world, the prime minister became a laughing stock globally as well as at home. (It was rumoured that his wife, Sophie Grégoire Trudeau, who has a flair for design, had played a key role in selecting the prime minister's wardrobe.)[60]

During the entire eight days, the prime minister had only one two-hour session with President Modi, giving rise to criticism that it was more a family holiday than a business trip. (The cost for the trip was $1.66 million.)[61] Not much of substance emerged on trade or anything else. Even the announcements of concluded commercial deals and investments were buried by the juicier photos of what the prime minister wore and by program glitches along the way.

Writing in the *Economic Times of India*, Canadian Candice Malcolm was notably harsh, saying that what went wrong was "narcissism paired with superficiality and poor judgment." She added pungently that the "prime minister's success to date can be traced more to his talents as a performance artist than to an understanding of statecraft, economics, or diplomacy."[62] While the team from Canada was hobnobbing with stars and starlets from Bollywood, business leaders from other countries were negotiating research and development partnerships on quantum computing in Bangalore.[63]

Not surprisingly, the Indian authorities seemed more interested in containing Sikh separatist activity in Canada than in promoting trade ties. Much of their concern is attributed to what they regard as unscrupulous ties between the Liberal Party of Canada and Khalistan (Sikh) separatists and extremists in Canada. Indian officials noted that Prime Minister Trudeau had attended a Khalsa (Sikh) parade in Toronto, given a speech, and been photographed standing in front of the Khalistan separatist flag. His predecessor, Stephen Harper, had studiously avoided this annual event while he was in office. Attempts to forge closer ties with India will inevitably be dwarfed in India by perceptions that Canada is indeed soft on the issue of Sikh separatism. This issue persists as a major obstacle to any aspirations for high-level engagement.

India will soon be the world's most populous nation, and it remains, warts and all, a vibrant democracy. As the World Bank recently recorded, India's accelerated growth began in 1991 at a rate of 5.4 per cent in the first twelve years, followed by four years of 8.8 per cent growth. After a brief downturn in 2008–09 due to the global financial crisis, the economy rebounded to about 7 per cent annually, faster than China's economy and with statistical supports less dubious than those provided by Beijing.

India is poised to become the world's third largest economy in 2032. Although Canada-India trade was a modest $9.8 billion in 2018, it represented an increase of $1 billion over the previous year and is 60 per cent higher than five years ago. Similarly, the total stock of investment was $4.5 billion in 2014 and is now estimated at over $30 billion.[64] As Joe Chidley writes, "If the Chinese miracle demonstrated the power of radical transformation and top-down economic engineering, India's miracle might end up being seen as a demonstration of the power of incremental change. There is not perfection, but progress."[65]

The major reforms initiated by Narendra Modi include a new inflation-targeting framework, the reform of energy subsidies, and measures to contain the financial deficit, to improve the business environment, and to strengthen a new insolvency and bankruptcy framework along with a federal sales tax. In what has been characterized as a move from "crony socialism to stigmatised capitalism," Modi has guided India to a limited market economy, one still encumbered by inflexible labour markets and trade liberalization. He is openly described as a "strongman with a ruthless streak."[66]

Essentially, Modi has cleaned up many of the messes he inherited. The problem of excessive bureaucratic oversight persists, and the problem of inefficient and politicized public-sector banking remains. Approaches to privatization, market liberalization, and competition have been more conservative than ambitious. Modi is also charting an aggressive, nationalist course in the country's longstanding dispute with Pakistan over Jammu and Kashmir, which brings its own attendant political risks.[67] Nonetheless, Martin Wolf believes that "we should be modestly optimistic about India's economic prospects over the next decade." An election could, of course, produce a chaotic coalition, but Wolf concludes, "Whatever happens ... India is an important country."[68]

Whether or how Modi's prescriptions will be sustained as India's democracy asserts itself is a good question, but it would be prudent to expect that India will be an even more compatible player for Canada in the decades ahead, one that should command more of a priority from Canadian exporters and investors. Attempts at deep diversification should give India pride of place but only if Canada can sublimate domestic political antics that run counter to the national interest.

If nothing else, Modi's dramatic victory in the May 2019 election should reinforce his ability to sustain economic reforms and should make India a more compelling partner for a strategic approach from Canada. It is even possible that a more constructive relationship with India may oblige China to adopt a more pragmatic tone with Canada as well. But the power of Modi's nationalist, populist appeal is the most important lesson of all to draw from the election, especially when combined with electoral verdicts in Australia and the European Union.

Given the resounding economic potential of Asia, as documented by Parag Khanna,[69] it is certain that any approach by Canada to diversify trade and investment should concentrate resources, energies, and time on the major democracies in the region and on other "friendly" countries, with India, Japan, Korea, Malaysia, and Singapore at the top of the list. The government has opened the door for Canada in Asia with the "mini TPP." It can also lead by orchestrating a deeper engagement with India. But, ultimately, it will be up to the private sector to break out of the North American cocoon and embrace the preferential market access available to Canada elsewhere.

5

Energy Development and Environmental Protection: The Elusive Search for "Balance"

The government of Justin Trudeau promised to balance the need for energy development with environmental protection. The effort proved futile. No pipelines to tidewater have been built even though the government purchased and then reapproved the Trans Mountain Pipeline while holding out the prospect for Indigenous investment. Major obstacles, including court challenges and protests, lie ahead. Canada is nowhere near meeting the goals of the Paris Accord. Energy and climate change policy are a bit like oil and water: they don't mix well. Successive governments have tried to shake the bottle in order to strike various kinds of "grand bargains" to build pipelines and appease environmental and Indigenous groups in the process. But no matter how hard the bottle is shaken, the two still separate, and national unity is compromised.

A national carbon tax became the cornerstone of Trudeau's climate change policy. In exchange for a carbon tax, the government agreed to support the construction of a pipeline to tidewater in order to promote Alberta's energy development. If there were early doubts that the grand bargain would work, the election of United Conservative Party leader Jason Kenney as Alberta's premier in 2019 struck its final death knell for reasons that are spelled out at greater length below. But as we argue in this chapter, there is no silver bullet to achieve carbon emission reductions aimed at mitigating climate change. There are political as well as practical obstacles, and efforts to forge a national consensus have not been helped by zealotry of theological proportions on both sides of the political divide.[1] Ultimately, a combination of different measures and solutions will be required.

Meanwhile, the need for Canada to develop its energy sector, which commands 10 per cent of its GDP, and to diversify its markets is more vital than ever.

ENERGY POLITICS: THEN AND NOW

In the 1950s and 1960s, the marketing of natural gas in Canada was a high-stakes political issue. In the words of Earle Gray, author of the *Great Canadian Oil Patch*, "Not since the founding of the Canadian Pacific Railway nearly a century before had Canada seen such a political maelstrom involving a private corporation as that which centred on the founding of TransCanada Pipelines Ltd. in the 1950s."[2] In order to get the pipeline built, TransCanada Pipelines asked the federal government to underwrite the costliest sections of the line through northern Ontario.

The federal government agreed to do so but only after securing the participation of the Ontario government in the venture and creating a Crown corporation to lay the northern Ontario portion of the pipeline. In Parliament, there was such a hue and cry about public funds being used to support a private venture that the Liberals were forced to invoke "closure" in order to stymie the opposition's attempts to filibuster the legislation. The political uproar, along with accusations that the government was using "Nazi" tactics to impose its will, helped to secure the defeat of the Liberals in the 1957 election. When it was finally completed in 1958, the pipeline was an engineering marvel, the longest in the world, and a striking symbol of national unity, to be rivalled only by the construction in the 1980s of a pipeline to bring natural gas from Siberia to western Europe. Following the recommendations of the Royal Commission on Energy, which was set up to examine problems in the regulation of oil and gas, the new Conservative government created a National Energy Board to regulate the energy sector and advise the government on energy-related matters.

Another major controversy erupted in the 1970s over a plan by TransCanada Pipelines and two US gas companies to build a pipeline that would carry natural gas from newly discovered oil and gas fields in the Prudhoe Bay area on the Alaska North Slope through the Canadian Arctic, southward through the Mackenzie Valley, across northern British Columbia, and then from Alberta into US midwestern markets. Adjoining oil and gas discoveries in Canada's Mackenzie Delta region made the pipeline even more attractive to investors.

At the outset, the Liberal government of Pierre Elliott Trudeau was enthusiastic about a northern gas pipeline, not only for commercial reasons but also because it viewed resource development in the North as a way for Canada to establish its sovereignty over its Arctic territories. However, it soon found itself in a ticklish political position due, in part, to its minority position in Parliament. New Democratic Party (NDP) leader David Lewis, whose party had held the political balance in Parliament since the 1972 election, charged that the plan to build a $5 billion natural gas pipeline down the "environmentally-fragile" Mackenzie Valley was "sheer madness" and strongly opposed the project.[3] The Conservatives also had doubts about the mammoth project. Opposition to the pipeline by the public and environmental groups also grew.

The government was in a tenuous position. In addition to agreeing to make public the recommendation of the National Energy Board to Cabinet on the plan before it would give the project a green light, the government also decided to hold public hearings on the pipeline to ensure that Indigenous and environmental rights would be protected. Supreme Court justice Thomas R. Berger was appointed head of the commission to conduct the hearings, a decision that was welcomed by the NDP and ultimately proved fatal to the project. After three years of community hearings, which comprised formal testimony by 317 experts and over 1,000 witnesses, the Berger Commission called for a ten-year moratorium on construction of a Mackenzie Valley pipeline.[4] Although this recommendation was not binding on the government, it was almost impossible for the government to reject it. The National Energy Board also rejected the Mackenzie Valley route on environmental grounds. The project was officially dead. Efforts to build a pipeline along an alternative route that would have followed the Alaska Highway also went nowhere. It was a cautionary tale on the fraught politics of pipelines.

In the early 1980s, energy politics, including energy pricing, taxation, and fiscal regimes, became a lightning rod for Western grievances and the growing alienation of Canada's Western provinces from Ottawa. The central planning aspirations of Ottawa proved disastrous for the energy sector and the economy as a whole, driving investment out of the country and exacerbating tensions with Canada's most important trading partner, the United States.

The Liberal government's 1980 National Energy Program (NEP), as it was then called, had several elements. Its centrepiece was a "blended" price for oil and natural gas, with a sharp increase in the federal proportion of oil and gas revenues. Consumers in eastern Canada, dependent on foreign oil, were also required to pay more as federal subsidies were eliminated. The most controversial element was the government's plan to Canadianize the oil industry through tax mechanisms that "rewarded" firms with a higher degree of Canadian ownership and through its creation of the federally owned Crown corporation Petro-Canada, which involved the acquisition and expropriation of foreign multinational companies operating in Canada. The NEP was greeted with howls of outrage in Alberta, Saskatchewan, and British Columbia. The Americans also strongly objected to the expropriation and foreign investment review provisions in the policy.[5] The NEP was so damaging and contentious that one of the first acts of Brian Mulroney's newly elected Progressive Conservative government was to abolish it in 1985.

Fast forward to the twenty-first century. Another storied energy policy and pipeline tale, complicated not just by local Indigenous and environmental politics but also by the national and global politics of climate change, has been equally bruising to national unity. Under the government of Stephen Harper, efforts to boost Canada's oil exports to the United States were stymied by the administration of President Barack Obama, which rendered a political decision to stop the Keystone Pipeline, a move that was applauded by American environmentalists. When Obama denied a permit for the project in 2015, the newly elected government of Justin Trudeau acknowledged the decision without comment, to the deep consternation of Western oil producers. The project was resuscitated by President Donald Trump days after his inauguration but continues to be thwarted by a variety of court challenges in the United States.

On 22 November 2015 the NDP premier of Alberta, Rachel Notley, announced a new climate and energy plan for her province. Her government would phase out coal-fired electricity generator plants over a fifteen-year period, cap carbon emissions from oil sands production, and impose a new carbon tax on Albertans. The announcement came just as Notley was about to attend newly elected prime minister Justin Trudeau's First Ministers' Meeting. It also came just before Trudeau and other Canadian leaders were to head to Paris to negotiate a new UN global agreement on climate change. As CBC News reported, Notley's climate and energy plan was "some of the most significant climate policy ever put forward by a government in Canada ... In doing so, she spared Trudeau from having to impose a solution on Alberta ... And what Notley put forward became a model for the federal backstop ... Trudeau leaned heavily on Notley's carbon levy and emissions cap to justify his government's decision to approve the Trans Mountain expansion."[6]

World leaders called the December 2015 Paris Conference "historic" and a "global U-turn."[7] When Prime Minister Trudeau addressed one of the early plenary meetings of the conference, he boasted that "Canada is back."[8] Canadian negotiators ensured the inclusion of human rights, Indigenous rights, and gender equality as well as a just transition for workers in the nonbinding preamble of a legally binding text. Environment and Climate Change Minister Catherine McKenna played an important facilitator role at the meeting and championed the goal of limiting temperature increases to 1.5 degrees Celsius. Under the pact that was reached in Paris, countries pledged to limit the rise in global temperatures to "well below" 2 degrees Celsius compared to preindustrial times, while striving to limit them to 1.5 degrees. Many saw the more ambitious target in the final text as one of Paris's more significant achievements. But as one seasoned observer of many climate conferences and meetings opined, Canada's leaders had fallen into a euphoria trap. "Paris," he said, "was a love and chowder society."[9]

On 22 April 2016 Prime Minister Justin Trudeau signed the Paris Agreement on climate change at a special ceremony at the United Nations in New York. "Today, with my signature, I give you our word that Canada's efforts will not cease," the prime minister said, adding that "[c]limate change will test our intelligence, our compassion and our will. But we are equal to that challenge."[10] In terms of concrete commitments, however, it was not clear that the government had really moved the dial on emission reductions. The government committed Canada to reducing its greenhouse gas emissions only by 30 per cent from 2005 levels by 2030, a goal set by the previous Conservative government as a floor, not a ceiling.

The government released the details of its Pan-Canadian Framework on Climate Change in March following consultations with the provinces, territories, and Indigenous peoples. The actual details of its carbon-pricing plan were subsequently laid out in its *Technical Paper on the Federal Carbon Pricing Backstop*.[11] The two key elements in the plan were a levy on fossil fuels and an output-based pricing system for industrial emitters. Under the plan, the federal government would return 90 per cent of the revenues it collects from its carbon tax to Canadians. As the *Financial Post* reported, rebates are to be determined when Canadians file taxes, either added to the refund payment or deducted from tax owing. The size of rebate is based on the number of persons in a household and whether or not they live in a metropolitan area. However, the size of the payments per household varies by province: it would be $248 in New Brunswick, $300 in Ontario, $336 in Manitoba, and $598 in Saskatchewan.[12]

While the government was laying the foundations of its carbon-pricing plan, it was also trying to thread the proverbial political needle on pipelines, thus rowing in two different directions at the same time. Although the Harper government had given its approval to Enbridge Inc. and its oil industry partners to proceed with construction of the Northern Gateway Pipelines project, which was to carry 525,000 barrels of bitumen from Bruderheim, Alberta, to Kitimat, British Columbia, the permit was revoked by the Federal Court of Appeal in June 2016 on the grounds that the government had failed to consult properly with First Nations about the project.[13] Trudeau had already promised that he would introduce legislation banning tanker traffic in the coastal waters of northern British Columbia, so it came as no big surprise when he permanently shelved the project in late November.

When Enbridge's proposal for the Northern Gateway Pipelines was rejected, Enbridge shifted its strategic vision south of the border with a US$28 billion purchase of Houston-based Spectra Energy Corp.

Canada's other major pipeline builder – TransCanada Pipelines – had been developing a proposal, Energy East, for a 4,500-kilometre pipeline "to carry 1.1 million barrels of crude oil per day from Alberta and Saskatchewan to refineries in Eastern Canada."[14] The proposal involved converting an existing natural gas pipeline to an oil transportation pipeline. It ran into stiff opposition in Quebec from environmentalists and the then mayor of Montreal, Denis

Coderre. Frustrated with a hostile political environment and an inconclusive regulatory process, TransCanada Pipelines abandoned its Energy East project after spending more than $1 billion on an inconclusive regulatory process.[15] Instead, it paid US$10.2 billion to acquire Columbia Pipeline Group – a leading network of natural gas pipelines in the United States.

Two days after terminating Northern Gateway Pipelines, Trudeau gave his government's approval to Kinder Morgan's Trans Mountain Pipeline expansion project and to Enbridge's proposed replacement of Line 3, a fifty-year pipeline from Alberta to the United States. Both plans involved expanding pipeline capacity along existing routes to allow for exports of more than 1.1 million additional barrels of oil per day, but as the projects' environmental critics complained, the consequence would be the production of anywhere between 23 million and 28 million tonnes of additional greenhouse gases annually.[16] As *Global News* reported, "Climate campaigners and indigenous groups immediately attacked the government's decision as a betrayal," and the Conservative's interim leader, Rona Ambrose, sagely observed that "the Liberals should have left Northern Gateway 'on the table' and must now actively promote the other approved lines ... I see very little prospect, politically speaking, that this pipeline will get built." The only politician who seemed happy about the decision other than Trudeau was Alberta's premier, Rachel Notley, who praised the prime minister for his "extraordinary leadership."[17]

However, Notley's unreserved enthusiasm for the prime minister would soon cool as pipeline construction stalled and the "grand bargain" on pipelines and climate change unravelled.

At the beginning of 2017, things were looking up for the start of construction of the Trans Mountain Pipeline after the Liberal BC government of Christy Clark announced that it had met the government's five conditions to secure coastal protection, First Nations participation, and economic benefits for all British Columbians. But with the July election defeat of her government by the NDP in a coalition with the Green Party, it was clear that trouble was brewing even though polls showed that a majority of British Columbians and Canadians supported construction.[18] With a minority government propped up by the Green Party, the new BC premier, John Horgan, stonewalled the approval process and launched a court challenge against the project. (The federal Green Party leader, Elizabeth May, also weighed in, saying that she was not opposed to the Trans Mountain Pipeline, just to its use to ship bitumen.)[19] With the project stalled yet again, Kinder Morgan announced on 8 April 2018 that it was halting construction and all "non-essential" spending on the project unless it could break the deadlock with the BC government. It gave Horgan a deadline of 31 May to make up his mind on the pipeline. This was no idle threat. Kinder Morgan and its investors were fed up with the constant delays to construction, and the federal government knew it. But everyone was surprised when Finance Minister Bill Morneau offered to indemnify Kinder Morgan against its losses and then, just two days before Kinder Morgan's deadline expired, made an offer to buy the pipeline outright for a generous sum of $4.5 billion and put the entire project under the control of a Crown corporation.[20] No economic rationale was provided for the amount the government paid, which Kinder Morgan cheerfully pocketed.

With exquisite timing, Kinder Morgan's shareholders voted to approve the federal buyout on 30 August, just as the Federal Court announced its decision against the pipeline's environmental approval, sending the National Energy Board back to the drafting table to conduct further consultations with the First Nations and a proper environmental assessment of the project's impact on the local killer whale population in Burrard Inlet, through which oil tankers would transit. The court ruled that consultations were not sufficient, hardly a legal verdict, but failed to say what would be. Kinder Morgan's investors had narrowly dodged a bullet. The same could not be said about the Trudeau government, which now had to defend itself for having squandered billions of taxpayer dollars on a project that was still a pipe dream.

After conducting more hearings and consulting with potentially affected parties, the National Energy Board recommended on 22 February 2019 that the federal government approve for a second time the long-stalled Trans Mountain Pipeline expansion. Noting that the project might have "significant adverse" impacts on the endangered killer whale population and local Indigenous communities, the 700-page report touted the project's compensating benefits for energy export diversification and economic growth.[21] Faced with a political hot potato in an election year, the government announced that it would conduct further consultations before making a final decision by June 2019 about whether to proceed with the pipeline. And if it was looking for political cover from the BC Court of Appeals, which reviewed proposed amendments to British Columbia's Environmental Management Act that would have granted the provincial government the authority to block the pipeline on putative environmental grounds, it did not get it. The court ruled that "the province's proposal to limit the amount of heavy oil flowing west to the ocean would be unconstitutional because only Ottawa has such oversight of the federally owned and regulated Trans Mountain pipeline."[22] It is unfortunate that Ottawa failed to assert legislatively its constitutional authority, which no less than a provincial court in British Columbia explicitly acknowledged. British Columbia said it would appeal the court's decision by taking it to the Supreme Court of Canada.

There were two other elements in the Trudeau government's environmental legislative strategy that bear mention because they will have an important impact on future pipeline projects and energy exports from Canada's West Coast. The first is Bill C-48, An Act Respecting the Regulation of Vessels That Transport Crude Oil or Persistent Oil to or from Ports or Marine Installations Located along British Columbia's North Coast,[23] which was tabled in the House of Commons in May 2017 to legislate a crude oil tanker moratorium on the North Coast of British Columbia and to set penalties for contravention of the moratorium. Since 1972 the federal government has had a nonlegally binding moratorium on crude oil tanker traffic through Dixon Entrance, Hecate Strait, and Queen Charlotte Sound.

It is worth noting that Bill C-48 would affect less than 15 per cent of the tanker traffic into Canada. The vast majority of tankers land on the East Coast and sail up the Saint Lawrence River to refineries in Montreal. Additionally, the bill would not restrict US tanker traffic through the Dixon Entrance and Hecate Strait. The sovereignty of both are matters of dispute between Canada and the United States.

The second important piece of legislation was Bill C-69, An Act to Enact the Impact Assessment Act and the Canadian Energy Regulator Act, to Amend the Navigation Protection Act and to Make Consequential Amendments to Other Acts.[24] The legislation would change the way major infrastructure projects are reviewed and approved, replacing the National Energy Board with a new Canadian

Energy Regulator and establishing new environmental review assessment processes to be carried out by a new federal Impact Assessment Agency. The bill was passed by the House of Commons on 20 June 2018 and subjected to more than 100 amendments in the Senate.

Both pieces of legislation were the butt of withering criticism. The *Financial Post*'s Diane Francis called Bill C-69 "a train wreck of politically correct nonsense ... [that] will impose onerous consultative and other burdens that will severely hobble all energy projects in future."[25] Groups like the Canada West Foundation were also highly critical of the bill for similar reasons.[26] A Fraser Institute study[27] criticized the basic premise of Bill C-48 with reference to international data showing that "even as more oil was transported by sea since 1970, spill frequency and volume declined precipitously. In fact, there has not been a significant spill in Canadian waters for more than 20 years."[28] The study also cited "a federal government analysis on marine oil spill preparedness, which estimated that a major spill of more than 10,000 tonnes was exceedingly rare and likely to occur once every 242 years. Similarly, a spill of 100 to 1,000 tonnes is expected to occur once every 69.2 years."[29] Perhaps more importantly, both pieces of legislation have generated serious fissures in the Canadian federation, almost a replay of the NEP controversy four decades earlier. As former Saskatchewan premier Brad Wall says, the statistics on support for potential independence or separatist movements in western Canada "should shock. They are an order of magnitude stronger than they were at the time of the NEP."[30] He cites Angus Reid polls conducted in February 2019 suggesting that "over 50 per cent of Albertans and Saskatchewanians ... strongly or somewhat supported their respective province 'joining a Western separatist movement.'"[31]

Alongside the government's new energy legislation came a slate of new climate change legislation. The government introduced new legislation for a carbon-pricing regime in its spring 2018 budget. Formally called the Greenhouse Gas Pollution Pricing Act,[32] the legislation received royal assent on 21 June 2018 as part of the Budget Act. It established the federal price on greenhouse gas (GHG) emissions, which would be applicable, as of January 2019, to any province or territory that requested it or that had not implemented its own carbon-pricing regime. When the bill was introduced, Quebec, Alberta, and British Columbia already had carbon taxes or cap-and-trade programs in place, so they were not covered by the legislation. Three other provinces were also in the process of introducing carbon-pricing mechanisms that met the federal government's criteria. Premier Brian Pallister's government in Manitoba briefly flirted with the idea of a carbon tax but then backtracked and said it would fight against the proposed plan in the courts. Saskatchewan and New Brunswick also opposed the plan.

The election of Doug Ford's Conservative government in Ontario in June 2018 redrew the battle lines on carbon taxes. Ford, who had opposed the cap-and-trade plan of the Liberal government during the provincial election campaign – a plan that forced large companies to buy allowances for their carbon emissions – moved quickly to revoke it soon after taking office. In Alberta, Premier Rachel Notley, who was heading toward an election, was also growing increasingly frustrated with the Trudeau government over the delayed Trans Mountain Pipeline. Unlike her electoral opponent Jason Kenney, who said he would immediately repeal the province's carbon tax if elected, she stood firm but called on the federal government both to overturn the tanker ban – she called it a "stampede of the stupid" and hurtful to "national unity"[33] – and to review Bill C-69. "They need to fix Bill C-69," she complained, "because in its current form, there is too much uncertainty and we're never going to be able to get these kinds of projects moving."[34]

As one headline shouted, Trudeau's "'grand bargain' on energy died" with Jason Kenney's United Conservative Party win in Alberta on 16 April 2019.[35] The federal government had already slapped a carbon tax on four provinces that had decided to defy Ottawa's climate change policy: Ontario, Manitoba, Saskatchewan, and New Brunswick. (Under the new tax, "[c]arbon pollution will initially cost $20 a tonne, rising by $10 a year until it reaches $50 in 2022.")[36] Now there was a fifth renegade province to tax as well. In addition to tabling legislation to scrap Alberta's carbon tax and roll back its climate change programs, Alberta's new premier announced that his government would launch a third constitutional challenge against the federal carbon tax, alongside Saskatchewan and Manitoba.[37] Quebec has since joined the attack essentially to protect provincial jurisdiction.

ASSESSMENT

The government's noble attempt to strike a balance between the economic need to develop Canada's abundant energy resources and the environmental need to meet the Paris Accord goals on climate change had clearly failed. Its "price on pollution," or carbon tax, had encountered stiff headwinds – some would say more of a hurricane – from five of the ten provinces. As the 2019 federal election approached, it had also not put one shovel into the ground to build a pipeline to tidewater, as the prime minister had earlier promised.

Even if implemented as planned, the federal government's carbon plan would not enable Canada to meet its Paris Accord obligations. But Canada is not alone. As of January 2019, not one of the G20 signatories was in compliance. In fact, every nation, except for Morocco and Gambia, is falling short of its Paris commitments.[38] Major polluters like China and India are nowhere near their targets and show little inclination to make the economic sacrifice adherence would compel. Under Donald Trump, the United States has walked away altogether, claiming the agreement imposed an unfair burden on the United States.

Trudeau and his team were clearly enamored with Nobel Laureate William Nordhaus's idea of a carbon tax. It was Nordhaus who in the 1990s developed the Dynamic Integrated Model of Climate Change and the Economy, which showed that if the governments of the world could implement a carbon tax to deal with the negative externalities of greenhouse gas emissions from human activity, emissions could actually be reduced. To achieve the target in the most recent UN report of the Intergovernmental Panel on Climate Change, which calls for limiting global warming to 1.5 degrees Celsius, Nordhaus's most recent model sets a carbon tax of $5,500 per tonne, which works out to a gasoline tax of $48 per gallon, a target that would be virtually impossible to achieve on political grounds alone.[39]

The Paris commitments were more modest than those contained in the panel's report. According to the Baker-Shultz Carbon Dividends Plan, the US could meet or exceed its Paris carbon reduction commitments with a carbon tax rate of $40 per tonne, which would increase annually based on a standard escalator rate plus inflation as measured by the Consumer Price Index. The plan's model showed that

US emissions could reasonably be around 32 per cent below 2005 levels by 2025. However, to mitigate the obvious political challenges associated with the plan, all of the revenues from the carbon tax would be returned to Americans as a dividend, and all other carbon regulations, including those affecting the energy sector, would be eliminated. There would also be border carbon adjustments to level the playing field with US trading partners.[40]

Investors in Asia no longer see Canadian energy as attractive. Canada has gone from being a "low-risk, high-reward" place for energy investment to the reverse – "high-risk, low-reward" – diminishing the potential of a sector that, for decades, had been a major growth engine for Canada, especially western Canada. The exodus is not confined to pipeline companies. The fire sale at $2.8 billion of Devon Energy Corp – an asset estimated to be worth $5 billion to $6 billion – to Canadian Natural Resources is a telling example of the foreign exodus from Alberta's tailspin. Encana's $7.7 billion purchase of Newfield Exploratory followed in the wake of similar strategic acquisitions in the Permian and Eagle Ford fields in the United States in recent years. Enerplus has made significant investments in the Bakken Formation, the Marcellus Formation, and the Denver Basin. Crescent Point is spending more on its Uinta and Bakken properties than in Canada. Baytex is doing the same in the Eagle Ford field in Texas. Even energy service companies like Precision Drilling and Akita Drilling are following the trend with increasingly more activity in the United States than in Canada. That is not surprising. Fourteen applications for new pipelines were submitted to US regulators for approval in the period 2017–19. Only one was submitted in Canada. The C.D. Howe Institute estimates that Canada lost $100 billion in potential oil and gas investment in the same period.[41] Royal Bank of Canada president David McKay has repeatedly warned that "Canada is at risk of squandering its energy advantage if it does not come together to tap the potential of its energy sector." New energy investments could add an additional 1 per cent of GDP, which is the equivalent of putting a new auto sector in place in Canada. It would also generate $200 billion in additional tax revenue over a ten-year period.[42]

What this strategic shift underscores is that, on energy, Canada has become a less competitive place to invest and do business. The problem is compounded by the high degree of economic interdependence between the Canadian and US economies. If Canada imposes higher carbon penalties than the United States, that trend will simply intensify. Carbon taxes and other costs related to climate change cannot be passed on to American purchasers. They come out of the bottom line of Canadian producers, making them less productive and less competitive. Alberta's economy is in a serious tailspin, with no ready avenue of redress because oil exports go only to the United States and trade at a substantial discount to the world price. Any diversification of oil exports will be stymied unless there is a policy framework and infrastructure that enable production and shipments to tidewater. Without pipelines to Canada's West and/or East Coasts, any notion of trade diversification beyond the US market will be illusory. Furthermore, rail transport of oil, which is both more costly and more dangerous, has doubled.

CARBON TAXES: A POLITICAL THIRD RAIL?

All agree that the climate is changing, that greenhouse gas emissions are accelerating, and that humans are primarily responsible. Differences do exist on the validity of eighty-year models, on predictions about the consequences, on the most effective and politically palatable way to reduce carbon emissions, and on the relative balance of commitments by major polluters. Smog levels in Beijing, Los Angeles, and New Delhi are harbingers of why action is needed. There are concerns as well about rising sea levels and extreme climatic events.

Carbon taxes, as many economists argue, may be the fairest way to spread the cost of adjustment and reduce emissions, but economic theory does not always jibe with political and economic reality, even though, as Andrew Coyne writes, "we're agreed we have to do something."[43] In British Columbia, for example, where carbon taxes have been in effect since 2007, carbon emissions increased by 5 per cent between 2015 and 2017, although in 2017 they were estimated to be at 2007 levels. As Dave Sawyer and Seton Stiebert point out, "high levels of economic growth have meant the carbon tax has had to work hard to keep GHGs in check," although they are at pains to point out, based on their modelling, that "[w]ithout the carbon tax, BC GHGs would be much higher today."[44] The other challenge, of course, is to ensure that such taxes remain revenue-neutral over time. As Charles Lammam and Taylor Jackson discovered, British Columbia's carbon tax, which when it was introduced was offset by reductions in other provincial taxes – including personal income taxes, corporate taxes, small business taxes, and the introduction of a low-income climate action refundable tax credit – is no longer revenue neutral. They calculate that "[i]f the available historical data are combined with the government's projections to 2018/19, then from 2013/14 to 2018/19, the carbon tax is projected to result in a cumulative $865 million net tax increase for British Columbians." If that tax were distributed equally among British Columbians, each "would pay $182 more per person, or $728 for a family of four."[45]

A similar story is playing out in Nunavut. The territorial government announced that it would plan to subsidize only half of the costs of its carbon tax, referred to as the "Nunavut carbon rebate." That means consumers would get only half of the money being returned to the territorial government by Ottawa. "We want to encourage Nunavummiut to do what they can to reduce their emissions. So we're not rebating the full amount," says Nunavut finance minister George Hickes. What is not returned to the people will be used "to fund other important initiatives."[46]

Philip Cross suggests that there are historical legacy obstacles to carbon taxes as well: "The enmity of Europeans to direct taxes has its historical roots in authoritarian rulers who used such taxes to fund unpopular wars. Given this background, it was easier for governments in Europe to sell consumption taxes to the public, although persistently weak incomes appear to be undermining support for a carbon tax to judge by France's recent 'gilets jaunes' protests." In the United States, "There is no national sales or value-added tax ... reflecting a hostility to indirect taxes that dates back to the Boston Tea Party and the American Revolution. In Canada, the GST [federal government sales tax] has always been unpopular. The Harper government was elected in 2006 on the promise of reducing the GST, and polls show most Canadians would follow British Columbia's 2011 referendum in voting against it if given the chance."[47] And, as Canada's own "yellow vest" protests demonstrate, a tax on all is patently unfair to some, notably those at the lower end of the income scale who depend on fuel for their livelihood.

There is also little evidence to suggest that the pain of a limited carbon tax would be severe enough to influence consumer behaviour, especially given the apparent inelasticity of gasoline demand.[48] Sport utility vehicles and trucks are still the most purchased vehicles annually in Canada and the United States, accounting for almost 70 per cent of vehicles sold in the United States in 2018.[49] If the taxes were raised in Canada to the level many consider essential to effect change – $300 per tonne or more – there could be a revolt that would make the "yellow vest" protests look like a picnic. When government's tinker with tax policy ostensibly to serve the "greater good," they rapidly learn that the tolerance of taxpayers has limits. The parliamentary budget officer estimates that a carbon tax of $102 per tonne would be needed for Canada to meet its Paris reduction goals. That is a tall order and not one that the Trudeau government was willing to accept in an election year. It remains committed to carbon tax policies that still fall well short of its Paris goals. The government is clearly as conflicted on this issue as are Canadians. A CBC News poll found that, "while nearly two-thirds of Canadians see fighting climate change as a top priority, half of those surveyed would not shell out more than $100 per year in taxes to prevent climate change, the equivalent of less than $9 a month."[50]

There is also a limit to taxes on corporations. As William Watson observes in the *Financial Post*, "You can try to take all carbon or corporate income taxes out of corporate profit alone, but if the rate of return in the industry falls below what's available elsewhere, capital will go elsewhere: to another industry, or another country, or both." The problem, he adds, is figuring out "how to bind governments to modest ambitions and revenue neutrality."[51] As was demonstrated by Canada and other countries on the Kyoto Accord – the predecessor to Paris – the "best combination for any individual country is global action combined with local inaction."[52] Posture over purpose is repeating itself again on the Paris Accord.

Interestingly, when CBC News asked Navius Research, a climate-modelling company, to project how close Canada could get to its Paris commitment if certain policies were ramped up, it concluded that even with a combination of the three most commonly discussed approaches – increasing the carbon tax, mandating sales of electric vehicles, and greening the electrical grid – Canada would still fall short of its 2030 Paris commitment. Navius Research's analysis suggests that "Canada needs a multi-pronged approach that addresses emissions in a wide range of sectors, beyond what people might normally consider."[53]

A SUPPLE CLIMATE STRATEGY

Mark Jaccard, one of Canada's leading climate change economists and modellers, likely has it right when he argues that a combination of flexible regulations and other mechanisms, including technological innovation, is ultimately what is required to reduce the bulk of carbon emissions because there is no silver bullet or magic formula in policy terms to address the problem. These methods, says Jaccard, can "get the whole job done – and need not cost much more than a pricing mechanism, if they're flexible enough ... to 'allow companies and individuals to determine their cheapest way to decarbonize.'" As an example, "a government can phase out coal plants, then let market competition determine the most cost-effective mix of low-emission replacements. Or phase out gasoline engines, then leave it to manufacturers and consumers to decide the resulting balance between electric, biofuel, and hydrogen vehicles."[54] It should also be recognized that "the oilpatch is by far the largest spender on clean tech in Canada, to the tune of $1.4 billion a year."[55] We know that "many oilsands plants are already emitting at or below the average [carbon] intensity for oil pumped in the United States."[56]

The policy challenge is also one globally of getting policies properly calibrated in two key sectors – power generation and transportation – that are among the main drivers of GHG emissions. Decarbonizing power generation presents one set of specific challenges, whereas electrifying the transportation sector occasions another.[57]

An instructive example is North Carolina, which successfully diversified its power mix while keeping electricity costs competitive and below the US national average (in contrast to Ontario, which has achieved neither). Traditionally reliant on coal for most of its electricity generation, North Carolina saw its natural gas electric generation surpass coal in 2016, with a growing contribution of renewable energy sources to the power generation mix, including solar (second only to California) and wind power generation. This change was achieved by legislating clean energy approaches to diversify the sources of power generation. North Carolina also realized that "renewable generation, such as from wind and solar, is not considered 'dispatchable' [i.e., the problem is the intermittent nature of electricity supply by wind and solar and the lack of available storage capacity] by utility planners, [as] it must be off-set with traditional generation sources and more continuous renewable resources." Investment in energy infrastructure, including "[g]rid modernization, reliable demand-side management programs, [and] voltage controls," has also been key to managing fluctuations in "the output from non-dispatchable energy sources."[58]

Globally, wind and solar currently contribute just 2 per cent of energy supply despite the billions of dollars invested in this technology. According to Mark P. Mills, a physicist at the Manhattan Institute, "a US$1 million investment in shale gas wells delivers fuel for six times the electricity produced of the same investment for wind or solar. To provide the same amount of electricity, the grid will need to be built far larger in countries, costing trillions of dollars." With regard to electric storage, Mills maintains that "the size of the necessary battery facilities required for large-scale renewable power will be immense and yet will still be unable to provide sufficient electricity to replace current demand." His point is that there will still be demand for fossil fuels even with the growing movement to electrify the transportation sector.[59]

North America's power-related carbon emissions have dropped as natural gas has displaced coal-powered plants, whereas emissions in Europe remain high because the growth of renewable energy was offset by Germany's closure of nuclear plants and its shift to more reliance on coal. That may have been a short-sighted decision because, as Bret Stephens of the *New York Times* suggests, something that might work on a scale and timeframe likely to make a difference for the climate is nuclear technology. But that "something" may also not have to be dependent on the nuclear technology we have now. The next generation of small-sized, molten salt (not uranium-based) reactors could offer the environmental and the energy advantages of nuclear power without the potential degrading disadvantages.[60] Beyond nuclear technology, Stephens suggests that "placing medium-sized bets on potentially transformative technologies not funded by regressive taxes or industrial subsidies" would be a better approach. In short, "let markets, not governments, figure out which ones work."[61] (The example of Rio Tinto and Alcoa discussed below falls precisely in this domain.)

Green energy also has a bigger role to play if governments can get the policy mix right and spur further innovation. Bjørn Lomborg's Copenhagen Consensus Center's analysis contends that a green energy research and development budget of around US$100 billion per year would be the most effective policy to combat global warming. The analysis suggests that resolving the technology deficit of switching from fossil fuels would be more effective than tax or cap and trade schemes. Lomborg and his fellow economists recommend pouring money into researching and developing clean energy sources like wind, wave, solar, and nuclear power, as well as more work on climate engineering, such as "cloud whitening" to reflect the sun's heat back into the outer atmosphere.[62]

Carbon capture is another promising innovation if it can be brought to scale. There are currently forty-three major carbon-capture projects operational or under development worldwide. In the United States nearly 160 million tonnes of carbon dioxide have been captured and stored. Most of the captured carbon goes into enhanced oil recovery (using carbon to extract more oil from a producing well). But it is a technology that can be used to capture carbon from the power sector to a much greater degree than is done now, especially since companies get a tax credit for carbon capture. The International Energy Agency projects that carbon-capture incentives of $40 per tonne could support storage of 450 million tonnes of carbon dioxide per year.[63] As Jan Christoph Minx and Gregory Nemet argue, "Meeting the climate goals of the Paris agreement is going to be nearly impossible ... Simply reducing emissions from their current level is unlikely to be enough to limit global warming to well below 2 degrees Celsius. In fact, we need to remove huge amounts of carbon dioxide – billions of tons per year – to meet these goals because we have repeatedly delayed our decarbonization efforts."[64]

Innovations in industrial processes will be critical. A good example from the corporate sector is Rio Tinto and Alcoa, which recently developed a technology for aluminum production – a high consumer of energy – with zero carbon emissions.[65] The Government of Canada, Government of Quebec, and Apple have invested in this innovation, with Apple alone providing $13 million to help facilitate the collaboration between Rio Tinto and Alcoa on the carbon-free smelting process and to provide technical support to the joint venture partners. We should also not forget about innovations in the energy sector to reduce GHGs. Mac Van Wielingen, for example, observes that "most people are surprised to learn that our oil sands emissions account for only 0.15 per cent of global emissions" and that "the industry has been focused on reducing its GHG output; emissions per barrel have decreased by 29 per cent between 2000 and 2016, and a report by research firm IHS Markit expects that will fall by another 16 per cent to 23 per cent by 2030."[66] The Dutch oil company Shell, which supplies about 3 per cent of the world's energy needs, is formally committed to reducing the carbon intensity of its energy products: "[I]n 2019, [it] set an unconditional three-year target to reduce [its] Net Carbon Footprint by 2% to 3% compared to 2016. This target setting will then be done annually, with each year's target covering either a three or five-year period. [Shell's] executives' pay is now linked, in part, to this target."[67]

Mark Carney, governor of the Bank of England, François Villeroy de Galhau, governor of Banque de France, and Frank Elderson, chair of the Network for Greening the Financial Services, have called on central banks and the financial sector to help smooth the transition to a low-carbon economy by (1) integrating the monitoring of climate-related risks into day-to-day supervisory work, financial stability monitoring, and board risk management, (2) leading by example by integrating sustainability into their regular business and risk-management frameworks, (3) bridging data gaps on climate risks, and (4) building capacity to assess climate-related financial risks.[68] The world's largest asset manager, BlackRock Investment Institute, has also urged investors not to ignore climate change and to "protect their portfolios as extreme weather events become more common and governments step up their efforts to fight climate change." According to BlackRock, investors "should incorporate measures of fossil fuel usage, water consumption and carbon emissions as a percentage of annual sales into their assessment when they decide which companies to invest in."[69] As the Global Commission on the Economy and Climate also stresses, investment in sustainable infrastructure must also be "supported by clear national and sub-national strategies and programmes. This is a central driver of the new growth approach. It requires integrating climate action and sustainability at the heart of growth strategies, investment plans, and institutional structures to facilitate the flow of public and private finance."[70]

As Edward Waitzer reports in *Corporate Knights*, following the recommendations of the Task Force on Climate-Related Financial Disclosures, "a group of three large Canadian pension plans called for enhanced climate disclosures from Canadian companies. The $270 billion Caisse de dépôt et placement du Québec has gone further, pledging to increase its climate solutions investments by 50 per cent and reduce its listed company carbon intensity by 25 per cent."[71]

Financial markets can clearly play a role in addressing climate risks by translating energy investments into financial costs and opportunities, but they can do so only if investors treat all energy producers equally; otherwise, investment and production will simply shift from one jurisdiction to another, and environmentally responsible producers, such as Canada, will be unduly penalized. The selective hypocrisy of some investors and financial institutions is problematic, to say the least. After announcing that it would no longer invest in Canada's oil sands or Arctic drilling, for example, Europe's largest bank, the Hongkong and Shanghai Banking Corporation (HSBC), whose global assets total more than US$2 trillion, announced along with BlackRock that it was establishing a dedicated Saudi Arabia investment fund seven weeks after the killing of journalist Jamal Khashoggi. HSBC was one of the companies involved in a bond sale totalling US$100 billion by Saudi Aramco, the state-backed oil producer. HSBC also defended its decision to continue to invest in the building of coal-fired electricity generation plants in Bangladesh, Indonesia, and Vietnam on the grounds that it needed to "appropriately balance local humanitarian needs with the need to transition to a low carbon economy."[72]

In terms of cost, a low-carbon future also does not have to cost the earth according to a major study by Citigroup. Calculating the cost of action versus inaction, the study finds that an "action" scenario "results in an undiscounted saving of $1.8 trillion" and that spending "more on renewables and energy efficiency" results in "savings in fuel costs in later years [that] offset earlier investment." This approach is vastly preferable to the "inaction" scenario, where "the potential liabilities of not acting are equally vast. The cumulative 'lost' GDP from the impacts of climate change could be significant, with a central case of 0.7%–2.5% of GDP to 2060, equating to $44 trillion on an undiscounted basis."[73]

THE CHALLENGE OF GETTING OTHERS ON BOARD

Even if Canada and like-minded countries adopt a diversified policy approach to mitigate the risks of climate change, there are formidable obstacles to getting major emerging market economies to do the same. Although China is making major investments in renewables, like solar energy, it is also boosting its reliance on coal by 25 per cent through the construction of hundreds of new coal plants. It is already the world's largest importer of coal, and its carbon emissions rose by almost 5 per cent in 2018. China's Belt and Road Initiative poses another existential frontier. It is funding infrastructure projects in over seventy countries from Central Asia to Latin America that could potentially account for over half of all new carbon emissions in the next few decades according to the World Economic Forum.[74] One of the reasons is that China has become the lender of last resort for energy infrastructure projects in countries that neither the World Bank nor other international institutions will fund because of their carbon footprint. China, for example, has earmarked more than US$20 billion for coal plants worldwide.[75] And China is not the only culprit, as Japan and North Korea are making similar investments in emerging economies, especially in Asia. As Gwyn Morgan notes, "South Africa, India, the Philippines, South Korea, Japan and China, all signatories to the Paris climate accord, are building a combined 1,800 new coal-fired power plants. Coal plants emit twice as much CO_2 as natural gas plants."[76]

Japan also has plans to add 36 coal stations to its existing 100 as it seeks to reduce its reliance on nuclear power after the Fukushima nuclear disaster. Its 2018 energy plan called for coal to provide 26 per cent of its electricity needs.[77] Faced with stinging international criticism, the Japanese government backtracked, indicating "that in principle it will not sanction construction of new large coal-fired power plants," but "about 30 projects remain, including facilities that will not be scrutinized for their impact on the environment."[78] Australia plans to end "its renewables subsidy program altogether by 2020, giving its abundant coal resources a major lift."[79]

One of the arguments for promoting Canada's natural gas and oil exports to China is that it may actually help to reduce its carbon footprint by reducing its dependence on coal. As argued by chemist Blair King and Wenran Jiang, president of the Canada-China Energy and Environment Forum, "the single biggest climate change challenge is China's heavy reliance on coal for power generation and transportation fuels. Replacing it with LNG [liquefied natural gas] and Canadian oil could result in substantial GHG reductions." It is important to bear in mind, as they note, that "China accounts for 28% of the world's GHG emissions, and a significant amount of that comes from coal. China accounts for half of all the coal used in the world. About 66% of China's power generation comes from burning coal. But coal is also used in China to produce gasoline and other fuels."[80] Groups like the Pembina Institute challenge this assertion on the grounds that Canadian exports will displace the development of clean and renewable sources of energy in China, but they do not dispute the GHG emission reduction gains to be achieved by substituting natural gas and oil for coal.[81]

A C.D. Howe Institute study comes to the same conclusion while stating its preference for a more rapid transition to renewables.[82] However, it fails to note that converting coal-fired plants to natural gas is a much simpler transitional step for an energy-hungry supergiant like China or other key Asian markets like India, Japan, and Taiwan. (And with wind and solar, the nondispatchable power problem still requires flexibility in power supply.) It is also a step that provinces like Alberta and states like North Carolina are successfully undertaking. As is the case with many debates about climate-mitigation strategies, the best solution should not be allowed to stand in the way of the good and what is feasible in the medium term.

A RESPONSIBLE AND REALISTIC POLICY ON CLIMATE CHANGE AND ENERGY DEVELOPMENT

Holding firm to aspirational Paris targets may give Canada the moral high ground on this issue and allow its politicians to dance in the Elysian Fields, but by moving in the opposite direction of the United States on environmental policy, Canada undercut a basic element of its competitiveness. Besides, if and when Canadians realize that the real price of compliance will be a tax of $300 per tonne or more, that moral high ground could become a dangerous perch. What Conrad Black has dubbed "this Frankenstein monster of economic stultification"[83] was rarely mentioned in the 2016 US election campaign and unravelled further when no clear consensus emerged from the 24th Climate Change Conference in Poland in December 2018. Jack Mintz also maintains, "It would make sense for Canada to have a carbon policy consistent with its major trading partners, most obviously the United States ... If Canada decides to go it alone in stopping oil and gas developments," which is "the direction we appear headed in now," then "resource provinces will get badly hurt – and so will Canada as a whole. We need a resource policy that allows for responsible development, just like [some] other countries have."[84]

Signals of alarm about the dire, long-range negative impact on climate change are unrelenting, but the political will is waning, and it is evident that some recalibration or rebalancing is in order. As Bret Stephens observes in the *New York Times*, "To have a diagnosis is not to have a cure, and bad cures can be worse than the disease. Those who think otherwise are in denial."[85] But the main problem is that without re-engagement by the United States on climate change and real, as opposed to aspirational, commitments by other major polluters like China and India, no cure will have much effect.

The ragged consensus emerging from the most recent climate conference in Katowice, Poland,[86] suggests, too, that a degree of political fatigue may be settling in on the climate debate. Without confident US leadership and concrete steps by major polluters like China and India, commitments to the Paris targets will continue to slide. It may well be a time for a reality check, for more diplomacy than zealotry on the topic, and for some recalibration of the best consensus for success.

It would be prudent for Canada to adopt as one of its primary goals a concerted effort to secure US re-engagement in the global climate initiative. To this end, Canada must show that it shares the United States' legitimate concerns about the unfair demands of the existing Paris Accord and must demand more precise commitments from major polluters, coupled with initiatives toward a plan of action that both North American countries could endorse without giving a competitive edge to either. This was precisely the approach that brought mutual benefit to the protracted debate about eliminating acid rain.[87] Such historical successes are worth repeating.

On energy, the government also needs to break the policy paralysis by acting legislatively in the national interest to assert its constitutional prerogative for interprovincial pipeline construction, to provide regulatory incentives for private-sector investment, and to reduce the scope for blocking techniques, if not outright vetoes, stemming from the courts, the provinces, and some Indigenous groups. Without energy innovation and development, Canada's governments will not have the financial ability to sustain health, education, and other social programs that are integral to the well-being of Canadians. Similarly, unless the federal government articulates a more positive path for responsible energy development, it will damage not only Canada's economic prospects but also the sinews that bind the country's regional differences. National unity is also the prerogative of the federal government, but the muddled policies on environment and energy have created serious fissures, most notably in western Canada, as evidenced dramatically in the 2019 federal election. Canada needs to establish a better balance on its shared continent in responding to the twin necessities of energy development and climate change mitigation. It is ultimately a question of leadership. By trying to walk in the middle of the road and dodge heavy traffic coming from opposite directions, the Trudeau government has exposed itself to being hit from both sides.

6

Democratic Alliances versus Authoritarians: Russia's and NATO's Future

At the height of the Cold War in the 1950s and early 1960s, policymakers and many Western intellectuals believed that the Soviet Union and its Communist allies, China included, would eventually succumb to the forces of liberalization and democracy as their economies and societies evolved and through the socializing effect of their membership in international institutions. It was called the theory of convergence, and it shaped the policies of many Western countries, including Canada, toward the Soviet Union and the post-Soviet successor states, Russia included, after the Cold War ended.[1]

In Western thinking, the theory of convergence was also central to the belief about the socializing role of liberal international institutions and the importance of the principle of universal membership. It was widely supposed that the admission of nondemocratic states to international institutions, including the Bretton Woods institutions, would have a moderating effect and encourage political liberalization in those states, which would otherwise be free riders, renegades, or revolutionaries intent on upsetting the international order.[2]

In supporting the principle of universal membership in the United Nations when that organization was founded, in actively promoting the Conference on Security and Cooperation in Europe and its successor body, the Organization for Security and Co-operation in Europe (OSCE), and in later promoting Russian membership in the G7 at the 1995 G7 Summit in Halifax and its admission to the World Trade Organization, Canada was an active proponent of the liberal internationalist ethos.[3] Promoting cooperation with the Soviet Union and then Russia, including in the Arctic, became a cornerstone of

Canadian policy, although cooperation in the North was infused by a pragmatic understanding that the world's two biggest Arctic states in geographical terms also had many shared interests.[4]

When he was the Speaker of Canada's Senate, Noel Kinsella observed in a speech to the Diplomatic Academy of the Ministry of Foreign Affairs of the Russian Federation on 7 November 2007 that cooperation between the two countries dates back to the Second World War, when the "Under Secretary of State for External Affairs [Norman A. Robertson] in 1942 tasked the newly-appointed Canadian Minister Dana Wilgress with obtaining as much information as possible on Soviet international civil aviation and development of the Far North." In fact, Canadian officials were so determined to reach out to the Soviets that they "endured a gruelling eight week trip – through Brazil, Ghana, Egypt and Iran – to reach Kuibyshev, today's Samara, the temporary wartime location of the Soviet Foreign Ministry." Formal bilateral relations between the two countries were established shortly afterward.[5]

Despite the ups and downs of the Cold War, efforts to forge better relations between the two countries continued: "In 1955, at former Soviet Foreign Minister Molotov's invitation, Lester Pearson became the first NATO Foreign Minister to visit the Soviet Union. Canada was the first NATO country to break a boycott imposed at the time of the Czechoslovak crisis [1968] by inviting then Foreign Minister Gromyko to Canada. Two years later [in May 1971], former Prime Minister Trudeau made a trip through the Soviet Union, promoting [the two countries'] ties as northern neighbours by visiting Norilsk, Murmansk and Leningrad."[6] Pierre Elliott Trudeau took the occasion to remind his Soviet hosts that Canada had reduced its troop levels in Europe by 50 per cent and, when signing a new protocol to promote closer ties with the Soviets, remarked that Canada was keen to diversify its relations because the United States posed a direct threat to Canada's national identity "from a cultural, economic and perhaps military point of view." Trudeau also openly expressed his admiration for the Soviets when he visited the Siberian city of Norilsk, which, he noted, had no Canadian counterpart. When General Wojciech Jaruzelski and the Military Council of National Salvation declared martial law in Poland in March 1981 to quash the overthrow of Communist rule, Trudeau raised more than a few eyebrows when he expressed his support for the Soviet-backed regime, stating that "if martial law is a way to avoid civil conflict, then I can say it is not all bad."[7] (Trudeau had previously invoked martial law and suspended civil liberties during the 1970 October Crisis, occasioned by the terrorist activities of the Front de libération du Québec.)

Trudeau's successors were much more cautious and guarded about the Soviets but nevertheless sought to promote closer ties, especially when the reformer Mikhail Gorbachev came to power and the Soviet Union began to disassemble. Following his own trip to Russia in 1989 to promote closer relations, which culminated in the Treaty on Concord and Cooperation of 19 June 1992 as well as number of major agreements on trade, economic cooperation, the mutual protection of investments, and sectoral cooperation in the North, Conservative leader Brian Mulroney became a champion of greater Western support for Soviet leader Mikhail Gorbachev's *glasnost* (economic openness) and *perestroika* (political restructuring) reforms, especially when they began to flounder. At the 1991 G7 Summit in London, Mulroney was one of the few Western leaders to engage Gorbachev and support his pleas for greater Western assistance. Mulroney also played a key role in arranging for the first meeting between newly elected president Bill Clinton and Russian leader Boris Yeltsin, who succeeded Gorbachev in 1993.

The strong foundation laid by Mulroney with Russia's new leaders would continue under his Liberal successor, Jean Chrétien. One of the notable achievements of the Chrétien era was the Global Partnership Program Against the Spread of Nuclear Weapons and Materials of Mass Destruction, launched at the 2002 G8 Summit in Kananaskis,[8] Alberta, as well as the continued development of Canada-Russia northern and economic relations.

Early in the tenure of Prime Minister Stephen Harper's government, relations were cool but cordial. Chairman of the Government of the Russian Federation Victor Zubkov paid a working visit to Canada in November 2007, during which he met with Governor General Michaëlle Jean and the Canadian prime minister. There were also regular contacts at the ministerial level between the Harper government and the Russians, notwithstanding the fact that Harper himself was no fan of Russian leader Vladimir Putin's increasingly autocratic ways. On 16 September 2010 Minister of Foreign Affairs Lawrence

Cannon visited Russia, and on 6 September 2013 Russian Foreign Minister Sergey Lavrov held talks with his counterpart John Baird on the margins of the G20 Summit in Saint Petersburg. Harper himself visited Russia twice: first for the G8 Summit in Saint Petersburg in 2006 and subsequently for the 2012 Asia-Pacific Economic Cooperation Forum in Vladivostok.[9]

However, relations turned decidedly sour following Russia's seizure of Crimea and its subsequent invasion of eastern Ukraine in 2014–15 and have not recovered since. In response to the invasion, Ottawa imposed sanctions against Russian individuals and legal entities no fewer than eighteen times, eventually extending visa and financial restrictions to 160 Russian citizens and 80 organizations. Activities between the two countries through the Intergovernmental Economic Commission, established in 1995, were also frozen, and direct military contacts were suspended. Russia retaliated by banning imports of Canadian agricultural products, raw materials, and food supplies, including fish, seafood, and pork. A number of Canadian citizens were also declared persona non grata and banned from entering Russia, including Foreign Minister Chrystia Freeland, whose ancestry is Ukrainian.

JUSTIN TRUDEAU AND RUSSIA

Although some thought that Justin Trudeau would follow in his father's footsteps by adopting a more conciliatory approach toward Russia, they were quickly disappointed. In fact, just days before the federal election of 15 October 2015, Trudeau bragged that "he would tell off Russian President Vladimir Putin 'directly to his face'" if he became prime minister. Trudeau went on to accuse "Putin of 'being dangerous' in eastern Europe, 'irresponsible and harmful' in the Middle East and 'unduly provocative' in the Arctic."[10]

But if that was Trudeau's view, it was clearly not shared by his first foreign minister, Stéphane Dion. During his short-lived tenure, Dion adopted a more sympathetic attitude toward Russia. He deliberately tried to reverse the policy of the previous Conservative government, which had cut almost all political ties with Moscow following Russia's annexation of Crimea and its support for pro-Russian rebels in eastern Ukraine, by openly promoting a policy of engagement with Russia.

In a speech he delivered at the University of Ottawa at the end of March 2016 that left many confused, Dion tried to outline his new foreign policy philosophy of "responsible conviction," a speech that we now know he wrote himself over the objections of the Prime Minister's Office. (It was reported that Trudeau's then foreign policy adviser, Roland Paris, implored Dion not to deliver it).[11] Dion signalled that the new Trudeau government would have a "new" focus on multilateralism and the United Nations and that there would also be a thaw in relations with Russia even as the Canadian government piled on new sanctions against Russia. Dion asserted that "Canada's severing of ties with Russia had no positive consequences for anyone ... not for Canadians, not for the Russian people, not for Ukraine and not for global security." He went on to suggest that "Canada must stop being essentially the only one practicing an empty chair policy with Russia, because by doing so, we are only punishing ourselves."[12] (The "empty chair" was a reference to the Harper government's 2014 response to Russia's military involvement in Ukraine, which included Canada's refusal to chair or host – or sometimes even participate in – multilateral meetings at which a Russian delegation was present.)

The shift toward engagement with Russia, especially in the Arctic, was delivered directly by Dion to Russian foreign minister Sergey Lavrov when the two met in Laos in June 2016 and was also underlined in an address marking the twentieth anniversary of the Arctic Council that was delivered on Dion's behalf at Carleton University by Parliamentary Secretary Pamela Goldsmith-Jones.[13] In an October 2016 interview with *Diplomat Magazine*, Dion again pressed his case for Russian engagement:

> When I became the minister of foreign affairs, all my counterparts were asking me to 'please, come with us and speak to the Russians. If you don't speak to the Russians, you'll never be relevant. You won't be able to help Ukraine, you won't be invited to the table, including in Syria.' It's not because I agree with [Russian President Vladimir] Putin, or the prime minister agrees with him. It's precisely because we disagree that we need to have strong dialogue. Canada will never recognize the illegal annexation of Crimea. Canada has been explicit in its condemnation of Russia's past acts of aggression, but also on areas where we think dialogue

can lead to improvements for us, for Ukraine and for global security. Deterrence and dialogue is our approach as one of the four framework nations, and it is our bilateral approach as well. It is important that allies remain united against Russian aggression towards Ukraine. When we are at the table, we can hold individuals to account, push for action and press for change. Engagement takes many forms and we are going to pursue every avenue in the cause of peace and stability.[14]

Some observers, like former Canadian ambassador to Russia Christopher Westdal, applauded what they saw as the stirring of an incipient thaw in Canada-Russia relations. "Multilaterally," Westdal wrote, "Canada's re-engagement with Russia can readily begin. In the world of the UN and its myriad agencies, of the Arctic Council, the OSCE, the NPT [Treaty on the Non-Proliferation of Nuclear Weapons], the NATO-Russia Council, the International Support Group for Syria and many more, Russia is unavoidable, its diplomats able and relentless. In all these settings, our delegations can start again with Russia's, seeking common ground, despite our withered bilateral links." "Bilaterally," Westdal further opined "we can start anew with a few basics, such as the resumption of normal diplomatic and Embassy functions and officials' policy consultations focused on concrete interests. We might begin with subjects relatively free of contention, such as anti-terrorism or cooperation in the Arctic."[15]

For a brief moment, it looked like the new Trudeau government might indeed have headed in the direction that Dion was urging. The *Toronto Star* reported that documents it had obtained through a freedom-of-information request showed that in August 2016 senior Canadian foreign affairs officials were also seriously contemplating a special, one-on-one meeting between Prime Minister Justin Trudeau and President Vladimir Putin. Although a direct, bilateral meeting of this kind never took place, Trudeau did meet with Putin on the edges of the 2015 G20 Summit in Turkey, where he reportedly told Putin directly to end Russia's "interference" in Ukraine.[16]

After barely a year in office, Dion, whose continued lecturing of the young prime minster and whose antagonistic, combative style rankled his Cabinet colleagues and senior officials in the Prime Minister's Office, was unceremoniously dumped in a Cabinet shuffle.

He was replaced by Chrystia Freeland, the minister of international trade and a rising star in the Cabinet, who became foreign minister in January 2016.

Freeland was no stranger to Russia. In her earlier career as a correspondent for the *Financial Times*, Freeland had played a key role in publicizing the arrest and subsequent murder of Russian lawyer Sergei Magnitsky and the nefarious actions of Russian oligarchs (and indeed Putin himself) who were enriching themselves at the expense of foreign investors who had rushed like lemmings into Russia at the end of the Communist era (and whose assets were subsequently seized or expropriated with the active collusion of Russian authorities).[17] While a member of the Opposition bench, Freeland had known the distinction of being one of the first Canadians to be put on Russia's travel ban list in retaliation against the sanctions that the Harper government had imposed on Russia. As *Global News* reported, "The day she was banned from Russia[,] Freeland responded on Twitter, saying she considered the sanction an honour."[18] Before becoming foreign minister, Freeland had pressed her negative views about Putin and the need for Canada to take a tough, uncompromising line in Cabinet, often clashing with Dion, who favoured a more conciliatory approach. That Freeland is a Canadian of Ukrainian descent meant that she was also the de facto representative in the Liberal government of 1.4 million Ukrainian Canadians.

With her appointment, the foreign minister and the prime minister were clearly on the same page when it came to Russia. Whatever softening of tone Dion had tried to bring to Canada-Russian relations with his public musings about the importance of engagement and conciliation evaporated with his departure. Following President Donald Trump's ill-fated meeting with Putin in Finland in July 2018, for example, Trudeau carefully sidestepped criticizing the president for reaching out to Putin but had harsh words for Putin himself: "Canada has been unequivocal in our condemnation of Vladimir Putin and Russia," the prime minister said, and he went on to "condemn Russia and the way Russia engages in international affairs." Trudeau was clearly echoing the view of most Canadians. A 2017 Pew Global Attitudes Project survey showed that 27 per cent of Canadians had a favourable view of Russia, with 59 per cent expressing an unfavourable view.[19]

THE END OF CONVERGENCE

It was not just Russia's actions in Ukraine that turned the dial on bilateral relations but also a growing sense generally among Canadian and other Western leaders that Russia under Putin was reverting to authoritarian rule and going back to Communist ways with the growing number of arrests, detentions, and even assassinations of Putin's critics, the mounting curbs on freedom of speech and association, and Russia's flagrant violations of state sovereignty and the international rule of law.

The cruel lesson of the second decade of this century is that democratic convergence is not happening. The world is no longer surfing what American political scientist Samuel P. Huntington once called the "third wave of democratization."[20] In fact, in Russia and elsewhere, we are witnessing a deeply troubling reversal of democratic fortunes. As Freedom House's 2018 annual report on the condition of global political rights and civil liberties shows, democracy around the world is in overall decline for the twelfth straight year.[21]

The policy implications of the end of convergence for Canada and other Western democracies are profound, and nowhere perhaps is the dilemma more keenly felt than in the case of Russia and how to deal with Putin.

This dilemma is compounded by American President Donald Trump's embrace of Putin. Trump obviously doesn't consider Russia to be as much of a threat to American interests as China and some of America's key trading partners. While musing openly about lifting sanctions on Russia and welcoming Putin back into the G8 fold, Trump has been bashing America's European and North American trading partners with steel and aluminum tariffs and launching a trade war with China. Trump's constant berating of US allies for taking a ride on American coattails, not just economically but also militarily, has also driven a deep wedge into the transatlantic alliance.

Some commentators believe that Trump is simply being naive when it comes to Russia. Others believe that Trump is beholden to Putin because Putin has the goods on Trump's former business dealings in Russia and/or because of the possibility that the Russians colluded with Trump's team to help him win the presidency, which was the subject of Special Counsel Robert Mueller's investigation into the

2016 US presidential election. Mueller's report explicitly acknowledges that the Trump campaign welcomed support from Russia.[22]

Notwithstanding the erratic behaviour of the American president vis-à-vis Putin, generally speaking there are three contrasting views about the severity of the threat that Putin's Russia poses to the West.

Russia in Decline

Some believe that Russia is a declining power and that the ill-health of its economy and unfavourable demographic trends underscore its core weaknesses. "Russia Is an Economic Pipsqueak," a headline in Washington's *The Hill* newspaper has opined. The article goes on to point out that there has been a lot of head scratching on Capitol Hill about President Trump's infatuation with Putin because of Russia's weak economic situation.[23] As the late US senator John McCain quipped, Russia is "a gas station masquerading as an economy" smaller than that of Canada.[24]

Despite having the largest landmass in the world (and eleven time zones), Russia's population of 144 million – down from its all-time high of 148 million at the end of the Cold War – is shrinking at roughly 0.4 per cent per annum. Low levels of life expectancy and the poor health of its population (especially males) are behind this trend. Comparatively speaking, Russia is only about the size of Germany's and Italy's populations combined, or slightly less than half the size of the US population.[25]

At US$1.55 trillion in 2017, Russia's GDP is a minuscule 8 per cent of the United States' GDP. Compare this figure with Canada's GDP in the same year, which stood at $1.65 trillion. It goes without saying that with a per capita GDP of less than $11,000, which is roughly the same as that of Turkey and Romania, most Russians are poor. The country also has one of the worst income distributions in the world. According to some estimates, 10 per cent of Russia's population control nearly 50 per cent of the country's wealth. Karl Marx must surely be turning in his grave. By comparison, during the Communist era the top decile of Russia's income earners took home only a quarter of the country's income.[26]

Nonetheless, Russia's income distribution figures are not all that different from those of the United States or France, which have the some of the highest levels of income inequality in the world. Bear in mind, however, that both countries are much richer than Russia as measured by their per capita GDP, which, comparatively speaking, means that those who are on the lower rungs of the income ladder are still generally better off than their Russian counterparts. Declinists also view Putin's growing unpopularity and the mounting opposition to his regime as further signs that Russia is weak and increasingly fragile.[27]

Russia Resurgent

Others disagree. Despite the puny size of its economy, Russia is still the world's second biggest military power. Russia and the United States are also more or less evenly matched in terms of their nuclear firepower as measured by the number of warheads they have in their strategic arsenals – 6,850 (Russia) versus 6,550 (United States). Some say that this parity explains why Russia still poses an existential threat to the United States even though the Cold War "ended" some thirty years ago.[28]

Russia has slightly over three-quarters of a million active frontline military personnel, 15,398 tanks, 3,429 aircraft, and 55 submarines. Compare that with the United States, which has 1.4 million active personnel, 8,484 tanks, 13,892 aircraft, and 72 submarines. With a defence budget of US$84.5 billion versus the United States' defence budget of US$601 billion (2015 figures), Russia is squeezing a lot more out of its defence dollars than the United States, even if the bulk of its military is comprised of conscripts compared to America's voluntary army.[29]

Thanks to a recent spike in the growth of the Russian economy (in spite of Western sanctions) because of a boost in the price of two key staples, oil and natural gas, which had plummeted to below US$40 a barrel in early 2016, and because of Russia's growing grain exports to China, Putin is now able to modernize Russia's military capabilities, including the three legs of Russia's strategic nuclear triad – intercontinental missiles, bombers, and submarines. Russia is also expanding its low-yield, nuclear tactical-weapon capabilities. In its nuclear-posture review, the Trump administration announced that it too will embark on a strategic nuclear-modernization program to keep America safe from its enemies, including Russia.[30]

But it is not just Russia's growing military capabilities that threaten the West according to those who believe that Russia is on the rise. It is also Putin's muscle-flexing and aggressive behaviour. The list is long: Russian incursions into eastern Ukraine, its seizure of Crimea, its continuous probes along the northern flanks of NATO and in the Arctic, its meddling in elections and sophisticated propaganda and disinformation campaigns, its poisoning of foreign spies and dissidents, and its growing influence in the Middle East, where it has backed Bashar al-Assad's brutal and murderous regime in Syria with its air power and other forms of support. (Although one must also ask whether Putin or Iran's ayatollahs have the wherewithal to rebuild Syria, they certainly share the responsibility with Assad.) All point to a Russia that is asserting its power and influence beyond its borders. What is also of concern is Putin's frequent reference to Russia's "invincible" nuclear arsenal. In his state of the nation address to the Federal Assembly on 1 March 2018, Putin showed a video animation of Russian missile attacks against Florida, where President Trump has his Mar-a-Lago resort.[31]

Russia the Aggrieved

A third school of thought believes that Russia is embarked on a "quest for status." In the words of Russian scholar Mikhail Troitskiy, this quest is not based on Russia's nuclear capabilities or its seat on the UN Security Council but rather on Russia's view of itself as a "retired superpower" that pulled out of the Cold War "voluntarily" as opposed to being "defeated."[32] However, instead of being "rewarded" for its cooperative stance on arms control after the Cold War, its support for the Western intervention in Libya, and its cooperation in intelligence sharing and counterterrorism, Russia was repeatedly snubbed as NATO expanded its membership to the borders of Russia and as the European Union reached out to countries like Ukraine and Georgia, which Russia views as being historically within its own sphere of influence.

According to this view, Russia also believes that the West has not lived up to its own commitments in the 1997 Founding Act on Mutual Relations, Cooperation and Security between NATO and Russia and in the 2002 declaration "NATO-Russia Relations: A New Quality."[33]

Troitskiy argues that Russia thinks it should have the right "to have a say about the membership of its post-Soviet neighbors in alliances" in which it is not itself a member.[34]

Russia is openly embracing China, a country with which it has historically had difficult relations, on the Machiavellian principle that "the enemy of my enemy is my friend." Putin also believes that the United States actively tried to undermine his own regime when there were major public demonstrations in Russia's major cities after the December 2011 parliamentary elections. After his own re-election to the presidency in March 2012, Putin quashed the protests and arrested opposition leaders, alleging that they were supported by the United States. As conceded even by former US ambassador Michael McFaul, who is no fan of Putin and has been highly critical of his regime, "Putin's anti-American campaign was not just political theater intended for a domestic audience: Putin genuinely believed that the United States represented a threat to his regime." Furthermore, "Putin was never inclined to believe in Washington's good faith. His training as a KGB agent had led him to distrust the United States along with all democratic movements" even though, "in the early years of his presidency, he had held open the possibility of close cooperation with the West. In 2000, he even suggested that Russia might someday join NATO," as did a number of Western analysts.[35]

As in most debates, there is some truth to each set of assertions. There is no question that the Russian economy is weak and thoroughly corrupt, although it is slowly recovering from its most recent financial crisis (2014–17), which saw the collapse of the ruble and affected both consumers and its struggling business sector alike. But notwithstanding its economic woes, Russia is still a formidable military foe to be reckoned with, and it remains a nuclear superpower. Putin's stance toward the West has also hardened – notwithstanding Trump's recent overtures and the fact that Putin's (and Russia's) insecurities given the country's decline may make it more dangerous, not less. The complete lack of trust between Russia and the West has prompted some commentators, like McFaul, to refer to the current situation not as a new cold war but as a "hot peace" because of Russia's incursions into its "near abroad."[36]

FORGING A NEW (AND MORE COHERENT) WESTERN STRATEGY

Despite disagreeing about Russia's capabilities and Putin's ultimate intentions, most informed observers agree that the West – and the United States, in particular – lacks a coherent strategy to deal with Russia. Trump's hastily conceived and disastrous Helsinki Summit with Putin in July 2018 is a case in point. The summit sowed "new disorientation and discord in American politics" according to CNN's Stephen Collinson while handing Putin "another win."[37]

There is no shortage of ideas about what the West's strategy toward Russia should be, but all ideas seem to converge on a number of common themes: (1) the strategy should be bipartisan and based on genuine dialogue and consultation between the United States and its allies, Canada included, (2) Western countries need to reaffirm their commitment to defending democracy and human rights and take effective measures to ensure that their own democratic institutions and electoral processes are not subverted by developing better resilience against cyber attacks and media manipulation by external actors, (3) the United States should recommit itself to defending its key allies in the Pacific and Europe while recognizing that stronger economic ties and security partnerships are but two sides of the same coin, and (4) the United States (and NATO) can pursue a policy of containment and engagement with Russia simultaneously but only from a position of strength and stability, not chaos or disarray.[38] It is perhaps also worth noting that despite all of the concern about Russian interference in democratic elections, China is seen by US intelligence officials as posing the major threat from cyber space.

Avenues of cooperation with Russia should include a renewed commitment to promoting nuclear nonproliferation and major reductions in strategic arsenals through arms control (not shredding the few treaties the West has with Russia), intelligence sharing and counterterrorism cooperation, and developing new rules to curb cyber attacks, including on critical infrastructure like power generation plants. In this regard, Trump's shredding of the Intermediate-Range Nuclear Forces Treaty and the earlier withdrawal of the United States from the Anti-Ballistic Missile Treaty are not only counterproductive but will also invariably provoke a new arms race with Russia. As

Michael Krepon writes, this "new age of nuclear confrontation will not end well." The United States and its Western allies have "manage[d] to survive the seven harrowing decades since Hiroshima and Nagasaki," but "[d]eterrence alone didn't produce this result; the combination of deterrence and diplomacy did. This safety net was the greatest unacknowledged achievement during the Cold War. It now has very little load-bearing capacity left."[39]

The West must also recognize that Russia seeks respect and a place in the global security order, a pursuit that is part of Putin's own appeal to Russians and his political base. The Russian bear cannot be put in a cage. It is just too big and right now angry. But it has to be tamed. Russia also has to understand that its quest for respect and status will come only if, in turn, it respects the sovereignty and the right of self-determination of other nations, including its closest neighbours, and that there will be penalties if it does not.

In 1953 the distinguished American nuclear physicist J. Robert Oppenheimer wrote, "We may be likened to two scorpions in a bottle, each capable of killing the other, but only at the risk of his own life."[40] What was true then about the world's two greatest nuclear powers is still true now. The continued risk of nuclear war should temper great power ambitions all around and provide real incentives to reduce that risk. But it is also the case that NATO can deal with Putin and curb his ambitions only from a position of strength, not weakness. As German Chancellor Angela Merkel stated before the 2016 NATO summit when she pledged to increase German defence spending and deploy troops in Poland and the Baltic states despite the strong objections of her own foreign minister, Frank-Walter Steinmeier, the principle of deterrence "is a deeply defensive concept."[41]

IMPLICATIONS FOR CANADA

In mid-June 2018, just before the NATO leaders' summit in Brussels, President Donald Trump wrote to Prime Minister Justin Trudeau to complain that there was "growing frustration" in the United States with NATO allies like Canada that have not increased defence spending as promised. "This frustration is not confined to our executive branch. The United States Congress has taken note and is concerned as well," Trump wrote.[42] Although Canadians did not appreciate the blunt way Trump delivered his message, it was certainly no different from that of previous American presidents, who had repeatedly called on NATO allies to spend more on security. His message certainly is no less different from and no less warranted than that of previous American governments. In the case of Canada, the reality is that its military is too small to either protect Canada or support its allies.[43]

The American public generally tends to support their presidents on this issue. A 2017 poll conducted by the Pew Foundation reported that 45 per cent of Americans believe that the country's allies should spend more on their national defence, 37 per cent say spending levels should stay about the same, and only 9 per cent think they should be decreased. But as Pew also reported, "there is a wide partisan gap on this issue, with 63% of Republicans calling for more spending from allies, compared with just 33% of Democrats."[44]

Canada currently spends a little more 1.2 per cent of its GDP on defence, well below the 2 per cent aspirational target (a goal to be achieved by 2024) that NATO countries reiterated for themselves at the June 2018 NATO summit – which amounts to a little more than Cnd$27 billion, a figure that is based on a new method of calculating such spending that includes some veterans' programs and money spent on information networks. By comparison, in 2017 the US defence budget of US$686 billion equaled 3.6 per cent of GDP, by far the largest of any NATO member. The combined defence budgets of all other NATO members totalled US$271 billion in 2017. Because most NATO members are small countries, only ten members spent more than US$10 billion. In rank order, these were the United States, the United Kingdom, France, Germany, Italy, Canada, Turkey, Spain, Poland, and (just barely) the Netherlands.[45]

The last time Canadian defence spending reached 2 per cent of GDP was when Brian Mulroney was in office. That level of defence spending allowed Canada to make a robust contribution to global security. In addition to its various NATO commitments, Canada participated in some sixteen peacekeeping missions in the late 1980s and early 1990s, including major peacekeeping and peace enforcement operations in the Balkans, Namibia, Cambodia, Central America, Somalia, and East Timor.[46]

Why should Canada spend more on defence? One of the main reasons was clearly spelled out by none other than Canada's foreign minister, Chrystia Freeland, in a speech she delivered to the House of Commons on 6 June 2017. As the *Globe and Mail* reported, Freeland "promised, in response to the Presidency of Donald Trump, a less United States-centric Canadian foreign policy, including making 'necessary investments in our military' because ... 'to rely solely on the U.S. security umbrella would make us a client state.'"[47]

Barely a day later, Canada's defence minister, Harjit Sajjan, unveiled his own much-awaited defence policy review. But as the *Globe and Mail* lamented, "The spin around it is finely spun, but beneath, the Liberal government's new military clothing is exceedingly modest ... The plan calls for the number of sailors, soldiers and air force personnel to increase by five per cent – over 10 years. [This includes the offer to pay bonuses to pilots since so many have already moved to Australia.] Canada's defence spending, among the lowest in NATO, will gradually increase from 1.2 per cent of GDP to 1.4 per cent, according to the government, or from one per cent to 1.2 per cent, as measured by many international observers. Either way, even if the Trudeau government wins a second majority government mandate, and then a third, Canada will still be nowhere close to meeting the NATO defence spending target of two per cent of GDP."[48]

There is little doubt that the global security environment is becoming more dangerous not just due to the continuing challenge posed by so-called "nontraditional" security threats, as in the case of extremist groups like the Islamic State of Iraq and Syria (ISIS), but also due to the revival of Cold War tensions as Russia and China flex their military muscle and try to re-establish their Cold War spheres of influence. As retired US admiral and former military commander of NATO James Stavridis wrote about NATO and Russian military exercises in the fall 2018, Russia's exercise was not only the largest one held since Soviet times, involving 300,000 troops and more than 1,000 military aircraft, but the exercise was conducted jointly with the participation of thousands of Chinese troops operating alongside Russian forces. Stavridis issued a blunt warning: "The message to the West is obvious: Russia and China might work together militarily against NATO in the East or the U.S. and its allies in the Pacific."[49]

There are other signs of troubling Russian behaviour. The Russian detention of a Ukrainian naval vessel and sailors from the Black Sea, whom the Russians alleged were trying to cross the Kerch Strait in violation of the terms of the Russia-Ukraine agreement on such passage, suggests that Russia is no mood to back down from "its strategy of seeking to destabilise and weaken Ukraine for domestic political as well as strategic reasons."[50]

A 2016 RAND Corporation war-gaming exercise showed that Russian armed forces would need only about sixty hours to occupy the Baltic states on NATO's northern flank and that NATO allies would not physically have the time to deploy troops to help Estonia, Latvia, and Lithuania. In response to the growing threat to NATO's newest members, the alliance deployed four multinational battalion-size battle groups on their territory, which include troops provided by Canada to Latvia.[51]

However, troop deployments and much-needed increases in military spending are not enough. As Russia (and China) build up their military capabilities and as geopolitical threats grow, Canada has to get serious about defence procurement and address its catastrophic procurement policies, which, for decades, have left its men and women in uniform poorly equipped and operating planes, helicopters, armoured personnel carriers, and ships that are years, if not decades, old – in some instances, so old that they are unsafe to operate. Even more embarrassing, Canada has antiquated CF-18 fighter jets that are being replenished by used versions of the same from Australia. There is no worse example of neglect than the shilly-shallying over fighter jet purchases.

As Canada's allies start to modernize their forces, Canada spins its wheels, hampered by an inefficient, politically driven military procurement process that shows few signs of improving despite many studies and reports on how to reform the system. There is ample culpability shared by all governments, Liberal and Conservative. As the *National Post* opined on its editorial page on 24 November 2018, in the debacle over replacing Canada's aging CF-18 fighter aircraft, "the urgency of replacing the CF-18s was as clear to the Harper Tories during their tenure as it is today. They didn't get the job done, and that's to their shame. But that failure has now been compounded and outdone by astonishing levels of Liberal government mismanagement ... The Liberal failures stemmed from their absurd campaign promise during the 2015 election to proceed with a fighter replacement process that was fair and transparent, but which also excluded the Conservative's preferred Lockheed Martin F-35, an advanced American stealth jet now entering service with several allied nations [for which Canada has already spent $700 million]. It was instantly obvious that the Liberal proposal was inherently contradictory: you can't hold a fair competition while excluding a clear front-runner."[52] By buying used Australian F-18s to fill the gap as Canada's aging CF-18s are retired before they fall out of the air, Canada, as the *National Post* noted, is spending "billions to augment a fleet that is already becoming obsolete, to avoid spending billions on replacing that augmented fleet just a few years later."[53]

A report by the auditor general of Canada was equally scathing and concluded that "National Defense did not manage the process to replace the CF-18 fleet with due diligence." It also criticized the government's $3 billion stopgap purchase of used Australian planes to augment Canada's CF-18 fleet on the grounds that the government lacked "a plan to deal with its biggest obstacles to meeting the new operational requirement: a shortage of pilots and the declining combat capability of its aircraft. Although National Defence has plans to address some risks, these investment decisions will not be enough to ensure that it can have the number of aircraft available daily to meet the highest NORAD alert level and Canada's NATO commitment at the same time."[54]

Canada's procurement and defence spending problems will be solved only when its political leaders shut the lid on the proverbial procurement cookie jar, which has too often been lifted to buy votes with the promise of jobs in different regions of the country. But they will not do so unless there is genuine public outrage and Canadians are dislodged from their general indifference toward the lamentable state of their armed forces. Vice Admiral Mark Norman's "real" crime when he was accused of compromising sensitive government data and dismissed as vice chief of the Defence Staff was his attempt to defend a decision to provide a supply ship for the Canadian Navy on time and on budget. As John Robson laments, "Canadian military procurement is inefficient even by government standards. But the main problem is we don't spend enough serious sums because we aren't serious. We keep promising NATO two per cent of GDP on defence, which isn't enough."[55]

However, as Canadian defence analyst David Bercuson argues, raising defence expenditures even in Canada (which is desperately needed) will not cure all of NATO's problems. NATO has had longstanding internal divisions, especially over its so-called "out-of-area" missions in the Persian Gulf, Libya, and Afghanistan, where some of its members chose to sit the mission out. During the Yugoslav Wars, NATO's bombing of Serbia and Serbian troops in Kosovo also rankled some NATO members even though that the conflict was right on NATO's doorstep and widespread atrocities were occurring. But the most serious problem today, as Bercuson notes, is an internal one involving the "swing to autocracy among some NATO members. Hungary, Poland, Romania, Turkey, and Italy are veering to the right, with Turkey having become a nation of one-man rule. The old saw that a NATO member had to be a democracy, adopted after the death of Spanish dictator Francisco Franco in 1975, seems to be going by the wayside. Which begs the question, if NATO is supposed to be bound together to fight as one, would Canadians countenance their military being used to defend Turkey today?"[56] It is a good question and not simply a rhetorical one.

There is little doubt that the growing democratic deficit among some of NATO's members poses a serious internal threat to alliance cohesion, especially if those members decide one day to opt out of the alliance because their leaders see greater common cause to be had with Russia or China and their autocratic rulers than with the democracies of the West. But this is not an entirely new problem for the alliance, and some historical perspective is in order. There were serious issues about internal political cohesion during the height of the Cold War as Communists fought for power in countries like Greece, which had joined NATO in 1952, and continued to do so even during that country's period of military junta rule from 1967–74. The Eurocommunist wave that swept through Italy, Spain, Portugal, and France in late 1960s and 1970s also threatened internal political stability and alliance cohesion. It was only when the influence of Moscow over the leadership of European Communist parties became apparent to the movement's supporters (and their sympathizers in the general public) that the Eurocommunist movement lost much of its earlier political momentum.[57]

It must be said that NATO, having been in existence for sixty years, is an outlier when it comes to longevity: no other formal alliance in history has lasted as long. That is all the more reason not to take the alliance's future for granted or to assume that Canada can shirk its own responsibilities, especially when it comes to raising defence spending and strengthening the alliance's deterrence capabilities and leadership at a time of growing geopolitical rivalry, turmoil, and internal alliance divisiveness. But at its root, NATO should be repurposed not just to deter Russia but also to stabilize other threats to global security, such as by countering cyber threats through higher levels of commitment and by imposing sanctions to curb lawless behaviour by rogue regimes.

7

In Search of a Middle East Policy

Nowhere is the "myth" about Canada as a "helpful fixer" as pervasive or more powerful than it is in the Middle East because that is where the myth was born. Myths are narrative threads that underlie a culture and are often invoked through the use of pungent metaphors intended to convey deeper truths about the world. For example, when the first governor of the bay colony of Massachusetts reminded his fellow Puritans that their community would be "as a city upon a hill" and that "the eyes of all people are upon us,"[1] little did he realize that more than 200 years later American presidents from John F. Kennedy to Ronald Reagan would invoke his words to remind Americans of their storied past and convey a vision of the future.

Canada's myth about its storied foreign policy past is centred, in part, on the role that Lester B. Pearson played at the United Nations to end the 1956 Suez Crisis, for which he was awarded the Nobel Peace Prize. When Justin Trudeau boasted, "Canada is back,"[2] he deliberately invoked the Pearsonian myth to promote the idea that Canada would return to its honest broker "roots" and multilateralist vocation, which, he argued, had all but been abandoned in the realpolitik policies of his predecessor – policies that Trudeau and his advisers believed were driven by naked economic self-interest and a militarized commitment to the US-led war against international terrorism.[3]

But as Trudeau soon discovered, myths all too easily vanish in the distemper of reality. Trudeau was not the first leader to learn that the hard way and surely not the last. As an editorial in the *Globe and Mail* opined, "For much of the period since the end of the Second

World War, Canada saw itself as an honest broker or helpful fixer, and the lead worshipper at the church of multilateralism. Despite the fact that Canada was at the centre of NATO and NORAD, military alliances designed to deter and if necessary fight the communist Soviet Union, successive governments and a large part of the foreign-policy establishment also came to see Canada as a kind of aspiring neutral. We were the middle power that invented peacekeeping, and found a selfless fulfilment in it. It came to be accepted by many Canadians as a defining national trait."[4] Many scholars have likewise noted the compelling attraction of the "middle power" narrative to Canada's foreign policy elites and political decision makers.[5]

In this chapter, we argue that Canada's scope for secondary influence on global issues like the Middle East hinges squarely on the degree to which Canada is perceived by others as an interlocutor in Washington. As this role is virtually nonexistent for Canada and most Western "allies" while Donald Trump occupies the White House, the pillars of Canada's foreign engagement will need to focus on realistic objectives like the defence of self-interest and assertions of intrinsic democratic and humanitarian values.

VALUES VERSUS INTERESTS

In a speech he delivered at Simon Fraser University in October 2016, former Australian foreign minister Gareth Evans welcomed the election of the Trudeau government, proclaiming that "one of the most comforting things to have happened is that ... Canadians seem to be again behaving like Canadians."[6] By that, he presumably meant that moral values would once against be at the centre of Canadian foreign policy and that the government would do "the right thing simply because it *is* the right thing."[7] He further remarked that the promotion of moral values is a "core foreign policy business, fitting squarely, when properly understood, within a national interests rather than just values-based framework." He argued that governments have to resist getting "increasingly drawn into the kind of *ad hocery* which has characterised ... so much of our international relations as well as domestic policy in recent years – lacking any kind of shape and coherence, lurching erratically from one position to another, and picking up and dropping aid commitments and treaty negotiation commitments and principled positions on policy issues like climate change as the domestic mood is perceived to change."[8]

However, Evans would have found little comfort in the way the Trudeau government handled the tension between "values" and "interests" in its policies in the Middle East. That tension exploded into full view in the seemingly contradictory policies of the government toward Saudi Arabia, characterized by its simultaneous refusal to cancel a longstanding arms deal with the Saudis, which rankled many human rights advocates, while openly decrying in a series of tweets by Foreign Minister Chrystia Freeland the Saudi government's arrest and detention of two female bloggers and human rights activists, one of whom was also flogged for her alleged crimes.

The Saudis were outraged by what they saw as a brazen attempt by Canada to interfere in their internal affairs. In retaliation, as *The Atlantic* magazine reported, the Saudis "declared the Canadian ambassador persona non grata and expelled him from the country ... froze all new trade and investment deals with Ottawa ... canceled educational exchange programs between the two countries, including scholarships and fellowships," which affected some 16,000 Saudi students studying in Canada, including many hundreds who were enrolled in Canadian medical schools, and suspended flights of the "Saudi state airline ... in and out of Toronto."[9] But politics was obviously at play. As *The Atlantic* further observed, "Canadian Prime Minister Justin Trudeau has upheld a $15-billion arms deal to Saudi Arabia that was concluded by his conservative predecessor in 2014, yet now he 'wants to defend himself from criticism of that decision by grandstanding and posturing on women's rights.'"[10] And the Saudi's continued to ship oil to Canada, including by tanker up the Saint Lawrence River to Montreal.

The ruckus didn't stop there. Following the brutal killing of journalist Jamal Khashoggi, the Canadian government, along with the US government, placed seventeen Saudi nationals – the fifteen men who had allegedly murdered Khashoggi, an aide to Crown Prince Mohammad bin Salman, who had reportedly ordered the murder, and Saudi Arabia's consul general in Turkey – on its Magnitsky sanctions list. Then, to further underscore its disapproval of Saudis, Foreign Minister Freeland personally welcomed to Canada eighteen-year-old Rahaf Mohammed Alqunun, a Saudi national, who was granted asylum after fleeing from her family because she was being physically abused by her father and forced into an arranged marriage.[11]

However, these showy displays of the Trudeau government's new gender-based foreign policy and commitment to human rights did little to appease those who wanted the government to take an even tougher line on the Saudis by cutting off all commercial defence ties. As the *Middle East Monitor* reported, "Relatives of 37 Saudis executed last week on alleged 'terror' offences have accused the Canadian government of being complicit in the brutal killing in which some of the bodies were nailed to a post in a public location for several hours in a 'crucifixion' position. Their anger was directed at the government of Prime Minister Justin Trudeau which has a $15 billion arms deal with Riyadh. Relatives of the victims claiming asylum in Canada called on Ottawa to stop the sale of arms to the regime, saying that continuing to do so makes Canada complicit in the kingdom's human rights abuses."[12]

The Trudeau government was obviously reluctant to cancel the deal – "the largest advanced manufacturing export contract in Canadian history," as the *Globe and Mail* pointed out – because it supported "thousands of jobs in Canada at a General Dynamics Land Systems–Canada plant in London, Ont., and suppliers across the country."[13] Jobs and two Liberal seats in the London area trumped human rights when push came to shove. A November 2018 survey by the Angus Reid Institute found that Canadians were pretty much evenly divided on the issue: 46 per cent thought that the ongoing multiyear deal should be cancelled, whereas 44 per cent thought that it should go ahead but that Canada should not sell arms to the Saudis in the future.[14]

A BITTER IRONY

When Canada's Conservative foreign minister John Baird told world leaders in a speech to the United Nations General Assembly that "Canada's government doesn't seek to have our values or our principled foreign policy validated by elites who would rather 'go along to get along,'" his critics were aghast.[15] When it came to the Middle East, the government of Stephen Harper was lambasted for its unflinching support for Israel and its opposition to Palestinian statehood – a criticism that overlooked the fact that Canada's opposition was conditional on the successful conclusion of a peace treaty between

Israelis and Palestinians.[16] Many of those same critics sniggered at the Conservative government's commitment to promoting gender equality through its maternal health policy for mothers, children, and newborns, which was announced at the 2010 G8 Summit in Muskoka, Ontario.[17] Although Baird's own so-called "dignity" agenda put him at odds with social conservatives within his party, he refused to back off on what he considered to be a fundamental principle of human rights.

In truth, there was a strong pragmatic cast to the Harper government's Middle East foreign policy (principled though it was on some issues) insofar as it was a policy that also sought to advance Canada's economic interests in the region. For example, the Harper government worked hard to strengthen Canada's relations with the Arab world as a complement to its strong position against unilateral Palestinian statehood and unwavering support for Israel.[18] Baird promoted deeper economic ties with the United Arab Emirates (following a brief spat over Canada's transport agency's refusal to give Gulf carriers Etihad and Emirates additional landing rights), Bahrain, Saudi Arabia, and Jordan, with which Canada concluded its first free trade agreement with an Arab country. Baird also launched a strategic dialogue with the Gulf's key regional body, the Gulf Cooperation Council, which included cooperation on counterterrorism and other initiatives to counter violent extremism.

The Conservatives took a hard line toward Iran and were roundly criticized for closing Canada's embassy in Tehran, a decision that has not been reversed by the Trudeau government despite Trudeau's earlier election promise to reopen the embassy and work to resume normal diplomatic relations. When there were major protests in Iran in 2018, for example, the biggest the country had seen since the Green Revolution in 2009, the Trudeau government called the violence "deeply troubling" while defending its refusal to resume diplomatic relations, saying that Canada will "continue to engage with Iran, on terms that we set."[19]

With the emergence of the Muslim Brotherhood in Egypt, Canada's guarded approach under the Conservatives was one that even liberal-minded Egyptians applauded. Unlike other Western nations, Canada did not recognize Syria's freedom fighters as the legitimate representative of the Syrian people because it had concerns about terrorist elements in their midst, the lack of representation of women, and whether the opposition was religiously and ethnically reflective of the Syrian people. Unnoticed by most of its critics, the Harper government also continued to support the Palestinian Authority's efforts to build the institutions and infrastructure for a viable Palestinian state, providing $5 million for economic growth and job creation in the West Bank and Gaza and another $25 million for humanitarian assistance, security reform, and assistance to the Office of the Quartet Representative. To those affected by the crisis in Syria, the Conservatives provided $316.8 million in direct humanitarian support and an additional $110 million for development projects in Jordan and Lebanon.

The irony is that after almost four years into its mandate, the Trudeau government was accused of being "Harper's pupil" not only for its arms sales to the Saudis but also for its "muted response to Donald Trump's move ... to pull out of the multilateral deal to curb Iran's nuclear ambitions," for abstaining on a UN resolution that condemned Trump's decision to move the US embassy to Jerusalem, and for being Canada's "most unequivocally pro-Israel prime minister since ... Stephen Harper," a fact displayed in a UN voting record that "'is among the most pro-Israel in the world and is markedly different than Canada's voting record under [Jean] Chretien and [Paul] Martin' ... During the two regular sessions of the UN General Assembly after [Trudeau] became Prime Minister ... Canada voted against 18 resolutions [attacking] Israel and abstained on only two."[20]

Refusing to "go along to get along" is clearly also part of the Trudeau playbook when it comes to the Middle East, although the Liberals would never publicly admit to it. The Trudeau government, at least rhetorically, has seen itself as being both more firmly "multilateralist" and aligned with the United Nations in its approach to international relations. Its problem is that its rhetoric has come back to haunt it because of its pragmatic stance on a number of issues, including arms deals with the Saudis and its "principled" pro-Israel policy.

THE CASE FOR CONSTRUCTIVE ENGAGEMENT

Most views on Canadian foreign policy in the Middle East, including the two views of seasoned practitioners discussed below, are premised on the assumption that, even in the chaotic political environment that obtains in this region, Canada can help to promote the norms, values, and principles of a liberal international order by supporting a diplomacy of constructive engagement. This approach includes promoting peaceful collaboration between disputants via track-two diplomacy and other kinds of peacebuilding and development-focused ventures, strengthening regional organizations, and supporting the formation of liberal social networks within states and between them.[21] Promoting pluralist ideals of social and religious tolerance and advocating the rule of law are also seen as vital to nation building and are premised on the idea that local elites and citizens will be receptive to these values even if they are not willing, at least initially, to accept every aspect of a democracy-building agenda.[22] But the real reason Canada wants to be seen as having a role is because the Middle East is a perennial flash point of global insecurity.

The late Michael Bell, who served as Canada's ambassador to Israel, Egypt, and Jordan, argued that on Israeli-Arab issues Canada's role as a "neutral" or "even-handed" player is simply not in the cards, as it would mean an abandonment of traditional Canadian values, "including tolerance, democracy, respect for diversity, and the rule of law." Instead, he championed the idea of "[f]air-mindedness as a Canadian leitmotif," which explicitly contains a concept of morality that, in addition to recognizing "the need for a legitimate and independent state for the Palestinians," would address "a secure and peaceful Jewish state for the Israelis." Bell also believed in the importance of protecting civilians on both sides of the conflict and that Canada needs to be "a strong proponent of negotiation over the resort to force."[23] He foresaw a vital and continuing role for Canada as chair of the Refugee Working Group, which was created several months after the Madrid Conference of 1991, an initiative led by the United States and the Soviet Union to relaunch the Israeli-Palestinian peace process following the Gulf War. Bell also worried that Canada's diplomacy in the region was too passive. When he was ambassador to Tel Aviv, he promoted the idea of a "dialogue fund," to be financed through Canada's aid program for the region, that would serve as a "bridge-building tool between Palestinians and Israelis,"[24] but that is the problem with Canada's aspirations in the Middle East:

they predictably go nowhere. Bell also thought that Canada could actively promote pluralism throughout the Middle East because it was not as threatening as democracy and that even authoritarian states, like Egypt, would be receptive to pluralist concepts of tolerance and diversity.[25]

Michael Molloy, a former Canadian ambassador to Jordan and a former peace process envoy, believes that Canada's pro-Israel stance in recent years has "deep roots" going back to the "horror Canadians felt at the fate of so many ... European Jews in the Second World War" and that this memory constitutes an "element of primal sympathy for Israel" among both Canadians and Americans.[26] Nonetheless, he also points out that for some governments, strong support for Israel was not allowed to get in the way when Canada's leaders believed Israeli leaders to be in the wrong. For example, in 2013 when Israeli agents used forged Canadian passports to assassinate a senior Hamas official, Khalid Mishal, who was living in Jordan, Canada expressed its strong disapproval by recalling its ambassador and demanding that Israel "refrain from using Canadian documents in the future."[27]

Molloy argues that Canada should dial back any ambitions about being a significant player in the Middle East because it "is not a superpower."[28] Canada can play a humanitarian role to protect refugees and those in need of protection – including by resettling refugees in Canada and by endorsing unconventional means, such as track-two diplomacy, to engage civil society in the peace process – but Molloy believes that a great deal more has to be done to engage the Canadian business community in the region. He notes that "a lack of interest on the part of the Canadian business community ... stems from factors such as proximity to other larger, safer, more predictable, and more accessible markets" and from the fact that "[i]in some parts of the Middle East, the private sector and supporting legal and financial sector are poorly developed."[29] Complacency is also a constraint, a view shared by others who have studied the opportunities for enhanced bilateral trade between Canada and the Middle East.[30] As CAE Inc.'s managing director in Dubai notes, Canadian firms have a habit of visiting, but if they do not strike an immediate dividend, they go home and seldom return.[31]

STRATEGIC SHIFT

Although the Middle East may have at one point been receptive to planting the seeds of liberal internationalism, the ground is much less fertile now. That does not mean that Canada should completely abandon any pretence of constructive engagement, but it should exercise a far greater degree of caution, recognizing its limited capacity for direct influence, especially as it no longer has a privileged position in Washington.

In the aftermath of the Arab Spring, during which citizens had taken to the streets of Cairo, Tunis, Tripoli, Damascus, and elsewhere to overthrow their rulers, many Western countries, including Canada, saw opportunities for diplomatic engagement, peacebuilding, democracy promotion, and the advancement of the rule of law and human rights.[32] At the same time, it was also apparent that many states in the region would require substantial levels of development assistance and foreign investment to rebuild their economies and forge new social and political compacts, especially if their newly formed governments were to succeed and extremists were to be kept in check. But none did succeed, and the extremists are now coming back.

Some also believed that regional organizations could, for the first time, play a more constructive role in fostering collaboration and regional stability in concert with international institutions. They saw in the UN-sponsored, NATO-led intervention in Libya in the spring of 2011 promising signs of regional institutional growth and engagement. Galvanizing the UN Security Council's resolution to "take all necessary measures ... to protect civilians" under chapter 7 of the Charter of the United Nations, including the establishment a no-fly zone, were prior resolutions passed by the Gulf Cooperation Council, the Arab League, and the Organization of Islamic Cooperation in support of collective action.[33] Arab states also contributed to the NATO-enforced no-fly zone over Libya. However, the precedent set by Libya proved to be short-lived because key members of the Security Council – Russia and China – did not want the precedent set by Libya to be followed in Syria, where they had a major stake in supporting the regime of Bashar al-Assad, and the Arab League's support for the Libyan bombing mission also quickly cooled.

In 2019 the Arab world looks quite different from the previous decade. Some Arab states – Yemen, Libya, and Syria – have experienced major state failure and descended into anarchy characterized by protracted violence and ongoing civil war. However, in other countries like Egypt, Jordan, Morocco, and the United Arab Emirates, the traditional state has proven remarkably resilient in fending off religious and populist pressures. In these countries, as Brookings fellow Shadi Hamid points out, political elites have maintained political legitimacy by draping "themselves in the flag of 'moderate' Islam," each with its own nationalist spin on the concept. In doing so, "they seek to counter domestic and regional ideological challenges emanating both from mainstream Islamist groups like the Muslim Brotherhood and from extremist organizations like the Islamic State of Iraq and Syria (ISIS)."[34] At the same time, these countries are resistant to external pressure for governance reforms and to opening up the political space because they fear jeopardizing the delicate status quo. As Hamid explains, "Pointing to the instability that the Arab uprisings wrought, authoritarian regimes argue either directly or indirectly that this is not the time for democracy, political reform, or anything that might challenge *haybat al-dawla*, or the 'the prestige of the state.' As part of the projection of religious soft power – by and through the state alone – they prioritize religious reform, including through coexistence forums and training programs for imams. In other words, this is not the time for anything rash, officials from these countries caution international audiences time and time again."[35] Arab regimes also like to remind their Western "allies" that by strengthening the state and building up their military capabilities, they are in a better position to deal with terrorist and extremist elements that also threaten the West.

A second important development is the mutable geostrategic environment. Under the administrations of both Barack Obama and Donald Trump, the United States has preferred to take more of a back-seat role as it slowly disengages from its traditional, front-seat driver position as the region's security enforcer, guarantor, and peacemaker. President Obama resisted pleas by key members of his own administration to become more deeply engaged in Syria's civil war and to back opposition forces that were supposedly more moderate. He drew "red lines" and then almost as quickly erased them as the situation worsened and Syrian president Assad slaughtered his own people, even resorting to the use of chemical weapons in violation of international law and a previous declaration that Syria had destroyed its stockpiles.[36] As Jeffrey Goldberg noted in his telling exit interview with Obama, "The message Obama telegraphed in speeches and interviews was clear: He would not end up like the second President Bush – a president who became tragically overextended in the Middle East, whose decisions filled the wards of Walter Reed with grievously wounded soldiers, who was helpless to stop the obliteration of his reputation, even when he recalibrated his policies in his second term. Obama would say privately that the first task of an American president in the post-Bush international arena was 'Don't do stupid shit.'"[37] To the extent that Obama "engaged" in the politics of the region, it was more of a "soft power" approach that focused on diplomacy, using a combination of carrots (normalization of relations) and sticks (sanctions) to secure a limited agreement with Iran in 2015 – known as the Iran nuclear deal framework – to dial back its nuclear ambitions while trying to restart the peace process between Israelis and Palestinians in 2013–14.

President Trump followed Obama's lead to further reduce the US military footprint in Iraq and avoid any kind of major military confrontation that would involve US troops. As Jack Thompson explains, he "encouraged [Middle Eastern states] to accept more of the regional security burden, resisted the temptation to send large numbers of troops to Syria and other hotspots, and – like Obama – tolerated Saudi Arabia's intervention in Yemen."[38] "Yet," says Thompson, "in key respects, [Trump] … departed from the policies of his predecessor. Relations with Riyadh … improved notably, whereas during Obama's presidency the US and Saudi governments were frequently at odds. Similarly, improving ties with Israeli Prime Minister Benjamin Netanyahu's government, which suffered during Obama's tenure, has been a priority. Trump [withdrew] from the 2015 deal designed to curtail Iran's nuclear weapons program – formally known as the Joint Comprehensive Plan of Action, or JCPOA – and reinstated sanctions on Tehran. Finally, Trump has shown no interest in promoting political reform or bolstering democratic norms – as he demonstrated soon after taking office with his so-called Muslim travel ban."[39]

While the United States took a step back in the Middle East, Russia manoeuvred to fill the vacuum, or as a headline in the *Washington Post* loudly proclaimed, "In the Middle East, Russia Is Back."[40] In 2015, Russia intervened in the Syrian conflict with troops, tanks, and combat aircraft to support Assad's besieged forces, which, along with Iran's support for the regime, helped to turn the war in his favour. Russia also promoted the sale of S-400 surface-to-air missiles to Turkey, to the consternation of Turkey's NATO allies because the missiles are also a threat to NATO F-35 fighter jets.[41] The US responded by cancelling Turkey's purchase of the F-35. Additionally, "Russian oilmen, arms dealers and financiers have been fanning out across the region, striking billions of dollars' worth of deals, reviving old relationships and forging new ones from Libya to the Persian Gulf."[42] But perhaps more importantly, Putin has leveraged Russia's role as a powerbroker in the Syrian conflict to reach out to all parties that have a major interest in its outcome, including Israel, Iran, Qatar, Saudi Arabia, Syria, and Turkey. It has also built stronger ties with Iran, which backs various extremist groups in the region.

In the twentieth century, America's interest in the Middle East, aside from its close relationship with Israel, was driven, in part, by the region's strategic importance as the world's major oil producer. Egypt's Suez Canal was also a key transportation corridor, which it remained long after the United Kingdom's and Europe's imperial powers relinquished their colonies in the Far East. In the twenty-first century, however, Alberta's oil sands, the discovery of major, new shale-oil reserves in the United States, and the invention of new "fracking" technology have turned North America into a self-sufficient energy powerhouse.

According to a US Energy Information Administration (EIA) forecast, American oil production will hit 13.1 million barrels a day in 2020. That constitutes a 19 per cent increase over the 2018 average production of 11 million barrels a day. With the discovery of new shale-gas reserves and the prospect of even more discoveries in Alaska, natural gas production is also expected to increase. The EIA forecasts that dry natural gas production will average 92.5 billion cubic feet a day in 2020, an 11 per cent increase over the 2018 average. In 2019, US daily oil production exceeded that of the world's two other major producers, Russia and Saudi Arabia, in part because

Saudi Arabia, along with other OPEC producers, had reduced production to keep oil prices high.[43]

At the end of the second decade of the twenty-first century, the Middle East and Africa (Nigeria, in particular) are not as important as they once were to North American energy supply needs. The region's strategic importance to the United States has correspondingly declined. With the rapid shift of economic power and global trade to the economic powerhouses of the Asia-Pacific, the Suez Canal no longer has the same geostrategic importance it once did. The opening of the Arctic Ocean may also further reduce the relevance of the canal in the supply chain. Today, roughly 50 per cent of global container traffic and 70 per cent of ship-borne energy pass through the sea lanes of the Indian and Pacific Oceans.

LESS ROOM TO MANOEUVRE

The above factors are important to any consideration of Canada's policy in the Middle East as it approaches the third decade of this century. Taken together, they underscore that there may be greater constraints on what Canada can do and correspondingly less room to manoeuvre and engage diplomatically (or militarily) compared to the past. First, when major Canadian "soft power" diplomatic interventions occurred in the past, as in Lester B. Pearson's intermediary efforts in the 1956 Suez Crisis and the role that Canada played in the Madrid Conference of 1991, when it agreed to chair the Refugee Working Group,[44] these initiatives were undertaken with the strong diplomatic support of the United States. That did not necessarily mean that Canada was always in lockstep with the Americans, but they were generally receptive to Canada's efforts because they too were deeply engaged and therefore welcomed support from their allies. Today, the United States has adopted a more unilateral approach to Middle East strategy and to geopolitics generally. It is reluctant to exercise its diplomatic leverage and influence even on disputes, like the Israeli-Palestinian conflict, where it has traditionally played a major intermediary role. It is also committed to reducing its military footprint and strategic presence in the region. As the United States disengages in the Middle East, a power vacuum is being created, but it is not one that can be easily filled by its allies, including Canada, which have even less influence than the Americans to bring to bear on local actors.

Like the United States, Canada is a close friend of Israel, but unlike the Americans, Canadians have comparatively little to offer in terms of military aid or security guarantees, notwithstanding Canada's free trade agreement with Israel, which was signed in 1997 and which both countries agreed to modernize in 2014. (Canada's two-way merchandise trade with Israel totalled a paltry $1.9 billion in 2018.)[45] Consistent support for the security of Israel, the only genuine democracy in the region, is warranted and should remain a cornerstone of Canada's Middle East policy.

In a part of the world where hard power is viewed as key to state survival, soft power and expressions of goodwill are of correspondingly less value – unless, of course, soft power is accompanied by hard power. Humanitarian and development assistance will always be welcomed by beleaguered and downtrodden Palestinians (and by others who are in the same position). But the Palestinians' fractured leadership makes negotiating with them problematic, and besides they are not looking to Canada to be their interlocutor. Canada should continue to lend its support to countries like Egypt that have brokered talks between Israelis and Palestinians in recent years. It can also add its voice to the disapproving chorus when violence erupts, as too often happens, and civilians are needlessly injured or killed. But Canadians should disabuse themselves of the notion that Canada has a major role to play in resurrecting largely broken peace diplomacy, if only because Israelis and Palestinians themselves have very little interest in going back to the negotiating table. There are even fewer points of access or leverage for a country like Canada in the brutal, ongoing civil wars in Yemen, Iraq, and Syria, apart from lending its full diplomatic support to wider international efforts to end these conflicts and offering assistance to refugees and other victims of war.

A similar logic applies to efforts to promote pluralism, the rule of law, and other kinds of "good governance" initiatives. Local elites must first be receptive to such entreaties; otherwise, they will stonewall and be hostile to what they consider an unwarranted intrusion or meddling in their internal affairs. In the aftermath of the Arab Spring, even the region's more moderate regimes have become extremely wary of embracing progressive governance reforms. They are playing defence against more radical Islamic elements within their own societies and doing so by reaffirming their commitment to Sunni precepts and Sharia law. To the extent that there is a willingness, for example, to recognize women's rights by allowing them to drive, as in Saudi Arabia, it is "about optics, not change." When it comes to basic rights, women "are entirely curtailed by the *Wali* and *Namus* practices, collectively known as the 'male guardianship' system."[46] In Saudi Arabia, limited social reforms have also been accompanied by a brutal crackdown on regime critics and human rights dissidents. The clear message that many Arab leaders, including the Saudis, are sending to the West is that they are not prepared to countenance major reforms in governance, human rights, or the rule of law. External guidance or remonstrations about such matters are neither sought nor welcomed.

In recent years, Canada's military engagement in the Middle Eastern (and North African) region has been modest and is likely to remain so, at least compared to the role Canada played earlier in Operation Desert Storm during the 1991 Gulf War or in the 2011 Libyan bombing mission, where a Canadian commander, Lieutenant General Charles Bouchard, directed the NATO-led air campaign. Under the Harper government, Canada lent the United States a small task force of six CF-18 fighter aircraft and two CP-140 long-range patrol aircraft to support the US operation against ISIS in 2014.[47] Trudeau ended the combat mission in 2016, fulfilling a promise made in the 2015 election. The mission was replaced by a reconfigured commitment and deployment of roughly 850 soldiers and air crew for the longstanding Operation Impact in Iraq and by up to 200 special forces soldiers to help train Kurdish Peshmerga and Iraqi troops in conventional warfare skills.[48]

Since the defeat of ISIS, the US-led coalition has focused its efforts on retraining local forces in counterinsurgency and counterterrorism, which also plays well to the Canadian army's skillset. After agreeing in the summer of 2018 to lead the NATO training mission in Baghdad, the Liberal government announced in March 2019 that Canada would extend its training and advisory deployment in Iraq until the end of March 2021. (Some interpreted the decision to extend the mission, along with Canada's 250-person training mission in Ukraine, as a way to deflect President Trump's criticism about Canada's "diminishing" role).[49] However, it is also clear that when the United States formally ends its military mission in Iraq, as President Trump promised he will one day do, Canada's commitment likewise will end.

HARD LESSONS IN TWITTER DIPLOMACY

There are some other more immediate lessons for Canadian diplomacy that emerge from the Trudeau government's handling of the Middle East file.

The first lesson is that ministers should be circumspect about resorting to social media to deliver diplomatic reprimands because both the content and mode of distribution to its intended recipient(s) are not always controllable or necessarily received in the manner they were intended. As former British diplomat Tom Fletcher cautions, "You can't replace diplomats with Twitter just because you no longer need to shout from a real balcony to reach crowds of people."[50]

When Chrystia Freeland tweeted on 2 August 2018, "Very alarmed to learn that Samar Badawi, Raif Badawi's sister, has been imprisoned in Saudi Arabia. Canada stands together with the Badawi family in this difficult time, and we continue to strongly call for the release of both Raif and Samar Badawi," she did not seem to realize that she had crossed a red line as far as the Saudis were concerned, not least because the tweet, in addition to being issued in English and French, was translated into Arabic by the Canadian embassy in Riyadh. If she did not know, someone in Global Affairs Canada should have. As David Ljunggren and his Saudi-based *Reuters* colleagues reported, "Two Gulf sources said it was the tweet from the embassy that upset Saudi officials the most. 'Matters were being handled through usual channels, but the tweet was a break with diplomatic norms and protocol,' said one of the sources, speaking on condition of anonymity because of the sensitivity of the issue. The sources did not clarify exactly how the tweet broke with diplomacy, but regional experts said it was the step of sending it to a domestic audience that would have angered Saudi officials."[51] The broken crockery was not limited to diplomatic hurt feelings. Matters quickly deteriorated, with Saudi Arabia selling off Canadian assets, suspending flights to Canada, boycotting Canadian wheat and barley, and ending the student exchange program.

Canadian officials were aghast at the Saudi reaction and immediately began to flail around to seek support for Canada's position. As an in-depth investigation into the matter by CBC News found, "in one email from the minister's office, a request was made to try and find any evidence of support from 'like-minded' groups or countries. Ninety minutes later, a staffer responded that that there was 'very little' to be found in terms of online backing from other countries."[52] The minister had phone calls with her counterparts in the United Kingdom, Germany, and Sweden, but to no avail.

Despite the calls, none of Canada's allies were prepared to rush to its defence or take up its cause. In terms of securing the actual release of Samar Badawi, as well as that of Nassima al-Sadah, a Shia human rights activist and writer who was arrested on 30 July 2018,[53] little was also achieved. The Saudis just dug in their heels. When Freeland met privately with Saudi officials on the edges of the UN General Assembly in New York in a bid to repair relations, Saudi Arabia's foreign minister, Adel al-Jubeir, told her that if Canada wanted to move on, it would have to apologize first and "stop treating the kingdom as 'a banana republic.'"[54]

The second lesson is that the government would have been wiser to have laid the groundwork and consulted with its allies before launching a Twitter attack. Going it alone is not a strategy if nobody is willing to back you up when push comes to shove. Sticking with old-fashioned "quiet diplomacy" might have been the better course regardless.

A similar case is instructive in this respect. Canada was successfully able to negotiate asylum for Asia Bibi, a Pakistani Christian woman who spent eight years in a Pakistani prison awaiting execution on false blasphemy charges. Although Bibi was eventually acquitted by Pakistan's Supreme Court, she could not leave the country even though her life was in peril from angry mobs who called for her death. The most that the government would say about the case during negotiations with the Pakistani government was delivered by Liberal member of Parliament Andrew Leslie, the parliamentary secretary to the minister of foreign affairs, in question period in the House of Commons: "With like-minded friends and allies, there are discreet and delicate discussions underway and I will not say anything further at this time."[55] And when Bibi finally arrived in Canada, there were no photo ops with ministers of the Crown or fulsome public statements by the prime minister to celebrate her arrival.

Saudi Arabia may be a more challenging country to deal with than Pakistan, not least because, as former White House staffer Ben Rhodes tweeted, it "Violates human rights, Oppresses women, Murders journalists, Meddles in the affairs [of] Middle Eastern countries, Is fighting a war that endangers millions in Yemen, and Has citizens who have financed/engaged in terror." However, its leadership may be amenable to persuasion as Saudi Arabia looks for friends, especially after its international reputation was marred by the brutal murder of journalist Jamal Khashoggi in its Istanbul consulate in October 2018, reportedly on the direct order of Crown Prince Mohammad bin Salman. Indian prime minister Narendra Modi was able to secure the release of 850 Indians held in Saudi prisons after quietly making the request to the crown prince during his visit to New Delhi.[56] Amnesty was also granted to 2,000 Pakistanis languishing in Saudi jails after a direct personal plea by Prime Minister Imran Khan.[57]

But the Sunni-Shia clash between Iran and Saudi Arabia is internally the epicentre of insecurity in the region. The US contretemps with Iran, which involves others, including Europe, Russia, and China, is a major question mark and could become a global flashpoint that would invariably affect Canadian interests.

MAKING A VIRTUE OF INCONSISTENCY

Middle East scholar Nathan Funk writes, "A virtue can be made of seeming inconsistencies in Canadian Middle East policy, but the effort to induce principles for policy making from past actions is likely to prove problematic if it is not informed by careful explanations for historical variation, and by reflection on current Canadian values and interests."[58] Funk, of course, is absolutely right. But sound policy is based not simply on drawing the right lessons from the past and calibrating Canadian values and interests accordingly. It also derives from a solid appreciation of the contemporary regional and global environment and the opportunities for and constraints on diplomacy that this environment presents, as we have argued here.

Officials also have to defend their decisions in an open and transparent way without obfuscation, buck passing, or blame avoidance, especially when interests and values conflict, as they did over the Saudi arms deal.

From the outset, human rights groups in Canada were opposed to the sale of light armoured vehicles (LAVs) to Saudi Arabia because it involved the supply of arms to a country that has one of the worst human rights records in the world. Both Conservative and Liberal governments wanted to see the deal go through because it supported thousands of Canadian jobs with General Dynamics Land Systems–Canada, which manufactures the LAVs. When human rights advocates offered video evidence that the Saudis were using the LAVs to attack civilians, the Trudeau government "defended" the sale by blaming the previous Conservative government for having negotiated the contract and saying its hands were tied. "As it turned out," *Global News* reported, "the Conservatives had actually only approved minor-level export permits for the vehicles; it was the Liberal's then-foreign minister, Stephane Dion, who signed off on $11 billion worth of armoured vehicles to Saudi Arabia." The government also said the reason that "it couldn't stop the deal was that doing so would subject Canada to economic fallout and financial penalties." That may have been true, but "documents from Global Affairs Canada made public [in 2016] suggest diplomatic and economic relations with Saudi Arabia were of greater concern than the potential 3,000 jobs in Ontario and unconfirmed, though potential, monetary penalty."[59]

The constantly shifting rationale for the sale was not the best way for the government to defend its policy. Worse still, both the media and Canadian public felt that they had been misled, if not lied to. No government will ever have the luxury of always being able to take the high road on matters of public policy. But the only way to make a virtue of inconsistency, especially when it comes to the Middle East, it is to do so plainly and with carefully reasoned decisions that provide a clear and transparent justification for what the government is doing or plans to do. Although many may not like the government's message, they may appreciate the forthright manner in which it is delivered.

With all the uncertainty in the Middle East, the opportunity for sermonizing is minimal. This is one region where, to quote Dean Acheson's assessment of Canada's approach to foreign affairs, acting as the "stern daughter of the voice of God" is risky.[60] Canada has interests to defend and values to support, but due to its limited capacity, Canada requires diplomatic circumspection at its best.

8

Finding Moorings in a Brewing Cyber Storm

Canadians now live in two worlds – the physical and the virtual – that increasingly meld into each other as the Internet of Things takes hold of the ordinary objects of daily life – cars, homes, and, yes, even clothes and toothbrushes. Already, Canadians inhabit the virtual world through cell phones, text messages, emails, Facebook, Twitter, Uber, apps like WhatsApp, and even the Weather Channel. But as everyone knows, digital interactions and data footprints go much further than a simple text or tweet. Whether through a cell phone app, an automatic teller machine, or a Fitbit, every tap of a key or flick of a wrist runs through the Internet, leaving a long digital trail.

Major sectors of the Canadian economy are also now largely managed by platforms that operate on the Internet. Affected infrastructure includes roads, railways, water and sewage treatment plants, air traffic control, banks, pipelines, and energy grids. Without the Internet, educational institutions, businesses, and governments would quickly grind to a halt. But all of these sectors are also vulnerable to cyber attacks. As noted by cyber expert Melissa Hathaway, who led the Cyberspace Policy Review for President Barack Obama after directing the Comprehensive National Cybersecurity Initiative for President George W. Bush and who has closely studied Canada's cyber vulnerabilities, "I don't think there has been a thoughtful analysis of what are the most strategic assets of this country from coast to coast and what are the powerhouses of the Canadian economy – oil and gas, the major ports, finance, telecom or silicon valley, etc. – and what is being targeted in terms of [both] cyber threats and theft of intellectual property." The problem, she says, "is there is no national vision." Canada "is ten years behind most developed economies in terms of thinking strategically about how it is economically dependent on the Internet and what it needs to do to make its economy secure and resilient. Canadians are taking too many things for granted and not looking at what is at risk."[1] This is the challenge that needs to be answered by a coherent strategy and clear lines of delivery and accountability.

THE HIDDEN WIRING OF THE ECONOMY

Both the Canadian and the global economies now depend heavily on the Internet, which is changing ways of doing business and transforming how people communicate and interact with each other. Without a hint of exaggeration, as one study notes, "The Internet is one of the major drivers of globalization in the twenty-first century; it is putting producers and consumers in much closer reach and, in the process, upsetting traditional ways of doing business ... Digital flows are cutting costs, improving productivity and positively affecting countries' growth rates around the world ... [C]ross-border Internet traffic, which has grown by a factor of 500 since the beginning of this century, could expand another eight-fold by 2025."[2]

But the dependence on digital has given rise to new vulnerabilities. Not only is there the danger that one's activities online are being surreptitiously monitored by government authorities like the US National Security Agency, as Edward Snowden revealed to a startled world in 2014, but there is also justifiable fear that the trillions of bits and bytes of data that speed across the Internet can be destroyed or manipulated with inestimable cost to the economy, reputations, and even life itself.

Like cancer, cyber attacks can take many different forms. They can be distributed denial-of-service (DDOS) attacks, where an army of bots shuts down a website by overwhelming its servers with access requests that cause the system to crash (although such attacks typically do not actually gain access to the data contained on the servers of the website itself), or they might involve sinister phishing attacks, where a user inadvertently downloads malware through an email or a website that disables the operating system of a computer or an entire network. If the network is responsible for managing and storing sensitive financial data or for operating critical infrastructure, such as an oil or gas pipeline, a transportation system, or a nuclear power plant, the damage from a well-planned cyber attack can cause major disruptions and perhaps even a major loss of life. This is no mere idle speculation. A Russian attack on Ukraine's eastern power grid in 2015 left many without heat or light in the midst of a very cold winter.

Stealing or destroying data and forcing systems offline obviously wreaks havoc upon communications and data flows, but there is also now a far more insidious threat that involves the actual manipulation of data as opposed to its destruction. Such manipulations can be used to distort the truth and can alter perceptions of reality, possibly with disastrous consequences for an economy, society, and even polity. As forewarned by Admiral Michael Rogers, former director of the US National Security Agency, "Our system – whether it's in the private sector or for us in the military – is fundamentally founded on the idea of trust of the data we are looking at. What happens if the digital underpinning that we've all come to rely on is no longer believable?"[3] This is a brave new world of fake news and so-called "deep fakes," where images, voice, and online video content can be manipulated for nefarious purposes.

Canada has suffered its fair share of different kinds of cyber attacks over the years. Canadian law firms, for example, have witnessed some of the worst security breaches, including cyber break-and-enters that could reveal sensitive information of clients to hackers. One of the biggest security breaches affected seven law firms that were involved in the takeover deal between BHP Billiton and Potash Corporation in 2010, where hackers were clearly intent on getting confidential information about the deal. Fingers were pointed at China's state-owned Sinochem Group, which was worried about the implications of the deal for global supply chains and control over potash. In 2011 another group of Canadian law firms was targeted by hackers because they were involved in a deal that included the Canadian acquisition of a Chinese company.[4]

In 2014 a series of highly publicized DDOS attacks crashed the websites of the Ottawa Police, the Supreme Court of Canada, and the Canadian Parliament.[5] The attack on the Ottawa Police was supposedly in response to its investigation into a teenager who was using his computer to report fake emergencies to dispatchers across

North America.[6] Even hospitals are not immune, as the Ottawa Civic Hospital discovered when 4 of its 9,800 computers faced a hacker's attempted malware attack.[7]

For cyber security, 2017 was a bad year. Not only were the social security numbers, birth dates, and local addresses of some 8,000 Canadians stolen in the Equifax credit data breach, which likewise affected 145 million Americans and some 700,000 Britons, but there were also thirty-three major, publicly reported cyber attacks on Canadian institutions. Those at the top of the list included the theft of 1.9 million customer email addresses along with 1,700 names and phone numbers from Bell Canada, 1 million addresses and phone numbers from Canoe Canada subscribers, information on 1.6 million Canadians and Americans who were users of a Vancouver-based subsidiary of PayPal, and the names, email addresses, and mobile phone numbers of 815,000 Canadian users of Uber taxi services. Customers at Loblaws, Shoppers Drug Mart, and WestJet were also advised that their rewards card points and/or rewards card information might also have been stolen.[8]

In June 2018 it was reported that the personal information of 80,000 Canadians stored in registries operated by the Revenue Canada may have been accessed unnoticed and without authorization over a twenty-one-month period. Revenue Canada had the dubious distinction of suffering more privacy breaches in a two-year period than any other department of the federal government.[9] In 2019 one in six Canadians were affected by the theft of personal and financial data from Capital One, prompting calls for much tougher penalties on financial and other institutions for failures to secure personal data.[10]

Some of the most highly publicized attacks have been ransomware attacks, where major institutions, such as universities or firms in the financial sector, were locked out of their computers unless they paid a healthy ransom, usually in untraceable Bitcoins, to get their computers unlocked. Two major Canadian universities – Carleton University and the University of Calgary – experienced ransomware attacks in 2016 and 2017, respectively. Calgary chose to pay the $20,000 ransom, whereas Carleton, which had backed up its data on another set of servers that were not subject to the attack, did not. Another university, Edmonton's MacEwan University, was duped into depositing almost $12 million in a fraudulent bank account in an online scam.[11] But these attacks pale in comparison to the 2017 WannaCry worldwide ransomware attack, which apparently originated in North Korea and targeted computers in many countries that were running on an older version of the Microsoft Windows operating system by encrypting files on those computers unless they paid a hefty ransom in the Bitcoin cryptocurrency.[12]

A 2018 National Exposure Index released by the private security firm Rapid7 reports that Canada ranked third on the list of "worst countries whose organizations and users have unsecured Internet services open to cyber attacks," whereas the United States was first and China second. Canada was followed in order by South Korea, the United Kingdom, France, the Netherlands, Japan, Germany, and Mexico. The countries were "ranked based in part on a scan of open ports to certain services ... relative to the number of allocated IPv4 [Internet Protocol version 4] addresses" – that is, operating systems that were using older versions of Windows Server Message Block operating systems.[13]

But it could get a lot worse. Major sectors of the Canadian economy from coast to coast are potentially vulnerable to cyber attacks. The Port of Vancouver, for example, could be disrupted by an attack similar to the one experienced by the Port of San Diego, which in September 2018 was subject to a major ransomware attack that disrupted the agency's information technology systems. Fortunately, the port's staff were proactively able to shut down systems that could have compromised normal port operations and public safety because it was able to rapidly mobilize a team of industry experts and local and federal partners.[14]

Canada's highly automated resource firms, including those in the energy sector, could suffer not only millions of dollars in damage, like the high-profile data theft from firms like Uber and Equifax, but also so-called "kinetic effects" resulting in injuries and even death if automated equipment such as remotely controlled bulldozers, diggers, heavy trucks, drilling equipment, or processing systems are comprised during operations. The accounting firm EY reports that "the cybersecurity risk to mining companies had jumped to third in 2017–18, from ninth the year before, on a top-10 work risk list because the 'attack surface' is getting larger as connected IT [information technology] and operational devices in a typical mine or ore transport system grow in the thousands."[15] The Canadian Security Intelligence Service (CSIS) has reached a similar conclusion and has warned energy companies about the growing risks of a combination of cyber espionage and bombings and cyber attacks against pipelines, oil storage and shipment facilities, and power transmission services.[16]

A 2018 survey by the Canadian Internet Registration Authority shows that Canadian small and medium-sized enterprises (SMEs), which are often said to be the backbone of the Canadian economy, are highly vulnerable to cyber attacks. The survey found that 66 per cent of firms with 250–499 employees had experienced cyber attacks in the past twelve months. "Overall, one in ten experienced 20 or more attacks."[17] SMEs are critical to the health of the Canadian economy. According to the Canadian Chamber of Commerce, they "employ more than 90 per cent of Canada's private sector workforce, make up 30 per cent of Canada's GDP, 25 per cent of our exports and account for 95 per cent of net job creation."[18] However, these firms are the most exposed to cyber-attack risks because they generally don't "have the resources to deploy complex security stacks and this makes them easier targets."[19] Furthermore, because of the critical role they play in supply chains in the manufacturing and services sectors, they can be conduits for cyber attacks on bigger companies, as was the case with the Target attack, which comprised the credit card credentials of some 40 million customers, because hackers were able to gain access to those files by stealing the login information of an Internet-connected heating, ventilation, and air conditioning system in Target stores. As the report by the Canadian Internet Registration Authority further notes, "It is estimated that 70 per cent of data breaches happen against companies with fewer than 100 employees which means that a problem that once only kept IT managers of large corporations up at night, will now be causing insomnia for many more."[20]

Many Canadian SMEs lack the resources to adequately train their employees in the basic protocols of cyber-security hygiene or to outsource cyber security to companies that specialize in this area, a market that may seem overwhelming because of the large number of different products and services that are potentially available. There needs to better and affordable access to basic cyber-security education for SME employees. At the same time, the insurance industry has an important role to play in assisting small businesses, especially since many policies do not cover errors of "commission" if, for example, an employee accidentally opens a phishing email or reveals a password or other sensitive information to a fake website. And sometimes data breaches are wilful, as discovered by the Quebec-based credit union the Desjardins Group when an employee leaked the information of "around 2.7 million people and 173,000 businesses, more than 40 per cent of the co-operative's clients and members," including "names, addresses, birth dates, social insurance numbers, email addresses and information about transaction habits."[21]

What is the security situation with respect to Canada's Internet service providers (ISPs), which are the "pipes" through which citizens and businesses access and use the internet? Canada's ISPs are far from the worst when it comes to security, but their security performance nonetheless remains somewhat underwhelming from a global perspective. According to data from CyberGreen reported in a study carried out by the Centre for International Governance Innovation, Canada ranks thirteenth in the world in terms of latent DDOS capacity. Adjusted for population, Canada is the seventh biggest potential originator of cyber attacks, just behind South Korea, the United States, Russia, Australia, Taiwan, and Italy.[22]

As the report argues, "this is cause for concern, because cybersecurity outcomes are highly interdependent. Ubiquitous interconnection entails that weak security performance by a single Canadian ISP jeopardizes not only that ISP's users, but also other individuals, other ISPs, other organizations, other countries, and, really, everyone else."[23] However, opinion surveys cited by the same study suggest that if Canada's ISPs decided to take remedial action in order to further ensure the security of their infrastructure, Canadians would be willing to pay more but only to those ISPs that clearly demonstrated that they could provide a reliable and secure Internet connection.

CANADA'S NEW CYBER-SECURITY STRATEGY

In June 2018 the Liberal government of Justin Trudeau unveiled its new cyber-security strategy for Canada. With a total investment of $500 million to be spent on cyber security over a five-year period, the government touted this expenditure as the single largest ever made on a problem that, in cyber crime alone, was costing Canadians over

$3 billion per year. Part of the funds were allocated to creating a new National Cybercrime Coordination Unit in the Royal Canadian Mounted Police (RCMP) to investigate cyber crimes that target the Canadian government and critical infrastructure. The government also established a new Canadian Centre for Cyber Security (CSE) to support leadership and collaboration between different government departments federally and provincially and with international partners. The government also promised that it would offer greater support to small and medium-sized organizations, which experience 71 per cent of data breaches, and that it would engage in a series of public consultations on how best to enhance cyber security in Canada.[24]

These initiatives have not come soon enough and are still inefficient and uncoordinated. As observed by Robert Hannigan, former director of British signals intelligence services, all Western countries, including Canada, are not winning the battle for cyber security. "If you look at two big trends," he notes, "the rise in the volume of attacks and the rise in sophistication, they are both alarming. On volume, particularly of crime, there were something like 317 million new pieces of malicious code, or malware [in 2016]. That's nearly a million a day, so that's pretty alarming. On the sophistication, we've seen, particularly, states behaving in an aggressive way and using very sophisticated state capabilities and that bleeding into sophisticated criminal groups. It's a rise in the sheer tradecraft of attacks." And it is not simply attacks against corporations and their global supply chains that corporations and governments alike have to be worried about but also attacks against the actual infrastructure of the Internet itself, including routers, switches, and the systems that manage Internet traffic.[25]

As discussed in chapter 4, China poses the major threat to the economy through its cyber attacks, which are also directed at stealing intellectual property and are the basis for the intelligence community's concern about Huawei's involvement in 5G network equipment. China was called out by Australia, the United Kingdom, Canada, and the United States for being responsible for state-sponsored cyber campaigns directed at stealing data from the military, government departments, and private companies.[26] As observed by Chris Krebs, director of the US Department of Homeland Security and Infrastructure Agency, "Russia's trying to disrupt the system, but China's trying to manipulate the system to its ultimate long-term advantage."[27]

But the real question is whether recent Canadian government initiatives are commensurate with the size and scope of the challenge. In the eyes of some, the creation of the Canadian Centre for Cyber Security was more of a move to try to consolidate bureaucratic power. Those same critics believe that Public Safety and Emergency Preparedness Canada has been marginalized in the cyber-security management equation and that there is now a new axis of bureaucratic competition between the CSE and the Department of National Defence.[28] There will be little clarity even with the passage of Bill C-59, An Act Respecting National Security Matters,[29] and there will still be competition among these different bureaucratic entities when it is passed. Canada will not have a proper cyber strategy until it identifies those sectors that are critical to the Canadian economy, identifies their different vulnerabilities, and then develops measures and creates clear oversight and responsibility to address those vulnerabilities. Further, although the levels of new funding in the budget for cyber security appear large, in practical terms they are relatively small, amounting to slightly more than $100 million per year over five years.[30] Most of the monies will be devoted to funding institutions instead of new operational programs.

The RCMP's newly funded cyber-crime centre also has mission overlap with the national cyber-crime centre. But there is no apparent deconfliction process, especially when it comes to sharing intelligence on organized crime, petty crime, and crimes affecting the national interest, nor is there evidence of bureaucratic or political leadership and accountability. There are offsets for shared services to help the CSE defend Canadian government services, including Revenue Canada, which has regularly experienced cyber attacks. Again, however, there is no overarching vision or responsibility in these initiatives, nor is there coherent leadership on how to secure the Canadian economy and create core centres of excellence. Instead, the new "plan" is largely tactically and bureaucratically focused. As Melissa Hathaway summarizes, a core strategic assessment should begin by asking four simple questions: (1) "What makes Canada strong?" (2) "What would make Canada weak?" (3) "Where do we [need to] focus our efforts?" (4) "How quickly do we need to do it?"[31] Canada must also ask whether it can attract top-flight IT employees to a sclerotic, bureaucratic institutional structure.

THE CYBER THREAT TO CANADIAN DEMOCRACY

When the US national security adviser at the time, John Bolton, met with Russian president Vladimir Putin in late October 2018, one of the clear messages he delivered to Putin was to stop meddling in US elections – a message his president was oddly reluctant to deliver. Bolton underlined that Russian interference, particularly in the 2016 US presidential election, had damaged Russia's own interests and also been "particularly harmful for Russian-American relations without providing anything for them in return."[32]

The list of Russian actions – all of which Putin has vigorously denied – is long. In 2015 the US Federal Bureau of Investigation (FBI) informed the Democratic National Committee (DNC) that one of its computers had been compromised by Russian hackers. The chair of Hillary Clinton's presidential campaign, John Podesta, had been the subject of a successful phishing attempt to get him to change his password so that someone could get access to his emails. In early June 2016, WikiLeaks founder Julian Assange announced that WikiLeaks had received hundreds of Clinton's emails, which it would publish on its website. Later that month, WikiLeaks published thousands of emails that it had secretly obtained from an unidentified source – likely Russian – that had been stolen from a DNC server. Some of those emails were so politically compromising that they forced the resignation of DNC chair Debbie Wasserman Schultz. In August hackers were able to get the personal telephone numbers and email addresses of leading Democratic congressional campaign members. There were more leaks and more compromising postings online, which again seemed to have Russian fingerprints all over them.

Then, exactly a month before the US election, the Department of Homeland Security and the Office of National Intelligence on Election Issues confirmed everyone's worst fears. In a joint statement, the two agencies declared: "The U.S. Intelligence Community (USIC) is confident that the Russian Government directed the recent compromises of e-mails from US persons and institutions, including from US political organizations. The recent disclosures of alleged hacked e-mails on sites like DCLeaks.com and WikiLeaks and by the Guccifer 2.0 online persona are consistent with the methods and motivations of Russian-directed efforts. These thefts and disclosures are intended to interfere with the US election process. Such activity is not new to Moscow – the Russians have used similar tactics and techniques across Europe and Eurasia, for example, to influence public opinion there. We believe, based on the scope and sensitivity of these efforts, that only Russia's senior-most officials could have authorized these activities."[33]

Regardless of whether Putin has hurt his own interests, he has sown deep dissension in the American body politic. Accusations not just of electoral interference but also of direct political collusion were the subject of a special inquiry led by former FBI director Robert Mueller. As Mueller's report underscores,[34] there is little doubt that there is a growing threat to democracy from the digital world, which increasingly seems to resemble a lawless Wild West. Congress ignored Mueller's core finding of Russian interference and focused instead on using the findings in its attempts to impeach President Donald Trump. However, it is not just American democratic institutions that are at risk but also democratic institutions everywhere, including Canada. But how serious is the threat, and should Canadians and their leaders be worried?

Canadian journalist John Ibbitson blithely wrote, "There is no reason why any foreign actor would want to interfere in Canada's election. The Liberal and Conservative parties are so closely aligned on every major foreign policy file that Russia, China or any other great power would achieve nothing by attempting to promote one party or undermine another."[35] Although there is little empirical evidence – at least in the public domain – of outside interference in Canada's federal election in 2015, the federal government has sounded the alarm and taken steps to protect Canada from the anticipated attempts of outsiders to interfere in federal elections by influencing public opinion. In November 2018, in a speech to the Halifax Security Conference, Canadian defence minister Harjit Sajjan underscored that Canada is anticipating that Russia has Canada in its sights for cyber attacks and fake news.[36]

There have also been a number of studies by academic and government sources reporting on the nature and extent of the threat of foreign meddling in Canadian democracy, including reports from the Communications Security Establishment, the Canadian Security Intelligence Service, and the Senate of Canada. A report by the Canadian Centre for Cyber Security, for example, concluded that although Russian online influence in Canada is less extensive and less successful than in other Western democracies, the Russian network is substantial and sophisticated. CSIS expects Russian disinformation techniques to continue, including masking attribution by creating so-called "independent" websites to conceal ties to the Russian government. Among the Russian online activities identified in the CSE report are trolling, promotion of extreme political views (both right and left), and activity related to Canada's Magnitsky Act.[37]

As noted by Allan Rock, former Canadian justice minister and attorney general of Canada and now a member of the TransAtlantic Commission on Electoral Integrity, "Russia has devoted much effort to stirring up its diaspora in Canada towards support for extreme positions. Twitter and Facebook are the principal platforms for the Russian operation, which is also broadening its ability to communicate in the French language (since 9 [million] of Canada's 34 million people are francophone). The Russian Television (RT) network recently launched a French language service."[38]

In 2018 Canada's Parliament created a new Standing Committee on National Security, whose mandate includes surveillance of online and other threats and ongoing, critical evaluation of Canada's capacity and strategies to counter them. But, as Rock also observes, "it is also somewhat ironic that some of the most aggressive cyber harassment Canadians have faced [has] occurred outside the country. Canada has contributed troops to the NATO Battle Group in the Baltic states, with almost 600 members of the Canadian forces now stationed in Latvia. On their arrival in the autumn of 2017, Canadian soldiers were met with a barrage of 'fake news' distributed by Russia on social media." Rock goes on to point out, "The false reports disparaged the Canadian soldiers, lied about their living accommodations and even claimed that a former officer jailed for life in Canada in 2013 for murder was in Latvia and commanding the Canadian contingent. In response, the Canadian military responded vigorously to the 'fake news,' undertaking a public relations campaign of its own, including the use of social media, to set the record straight. Perhaps the Russians got the message, because their disinformation efforts against Canadian troops in Latvia diminished in the ensuing months."[39]

Cyber threats to democratic institutions and policy come in many forms. To be sure, the actions taken by authoritarian regimes, like Russia and China, to tamper with electoral systems, hack into political party computers, steal emails and other kinds of information, sow discord by spreading rumours and fake news through online disinformation campaigns and social media, and reveal embarrassing personal details of politicians and celebrities, among other tactics, are mounting, especially when there are willing accomplices in the body politic who see partisan gain from supporting such activities.

But there are other threats from those corporations that harvest personal data from social media platforms like Facebook and then sell that data to political actors without user consent. In late 2009 Facebook changed its privacy settings to make more information public by default. In 2010 Facebook's founder and CEO, Mark Zuckerberg, merrily stated that privacy is no longer a social norm: "People have really gotten comfortable sharing more information and different kinds but more openly and with more people."[40] His words would later come back to haunt him.

The 2018 Cambridge Analytica scandal erupted when a company that had developed an app for Facebook, ostensibly for research purposes with the informed consent of users, exploited its access to Facebook accounts to collect all kinds of personal data that it subsequently harvested to develop psychological profiles of each individual. The information was then sold and used to direct highly targeted advertising in political campaigns. The scandal, which was revealed by a young Canadian whistleblower, Christopher Wylie, who had worked for Cambridge Analytica, was deeply embarrassing to Facebook and Zuckerberg, who found himself summoned to appear before Congress (which he did) and a British parliamentary committee (where he was a no-show) to apologize for his company's actions and the egregious breach of privacy of Facebook users.[41]

The Cambridge Analytica scandal, however, may just be the tip of the iceberg when it comes to managing the risks users confront when they go online and how their personal data are collected and manipulated by the deceitful or the unscrupulous. When nude photos of actress Jennifer Lawrence were leaked online without her consent, she complained to *Vanity Fair* that the event was no less than a sex crime. "Just because I'm a public figure, just because I'm an actress, does not mean I asked for this," she said.[42]

The digital world permits enormous freedom of expression and for all kinds of content to be posted and communicated online. In most liberal democracies, however, at least until recently, there has been little regulation of online content. Stories that are patently untrue can go viral in nanoseconds. For example, in January 2017, YourNewsWire – a website based in Los Angeles – reported that the Canadian singer "Justin Bieber told a Bible study group that the music industry is run by pedophiles" and that according to a study by National Public Radio, "twenty-five million fraudulent votes had been cast for Hillary Clinton."[43] Both stories were untrue.

Hate speech and harassment are also major problems. As *New York Times* writer Frank Bruni stated in 2018 in the aftermath of a murderous attack on a Jewish synagogue in Pittsburgh and in response to Cesar Sayoc's alleged mailing of pipe bombs to prominent Democrats, the Internet "creates terrorists. But well shy of that, it sows enmity by jumbling together information and misinformation to a point where there's no discerning the real from the Russian."[44]

At the same time, maintaining diversity of content and allowing different voices to be heard are also growing challenges because of the overwhelming market dominance of a small number of online platforms like Facebook, Twitter, Google, Amazon, and in the entertainment world, Netflix. These tech giants enjoy oligopolistic, if not monopolistic, control in cyber space. Further, the algorithms that manage and curate online content on these platforms generally tend to be written by young, white males who have limited world experience and lack the kind of educational background that would expose them to different cultural viewpoints and processes of moral reasoning. There are already moves in the US Congress to address the concerns about monopolistic controls and some calls to break up the digital giants. The US Justice Department has also initiated a broad antitrust review of major technology companies.[45] However, confronted with the growing threat of regulation, companies like Facebook are already taking a combination of pre-emptive and defensive measures to evade antitrust enforcement and protect their business model.[46]

The lack of transparency in the way "big data" are harvested and curated by major Internet platforms also means that the general public and regulators have little knowledge of corporate business models and how data are manipulated and marketed. Algorithms are closely kept trade secrets, much like the formula for Coca-Cola.

Some knowledgeable observers now question whether democracy can actually survive in a world of "big data" and artificial intelligence. As the prestigious journal *Scientific American* explains, "Today, algorithms know pretty well what we do, what we think and how we feel – possibly even better than our friends and family or even ourselves ... The more is known about us, the less likely our choices are to be free and not predetermined by others. But it won't stop there. Some software platforms are moving towards 'persuasive computing.' In the future, using sophisticated manipulation technologies, these platforms will be able to steer us through entire courses of action, be it for the execution of complex work processes or to generate free content for Internet platforms, from which corporations earn billions. *The trend goes from programming computers to programming people.*"[47]

In George Orwell's novel *Nineteen Eighty-Four*, a big face gazes down from a wall with a caption that reads, "Big Brother Is Watching You." In today's world, Orwell's Big Brother seems archaic and clumsy. Governments and private entities have far more sophisticated tools at their disposal. *Scientific American* calls this the politics of "big nudging," which entails large-scale government efforts to direct citizens toward preferred kinds of behaviour. "The new, caring government is not only interested in what we do, but also wants to make sure that we do the things that it considers to be right ... To many, this appears to be a sort of digital scepter that allows one to govern the masses efficiently, without having to involve citizens in democratic processes. Could this overcome vested interests and optimize the course of the world? If so, then citizens could be governed by a data-empowered 'wise king,' who would be able to produce desired economic and social outcomes almost as if with a digital magic wand."[48]

We may think that we are still far off from this kind of world. However, authoritarian regimes like China are already moving quickly to harness these technologies for nefarious purposes. Using facial-recognition technology, China is deploying surveillance cameras and control of the country's digital space to monitor the physical movements and online behaviour of all 1.4 billion of its citizens. As the *Business Insider* reported in 2018, "China's facial recognition surveillance has already proven to be eerily effective: Police in Nanchang, southeastern China, managed to locate and arrest a wanted suspect out of a 60,000-person pop concert."[49] Artificial intelligence and digital technologies, it seems, really are ready-made for dictators.

It comes as no surprise that citizens everywhere are becoming increasingly mistrustful of governments, Internet companies, and social media platforms when it comes to their own data and privacy. A CIGI-Ipsos global survey of public attitudes in twenty-five different countries conducted in 2017–18 found that cyber criminals (82 per cent) and Internet companies (74 per cent) are the largest sources of distrust online, more so than even governments. The figures for Canada are 82 per cent and 75 per cent respectively.[50] (The survey was conducted before news of the Cambridge Analytica scandal erupted.) Interestingly, despite the identification of Internet companies and social media platforms as common sources of distrust, less than a quarter (23 per cent) of respondents pointed to control by corporate elites as a reason for their distrust.

An overwhelming majority (68 per cent) of those surveyed also exhibited high levels of distrust toward social media. In Canada 71 per cent agreed that social media companies contribute to their distrust of the Internet. Much of that hostility in Canada also appears to be directed at the social media giant Facebook. As a January 2019 Nanos survey for the *Globe and Mail* reported, "Canadians hold strongly negative views of Facebook's approach to protecting personal data and are concerned the social media giant will have a negative impact on the 2019 federal election … The survey found more than seven in 10 Canadians think Facebook does a poor or very poor job of monitoring how the platform is used to influence politics. It also found that more than eight in 10 Canadians think Facebook is untrustworthy or somewhat untrustworthy with people's personal data. Also, more than six in 10 Canadians say Facebook will have a negative or somewhat negative effect on the next federal election."[51] Further, as a major report by Allan Rock underscores, "In Canada, even if disinformation is discovered, there is no guarantee that platforms will quickly remove it. For example, Facebook was alerted by a member of the House of Commons' Standing Committee on Access to Information, Privacy and Ethics about a false story regarding the Canadian military in Latvia but only removed the post a month later after it was prompted again to remove it."[52]

On the one hand, the Internet and the digital world have created unparalleled opportunities for freedom of expression, communication, commerce, and the dissemination of knowledge. Such opportunities are vital to a vigorous, prosperous, open society and to democracy itself. On the other hand, the rapid evolution and growth of the digital ecosystem have led to major abuses and mounting public concern that the digital space needs gatekeepers to prevent such abuses and a further erosion of democratic institutions.

REGULATORY CHALLENGES

Regulation of the digital space is "inevitable," as concluded by a 2018 report jointly produced by the Centre for International Governance Innovation and Stanford University's Digital Policy Incubator. The report, entitled *Governance Innovation for a Connected World: Protecting Free Expression, Diversity and Civic Engagement in the Digital Ecosystem*, argues that the challenge is essentially one of learning how best to apply the norms, standards, and rules of the non-digital world – also sometimes referred to as the "analogue world" – to the digital.[53] In his summation of the report, Bill Graham points out, for example, that "the non-digital world widely accepts that governments legitimately set ground rules in many sectors, for example, telecommunications common carrier regulation, transportation safety rules, broadcasting regulation, and radio frequency allocation and spectrum management rules, among others."[54] The report argues that the digital world increasingly needs similar kinds of regulation and legislation. However, in this new environment, Graham notes that "civil society will need to get over its long-standing aversion to having government intervene to control the behavior of internet platforms and users. Acceptance may be difficult to achieve because of fears that regulators may not take sufficient care to understand the fast-moving environment. The concern is that government may regulate to solve today's (or yesterday's) problems without considering that today's dominant players can be replaced, which would rapidly make those regulations obsolete and could even work to impede innovation. The question is really how to avoid undesirable or unintended outcomes."[55] Parenthetically, it is not clear that we have trust in the capabilities of regulators to oversee a rapidly changing industry or in government officials to regulate online content and the legitimate boundaries of free speech.

Prior to the 2019 federal election, Canada was unique in the democratic world for having a minister for democratic institutions with clear political responsibility to protect Canada's democratic processes, as well as a minister of digital government. The country also has a long tradition of strong election laws, including spending limits, with processes overseen by a chief electoral officer reporting to Parliament. That foundation was strengthened with the passage of Bill C-76, The Elections Modernization Act, which provides additional safeguards, including an outright ban on foreign paid political advertising.[56] (As noted above, Canadian law and policy have also begun to deal with cyber threats, including $500 million in the federal government's 2018 budget to consolidate and build on cyber-defence capacity across government through the new Canadian Centre for Cyber Security.)

All democracies are wrestling with the issue of foreign manipulation of Internet-based platforms to distort the political conversation during elections and to deceive voters through false information. This manipulation includes hacking and leaking, bot farms and trolls aided by the online equivalent of what Soviet leader Joseph Stalin called "useful idiots," and "deep fake" videos that are also intended to confuse and deceive. Clearly, no single country or political jurisdiction can deal with these cyber challenges on its own because there are no real "borders" – or at least controllable ones – in cyber space.

Canada has shown international leadership by promoting the development of a Rapid Response Mechanism, which it first proposed at the 2018 G7 Summit in Charlevoix, Quebec, and by continuing as chair of that initiative so as to ensure follow-through in coordination, information sharing, and collaborative development of best responses.[57] Nevertheless, there is still a great deal that has to be done to defend Canada's democratic institutions, including enhancing "cyber literacy" by making citizens aware of the risks of manipulation, distortion, and misinformation through social media and other online platforms. Fundamentally, Canada is confronting an old Cold War threat, namely "disinformation," but in a new and vastly more powerful guise.

DOES CANADA FOLLOW EUROPE'S LEAD?

Deciding upon and setting limits, especially when it comes to hate speech and online privacy, are not easy tasks. Europe is clearly leading the way, although not without controversy. Germany has introduced legislation banning hate speech online. The law known as NetzDG (Act to Improve Enforcement of the Law in Social Networks) was introduced to deal with the growing problem of hate speech online, much of which was directed at the major influx of refugees into Germany. Under the law, social media platforms with more that 2 million subscribers are required to remove illegal hate speech content within a twenty-hour period after receiving a user complaint, or they will suffer very stiff fines that could be as high as 50 million euros.[58] A variety of concerns have been raised about the law. The legislation appears to be directed at American-operated social media platforms because of the high subscriber threshold. Because the fines are so hefty, freedom-of-speech advocates worry that media platforms will err on the side of caution and take down posts that fall into the "grey" zone, namely those that are controversial but not necessarily threatening to any group or person. For some, asking media companies to police hate speech online through their algorithms gives them too much power in the absence of proper oversight, accountability, and transparency mechanisms.

The European Union's General Data Protection Regulation, which went into effect in May 2018, has global ramifications, including for Canada. Under the law, which imposes uniform data privacy and data protection regulations right across Europe, companies are held accountable for the way that they handle personal data associated with EU residents, regardless of whether or not they are incorporated into the European Union, with penalties for noncompliance running as high as 4 per cent of global revenue or 20 million euros, whichever is greater.[59] European residents also have a legal right to access, correct, and erase their data, as well as to move it to another service provider if they so choose. Companies are required to report breaches involving EU resident data to data protection authorities within a seventy-two-hour period and to notify those individuals directly about the data breach. The law also encourages corporations to review the way that they handle and manage data on a regular basis and to take remedial measures to strengthen security and privacy in their administrative and technical operations as necessary.

Many countries, including Canada, are studying these requirements to determine whether they should introduce similar requirements for the way that data is handled, managed, and distributed. (This could also be an important task for NATO.) An excellent series of recommendations to help policymakers steer their way through the digital labyrinth is offered in a report that was developed jointly by Edward Greenspon of Canada's Public Policy Forum and Taylor Owen of the University of British Columbia entitled *Democracy Divided: Countering Disinformation and Hate in the Digital Public Sphere*.[60] For example, it urges publishers of online content to identify themselves; Internet companies (or online intermediaries) to be held legally responsible for content they publish on their websites; all forms of advertising (including political advertising) to be transparent in terms of their source and funding; algorithms to be subject to regular audits by external, "independent authorities" and the results made publicly available; noncriminal remedies to investigate and respond to hate speech online; and independent panels to investigate disinformation (i.e., fake news) and hate speech online. Educational programs to promote digital literacy and greater public awareness and literacy are also encouraged by the report.[61]

Some of these recommendations are sensible, but others may not be well received. Internet and social media companies will fight tooth and nail against having algorithms – their most cherished trade secrets – scrutinized or validated by outsiders. Depending on how it is done, policing "fake news" could curb freedom of expression and thought, although it is important to remember that freedom of expression is a right but not an absolute one. The Canadian Charter of Rights and Freedoms protects free speech but does not preclude reasonable limits, as the example of hate speech provisions in Canada's Criminal Code attests.

Historical perspective is in order. "Fake news" and the manipulation of the "truth," especially in the political arena, are not new phenomena. Orson Wells's broadcast "The War of the Worlds," which terrified radio listeners, was one of the first examples of "fake news" in the modern era. So too were Nazi propaganda campaigns and censorship, which were far less benign and aided Adolf Hitler's rise to power. As we debate the need to police the Internet and social media, it is important to remember Justice Louis Brandeis's observation that "[p]ublicity is justly commended as a remedy for social and industrial diseases. Sunlight is said to be the best of disinfectants; electric light the most efficient policeman."[62] But you still need good laws and intelligent police officers to enforce them, which means that Canada is also going to have to deal with the businesses that own social media platforms and make them more accountable for curating the content on their platforms so that what gets posted or distributed is in accordance with Canadian laws.

In his testimony at the hearings of the International Grand Committee on Big Data, Privacy and Democracy in Ottawa in May 2019, when politicians from Canada and ten other countries gathered to consider how best to protect citizens' privacy and their democracies in the age of big data and social media, Jim Balsillie noted, "Disinformation and fake news are just two of the many negative outcomes from unregulated attention-based business models. They cannot be addressed in isolation. They have to be tackled horizontally, as part of an integrated whole. To agonize over social media's role in proliferation of online hate, conspiracy theories, politically motivated misinformation and harassment is to miss the root and scale of the problem."[63] In other words, to return to our discussion of competitiveness in chapter 3, global market concentration in online social media platforms lies at the root of the problem.

Canada's legal and institutional structures are also not well equipped to deal with firms that operate in a cyber world that has no borders. But that is no excuse for inaction. Balsillie offers a number of useful suggestions to help make these firms more accountable. They include, among other things, eliminating the "tax deductibility of specified categories of online ads ... so that tax incentives favour subscription models for online services"; imposing a complete ban on "personalized online advertising for elections" to reduce the risks of voter manipulation and "sale to the highest bidder during an election"; implementing "strict data governance regulations for political parties," including the application of "privacy regulations to political parties regarding access to personally identifiable information" and "transparency of all commercial and technical relationships between political parties and social media companies"; and adding "explicit personal liability alongside corporate responsibility to affect CEO and Board of Director decision-making," including "adding annual signed CEO and Board certifications similar to those required for Sarbanes-Oxley compliance. This 2002 Act was designed to better protect investors by improving the accuracy and reliability of corporate disclosures in the wake of various accounting scandals."[64] As Basillie attests, "personal liability ... immediately changes behaviour to one of greater prudence and caution."[65] In other words, preserving the integrity of democratic institutions is not just a security issue but also one of fostering corporate social responsibility and getting serious about regulating "unregulated attention-based business models."[66]

If Canada expects to support global initiatives to combat cyber attacks and regulate digital empires, it needs a more coherent strategy and clear lines of responsibility – bureaucratic and political – at home. The scattershot process now in place will doom Canada to irrelevance.

9

Immigration and Refugees

Although Canada is a nation of mostly settlers and immigrants, the positive narrative that immigration is critical to the vitality of Canada and its future economic growth and prosperity has been undermined by the ineffectiveness of the policies of the government of Justin Trudeau in managing an influx of cross-border asylum seekers and refugees during its tenure. The government's hyperbolic rhetoric and welcoming policies on immigration and refugees have not been matched by its performance in expeditiously processing asylum seekers or ensuring that those who come to Canada under dire circumstances receive the support they deserve to find jobs and integrate into Canadian society. As a consequence, immigration and refugees have become a "hot button" political issue, although it is also undeniable that Canadians have been influenced by what they see on their own borders and to some extent by what they see happening in Europe and the United States, particularly the parlous conditions on the US border stemming from inaction on the closing of asylum loopholes.

Since the refugee crisis in Syria and North Africa first erupted in 2010–11, the European Union has struggled to manage its impact as some 3.2 million refugees and asylum seekers have crossed the border into Europe. Some countries, like Germany, Italy, Greece, and Turkey, were initially welcoming and opened their borders to the refugee influx, whereas others, like Czechoslovakia, Hungary, and Poland, turned them away. But the welcome mat is now being rolled up as Europe's leaders confront a growing backlash from their own citizens, even in countries like Germany that have been welcoming to refugees, because of the fear that governments have lost control over their countries' respective borders and have struggled to manage the strain on their social services. Even a Western democracy like Australia, once a champion of refugee rights and legal due process, is denying refugees asylum, instead putting them in camps on remote islands in the South Pacific where living conditions, according to many informed observers, are deplorable and subhuman. As indicated below, there is strong evidence that public attitudes in Canada are hardening in the face of abuse of Canadian laws, but at the same time, there is recognition that Canada needs more immigrants to replenish its aging demographic and to bolster sagging productivity.[1]

THE IMMIGRATION CHALLENGE

Canada may have a young prime minister compared to his Mexican and US counterparts, but the same cannot be said about the rest of the population. Canadians are the golden oldies, relatively speaking, of North America. The median age of the Canadian population in 2017 stood at 42.2, compared to 28.3 for Mexico and 38.1 for the United States. As well, Canadians on average tend to live longer than their North American counterparts. In 2019 the country ranked seventeenth in the world, with Canadians having an average life expectancy of 82.4 years, which was 3.5 years longer than Americans and 7 years longer than Mexicans.[2] With Canadians living longer, however, there is greater pressure on social services, healthcare, and all the public services that are required to care for an older population.[3] But it is not just replenishing an aging population that poses a challenge; Canada also faces major skilled labour shortages in just about every key sector of the economy: engineers, technicians, information technologists, pilots, nurses, doctors, and so on. And these shortages will only grow as technology and advanced services come to play an increasingly important role in Canada's economy.[4]

Projections suggest that the costs of two key income transfer programs, Old Age Security and the Guaranteed Income Supplement, will increase by 47 per cent between 2017 and 2047 because a larger share of the population will be eligible for such programs. Healthcare costs will also increase. Right now, seniors consume more than four times the healthcare costs of Canadians aged fifteen to sixty-four. At the same time, Canada's labour-force participation rate will have shrunk from its peak of 67.6 per cent in 2008 to roughly 61.0 per cent by mid-century, which points to slower growth and lower government revenues. Although the government of Stephen Harper tried to reduce the squeeze on the public purse by raising the age of eligibility for Old Age Security and the Guaranteed Income Supplement to sixty-seven in 2029, the Trudeau government restored the age of eligibility to sixty-five, unlike other countries in the Organisation for Economic Co-operation and Development that have taken measures to raise the eligible age for government income support.[5]

Some argue that Canada should aspire to grow its population to 100 million by the end of this century.[6] This view is challenged by others on the grounds of the country's environmental sustainability, a proposition that is hotly debated. But what is clear is that without a healthy influx of immigrants and the social capital that comes with them, the Canadian economy will shrink, acute labour shortages will mount, and the ability of the government to provide social services to Canada's aging population will be severely compromised. A study by the Conference Board of Canada points out that "immigration's share of annual population growth will rise ... to 100 per cent by 2034 – when the number of deaths is expected to exceed the number of births."[7]

Under the Trudeau government, Canada plans to increase its annual immigration targets from 330,800 in 2019 and 341,000 in 2020 to an eventual annual intake of 350,000, its aim being to settle 1.3 million new permanent residents by 2021. These targets were announced in Immigration, Refugees and Citizenship Canada's October 2017 report to Parliament.[8] In addition to increasing the number of skilled worker immigrants under the economic immigration programs managed by the federal Express Entry economic system and Canada's Provincial Nominee Programs, the government raised the number of immigrants accepted both in the family and refugee category and in the humanitarian category, where the contribution to productivity is less assured.[9]

But what is surely worrying is that public support for immigration is eroding, in large part because of the surge of irregular asylum seekers across the Quebec border since the election of President Donald Trump. A major poll undertaken by Ipsos clearly shows that only 38 per cent of Canadians believe that immigration has had a positive effect on their country. That figure is higher than in the United

States (35 per cent) but lower than in the United Kingdom (40 per cent), where immigration has been one of the central motivating factors among supporters of Brexit. Forty per cent of Canadians in the same poll agreed with the statement "Immigration is causing my country to change in ways that I don't like." The numbers were 46 per cent and 43 per cent for the United States and the United Kingdom respectively.[10] But Canadians are clearly conflicted because 43 per cent also agreed with the proposition that immigration is good for the economy, whereas 47 per cent agreed in the United Kingdom and 42 per cent in the United States.[11] The majority of Canadians (51 per cent) want the country to admit immigrants who are educated and can fill categories in professions where there are shortages (e.g., doctors).[12]

Darrell Bricker of Ipsos concludes that "Canadian views on immigration [are] mixed. We look good in comparison to rest of the world, not as good on our own." He believes that the "potential for [a] populist/nativist backlash in Canada [in the] short term, [is] middling to low." However, there is "[s]ome kindling on the ground but [it] lacks essential elements for combustion." Bricker also makes the important observation that public attitudes in Canada will be shaped by whether or not governments effectively manage the flow of migrants across the border with the United States. He further points out that the political narrative about immigration "needs to evolve past country benefit, test of compassion, to positive community/personal impact." Governments will increasingly have to demonstrate that immigration is "[n]ot just good for us, [and] them" in the collective sense but also good for Canadians in terms of their own personal livelihood.[13]

A U-TURN

To many, it looked like a U-turn. And it was. In April 2019 Prime Minister Justin Trudeau's Liberal government buried tough, new immigration measures on asylum seekers entering Canada at "unauthorized" border crossings in Bill C-97, The Budget Implementation Act. Under the new legislation, claimants' access to a hearing by a refugee tribunal would be severely restricted. Claims by those who had already filed a refugee claim in another country such as the United States would also be disallowed.

The Liberal government's erstwhile supporters in the refugee-advocate community of nongovernmental organizations were outraged. Amnesty International Canada (English Branch), the British Columbia Civil Liberties Association, the Canadian Association of Refugee Lawyers, the Canadian Civil Liberties Association, and the Canadian Council for Refugees wrote a letter to the prime minister excoriating his government for including "an unexpected, substantial and deeply troubling reform affecting the human rights of refugees in the omnibus *Budget Implementation Act*, Bill C-97."[14] The group went on to point out that the measure would end up "depriving certain refugee claimants of access to full and independent refugee hearings" and that it was "harsh and unnecessary." It argued that "stripping crucial and hard-won human rights protections from people in a budget bill is undemocratic and means that Parliamentarians will be deprived of the ability to properly consider the effects of the change on vulnerable people, and its unforeseen consequences on the refugee determination system."[15]

But it was not just civil society groups that were incensed. *National Post* political affairs columnist Andrew Coyne called the "draconian shift in policy" simply "breathtaking." He pointed out that "what is wrong about the new Liberal policy is not that it is hypocritical, but simply that it is wrong: arbitrary, inhumane, and vastly unnecessary."[16] *Globe and Mail* columnist John Ibbitson, however, welcomed the government's new immigration plan on the grounds that "the core purpose of immigration is to stoke the economy and prevent population decline" and that "[t]he intent of deterring crossings at unauthorized places should be to bolster the overall system."[17] Absent from the criticism of the change in government policy are solutions that address concerns about the strain on municipalities and social services, which have been raised by local officials.

It also came to light that the government's border security minister, Bill Blair, had written to the US homeland secretary to initiate talks about closing a loophole in the Safe Third Country Agreement, which went into effect in 2004. Under the agreement, each country declares the other country a safe haven for refugees, preventing most refugee claims at the US-Canada border. However, claimants crossing the border at unauthorized or "irregular" locations can file asylum claims after entering Canada and, under existing Canadian law, cannot be turned back by law enforcement officials.[18]

This loophole was exploited by those whose temporary status in the United States had to be taken away as well as by a wave of asylum seekers who crossed the border in large numbers in the period 2017–19 after Donald Trump imposed a travel ban on seven Muslim countries, which was followed a little more than year later by his "zero tolerance" policy on illegal immigration. (This was a different situation from the discovery by Canadian authorities of an elaborate "human smuggling operation" to bring nearly a thousand Chinese migrants across the Canada-US border via the Peace Arch Park, which straddles the international border between Surrey in British Columbia and Blaine in Washington State.)[19]

What a different picture of a government that a mere three and a half years earlier had gone out of its way to roll out the red carpet for Syrian refugees. The prime minister personally welcomed Syrian families arriving at Toronto Pearson International Airport on 11 December 2015 and stated, "Tonight they step off the plane as refugees. But they walk out of this terminal as permanent residents of Canada with social insurance numbers, with health cards and with an opportunity to become full Canadians."[20] As the headline of an editorial by *New York Times* columnist Nicholas Kristof gushed, "Thank God for Canada! Our Boring Neighbor Is a Moral Leader of the Free World." In addition to praising Canada's foreign minister, Chrystia Freeland, for standing up for women's human rights when Canada granted asylum to a young Saudi woman, Rahaf Mohammed Alqunun, who had fled to Bangkok to escape being murdered by her family, Kristof praised Canadians for "stepping up" during "the worst of the Syrian refugee crisis" when "President Barack Obama admitted just 12,000 Syrians and ... Canada accepted 40,000 Syrians."[21] In fiscal year 2018, the Trump administration accepted only sixty-two Syrians.[22]

Some also blamed the prime minister for unleashing the "flood" of asylum seekers with his tweet on 28 January 2017: "To those fleeing persecution, terror & war, Canadians will welcome you, regardless of your faith. Diversity is our strength #WelcomeToCanada." But as time would soon tell, Trudeau's "welcome mat" was a naive impulse. Little thought or planning had occurred regarding how to receive and assimilate so many and how to pay for them. The municipalities and provinces were left holding the bag. As *Financial Post* columnist Diane Francis points out, "Before the tweet, border officials prevented 315 people a month from illegally crossing the border. Post-tweet in 2017, about 18,149 illegally crossed the border, then claimed asylum as refugees – even after entering illegally – and were allowed to stay, get welfare, education, housing, healthcare and work permits. By May 2018, the number of refugee cases pending [had] jumped to 54,906 from 18,348 in December 2016. That's the population of Grande Prairie, Alberta or Granby, Quebec."[23] However, the peak came in August 2017 when almost 6,000 asylum seekers were greeted at unauthorized crossings by the Royal Canadian Mounted Police, although the numbers declined steadily in 2018 and by early 2019 had fallen to 1,696 in January-February compared to 3,082 in the same period the previous year.[24]

WHERE THE GOVERNMENT FAILED

Clearly, broader political and electoral considerations were at play in the government's decision to clamp down on asylum seekers and what Blair disparaged as "asylum shopping," a phrase that further outraged the government's critics.[25] Craig Damian Smith at the University of Toronto called Trudeau out for wanting "to shore up Liberal support in Quebec and in the 905 suburbs around Toronto, where anti-refugee sentiment boiled over into protests against asylum seekers," and although the new policy would "cause some advocates for refugees to sour on the Prime Minister, there are not enough of them to matter electorally."[26] Public concern was fuelled by the impact of the influx on public housing, healthcare, and education facilities in Montreal. Similar pressures were also evident in Toronto.

The Trudeau government was clearly running scared as it desperately tried to straddle being tough and being tolerant. Canadians were becoming increasingly concerned about the government's asylum and border management policies and how economic migrants were jumping the queue and abusing the system. In a September 2018 Angus Reid national poll, 67 per cent said they thought the refugee situation was in a crisis, whereas 71 per cent wanted to see greater investment in border security than in assisting those entering Canada through "irregular" points of entry. These concerns crossed traditional party lines, with many of those surveyed believing that Conservative leader Andrew Scheer would prove to have a better handle on the issue if he became prime minister. At the same time, some observers blamed the media for stoking anti-immigration fears and fostering the perception that Canada was being "invaded."[27] However, another national poll in 2018 found that there was mounting concern over "irregular" migrants who were entering Canada at unofficial border crossings to seek asylum since it was believed that they were "exploiting the system to get express entry into Canada and that security procedures [had] been compromised as a result."[28]

As it struggled to manage the growing number of cross-border asylum seekers, the Trudeau government was learning a sober lesson that leaders in other Western democracies, especially in western Europe, had already absorbed: the majority of citizens in an otherwise tolerant and open democratic society will generally be welcoming toward those seeking refuge provided the numbers and the costs are manageable and the flows are conducted in an orderly way. But when a government is seen to be losing control over its borders and cannot effectively manage the flow and needs of asylum seekers, it will place itself in political peril. Canadians are no different from Europeans or Americans in believing that if they cannot secure their borders, they are not citizens of a "real" country.

It was not just what was happening at the border that was a problem; it was also the government's inability to process asylum claims in a timely manner and, as further discussed below, the difficulties that those among the most recent influx of refugees were experiencing finding jobs and integrating into Canada's economy. The government's lofty rhetoric about Canada being a safe and welcoming haven for refugees was not matched by its performance on implementation.

A 2019 report by the Office of the Auditor General of Canada delivered a scathing indictment of the government's record in processing asylum claims. It found that there was a backlog in December 2018 of "71,380 claims waiting for protection decisions" and that "[f]ewer than 20% of claimants [had] received a hearing for a protection decision within the required 60 days. Half the protection decisions were made at the hearings themselves. The remaining protection decisions were normally provided within 25 days of the hearings. In February 2018, the Board announced that it would set aside the 60-day requirement, as permitted by immigration regulations, and schedule hearings according to when claims had been made. By the end of December

2018, the expected wait time for a protection decision had reached two years."[29] The report concluded, "Overall, we found that Canada's refugee determination system was not equipped to process claims according to the required timelines. Despite reforms introduced in 2012 to speed up decision making, the system was again faced with a significant backlog of unresolved claims." Many of the inefficiencies were bureaucratic and the result of "significant gaps in information sharing and duplication of effort among the three main organizations involved in the claims process: the Canada Border Services Agency; Immigration, Refugees and Citizenship Canada; and the Immigration and Refugee Board of Canada ... [T]he organizations used different information technology systems, with limited interoperability. Although the organizations shared some information electronically, they still relied on paper and faxes to share specific claim information. In addition, few claims that were eligible for faster processing received quicker decisions. As a result, claims that could have been fast-tracked tied up the system instead."[30]

The record of refugees finding jobs has also been quite mixed. A major study by Statistics Canada on the labour market outcomes of some 830,000 refugees who entered Canada from the 1980s to 2000s found that the earnings of refugees from different countries varied greatly: "Ten years after entering Canada, the refugee groups with the highest earnings (i.e., from the former Yugoslavia, Poland and Colombia) earned roughly double what those with the lowest earnings did (i.e., from Somalia, Afghanistan, Pakistan and China). Differences in outcomes were accentuated by the fact that groups with low (high) employment rates tended to have low (high) earnings levels among the employed, and groups with high employment rates tended to have high earnings among the employed. Furthermore, male and female refugees from the same country tended to have similarly low (high) relative earnings. These high correlations in men's and women's earnings across groups tended to exacerbate any poverty issues for refugees with low earnings."[31] The study also found that "[p]rivately sponsored refugees earned more than comparable government assisted refugees during the initial years in Canada. However, this advantage disappeared after a decade in the country."[32]

Recent statistics also show that an alarming number of refugees become homeless despite government assistance. Reports released by Employment and Social Development Canada show that in 2016 there were 2,000 refugees in shelters across Canada and that in 2018 an estimated 40 per cent of those in Toronto shelters were refugees or asylum seekers.[33]

In another study of the 25,000 Syrian refugees who settled in Canada during the period 2015–16, the initial numbers were not especially encouraging.[34] It found that "Syrian refugees had a lower employment rate than other refugees, largely because they had been in the country for a shorter period of time ... Among Syrian refugees aged 20 to 59 who arrived in 2015 and 2016, 24% of males and 8% of females were employed on Census Day (May 10). This compared with 39% of male and 17% of female refugees from other countries."[35] One of the major obstacles to labour integration is language proficiency: "In 2016, 55% of Syrian refugees did not speak English or French, compared with 28% of refugees from other countries."[36] Many of the Syrian refugees were also young families with children and fewer working-age males. Clearly, a much greater investment has to be made to provide proper language training for new refugee entrants so that they can enter the labour market more quickly and become productive members of society. Fixing a broken system for processing asylum and refugee claims is also a top priority.

TACKLING THE GLOBAL REFUGEE CRISIS

Canada also has a role to play in addressing the global refugee problem in both its "downstream" and "upstream" dimensions. Most of today's major refugee crises are caused by a combination of conflict and bad leaders who persecute their own people. The failure of the West and the United Nations to nip these conflicts in the bud and to hold regimes accountable for human rights abuses of their people lies at the root of this crisis. As Western and other societies reach the limits of their ability to accept new waves of refugees and asylum seekers and to quell the nationalist-populism fervour, they will have to impose greater responsibility on rogue regimes to fix their own governance problems and will have to hold them accountable.

Globally, the sheer numbers are staggering. Overall, there were 70.8 million forcibly displaced persons worldwide in 2018 as a result of persecution, conflict, violence, or human rights violations. More than 41 million of those were internally displaced persons (IDPs), nearly 26 million were refugees living outside their home countries, and another 3.5 million were asylum seekers awaiting classification.[37] Palestinian refugees numbered 5.5 million.[38] However, what tends to be overlooked is that 84 per cent of the world's refugees live in low- and middle-income countries; in other words, the vast majority live in places that can least afford to accommodate them.[39] Two-thirds live in protracted situations of displacement. In the early 1990s, it took an average of nine years to resolve the displacement of refugees, whereas it now takes twenty years and for some much longer.[40] Generations are born and grow into adulthood in the precarious, sometimes dangerous, always underfunded circumstances of the refugee "camp" or IDP settlement. In point of fact, most forcibly displaced are living not in camps but in urban environments. That may sound more humane, but the problem is that they essentially become invisible – and thus hard to reach with the assistance they may need. Most cannot work, so they become destitute. They do not qualify for local services and programs, so they live marginal existences and are forgotten. As many as 1 billion people may be forcibly displaced by a combination of devastating droughts and/or floods, extreme weather, and the destruction of arable land and potable water supplies. Under some scenarios, one in nine human beings will be on the move by the middle of this century.[41]

Uganda offers an instructive example of the kind of problem that low-income countries face. Uganda is hosting at present the highest number of refugees in its history – more than any other country in Africa and the third largest number globally. Among the 1.37 million refugees in Uganda, 84 per cent are women or girls, and 62 per cent are children.[42] Although the vast majority of refugees (over 1 million) arrived from South Sudan, Uganda also hosts refugees from the Democratic Republic of the Congo (236,572), Burundi (39,041), and Somalia (35,373).[43] In comparison, Canada accepted 28,000 refugees in 2018, down from a record-breaking 47,000 in 2016.[44]

Uganda's GDP in 2018 amounted to a paltry $27.5 billion in a country of 43 million, versus Canada's GDP of $1.7 trillion in a country of 37 million. Average per capita income in Uganda was $643, versus $46,261 for Canada. Total government expenditures amounted to

$5 billion, versus $665 billion for Canada. At the best of times, the Ugandan economy and Ugandans themselves are struggling.[45]

What has made the influx of South Sudanese refugees especially challenging has been the suddenness of their arrival: more than 512,000 arrived in Uganda from South Sudan in the period July 2016 to January 2017 alone.[46] Although the flow of refugees into Uganda slowed in early 2019 to 190 per day, the situation remains dynamic and unpredictable.[47] And there are major shortfalls in funding. In 2018 the operations of the United Nations High Commissioner for Refugees (UNHCR) in Uganda had received "just 38 percent of the required US$1.4 billion requested to support South Sudanese refugees."[48]

Uganda's challenge is an egregious example of the problem that the global community now confronts. Unlike Uganda, many countries, including some in the developed world, are not honouring their commitments to assist refugees under the 1951 Convention Relating to the Status of Refugees. Some countries will not take refugees, nor are they prepared to step up to the plate to help those countries that do. Calls for more money to help the UNHCR and refugee-hosting countries have gone unanswered, and existing pledges of financial support remain unfulfilled. It is sometimes remarked that the world finances refugee assistance as if it were a charity ball.

Some countries also want to send refugees home before it is safe for them to do so, and in other countries, terrorist groups are exploiting refugees for their own selfish partisan ends. In Lebanon, for example, Hezbollah has taken over the return of Syrians, sending them to areas where they are recruited as human shields and using them to establish territorial eminent domain.[49]

A key feature of the challenge relates to gender. More than half of the forcibly displaced are women and girls. Half of all forcibly displaced are under eighteen. Women's reproductive health needs are rarely provided for. On the Venezuela-Colombia border, for example, women and girls are frequently subject to sexual abuse and are conscripted into prostitution rings by criminal gangs and narcotraffickers. In 2017 the level of funding for the UNHCR's budgeted needs fell short by 43.3 per cent.[50] And where money is provided, its distribution is unequal: IDPs, who are twice as numerous as refugees, receive 14 per cent of the total made available for refugees. The distribution of funding is also inequitable and sometimes makes no sense.

The UNHCR's global annual budget is US$7.3 billion. In comparison, Sweden spends $7.1 billion annually to manage its 163,000 asylum seekers (i.e., to classify, process, feed, house, and track them).[51]

It is also apparent that those who are attempting to escape violence and persecution are taking riskier and riskier journeys to get away. And many don't make it, as attested by the tragic, gut-wrenching image of the body of a three-year-old Kurdish boy, Alan Kurdi, washed-up on a beach after he drowned in the Mediterranean Sea as his family tried to make their way to Canada.[52]

Although the refugee challenge is daunting, it is one that must be met with proper resourcing and policies that are directed at tackling the root causes of refugee crises, which are often political. Even at their current record number, refugees comprise a tiny percentage of a global population that had reached 7.7 billion people by September 2019.[53] Structural reform of the global refugee system is essential, although not easily achieved. The most urgent features of this reform are long overdue: new funding mechanisms that are not dependent on voluntary contributions; each country paying its fair share; and a level of resources for both refugees and host countries that is stable and predictable. The global refugee system also needs new oversight and accountability mechanisms that strengthen state obligations and ensure better state compliance with 1951 convention commitments.

MAKING BAD REGIMES ACCOUNTABLE

Political accountability is not simply a downstream problem. It also runs upstream to those states that are responsible for the crises that create refugees in the first place. Such crises do not simply "happen." Refugees are people fleeing from violence, political persecution, and other human rights abuses by dictators and despots. They are the victims of bad governance and corrupt leaders who have actively targeted different ethnic communities and religious groups often with the aim of "ethnic cleansing," as in the case of Myanmar's Rohingya population, whose members have long been the victims of government efforts to force them out of their homes and off their lands. The list of countries where repressive and autocratic leaders have provoked a mass exodus of their own people includes Syria, Libya, South Sudan, Myanmar, Venezuela, and Burundi. As observed by the

World Refugee Council's report *A Call to Action: Transforming the Global Refugee System*, "Even when the causes of displacement are well-known and where individuals responsible for the displacement can be identified ... there is little accountability. The lack of accountability for causing displacement means, in turn, that political leaders and insurgent groups alike can act with impunity – without regard for the immense suffering caused by their actions."[54]

Not only are there clear prohibitions against forced displacement in international law, but the UN Security Council clearly has a key role to play in enforcing those laws and holding bad leaders to account for their actions. If they are not held accountable in their own national courts, the international community should avail itself of the tools that are available through the International Criminal Court or the courts of more progressive governments where the rule of law obtains. Syria's Bashar al-Assad should be number one on the list. There should also be a focus on prevention by looking for early warning signs of mass displacement and a demand that the Security Council do its job and act accordingly instead of tending to the national interests and allegiances of the its five permanent members: China, France, the United States, the United Kingdom, and Russia.

One potential means to enhance accountability is to take the purloined assets held offshore by corrupt leaders, which have already been "frozen" either through a UN Security Council resolution and/or under Magnitsky-style legislation,[55] and repurpose those assets to assist the victims, namely those whose human rights have been violated by the actions of their leaders, as further discussed below. Downstream, greater effort should also be made to name and shame member states who are not living up to their responsibilities under the 1951 Convention Relating to the Status of Refugees. These states include countries that are not honouring their financial commitments to the UNHCR, countries that refuse to accept and resettle refugees, and countries that subject refugees to inhumane treatment, in direct contravention of the convention.

New sources of funding are also required to meet the growing needs of the UNHCR and other agencies that provide humanitarian assistance to refugees. Compulsory assessments, as in the case of UN peacekeeping contributions, which are calculated to reflect the size of each member state's economy as recommended by the Canadian-led

World Refugee Council, would be an important step toward stabilizing funding and budgets in the UN system.

Another challenge is to help refugee-hosting states grow their economies through trade and flexible debt management policies so that refugees living in those countries can secure meaningful employment alongside the local host population. Jordan, for example, has been granted trade concessions by the European Union for those sectors of the Jordanian economy that hire refugees. There is a strong case to be made for multilateralizing trade concessions to all low- and medium-income refugee-hosting states through the World Trade Organization (WTO), which addressed the issue in general terms in its *Aid for Trade Global Review 2017*.[56] As Canadian trade lawyer Lawrence Herman argues, special trade concessions to refugee-hosting countries could be provided through the "Decision on Differential and More Favourable Treatment, Reciprocity and Fuller Participation of Developing Countries," a waiver adopted in the General Agreement on Tariffs and Trade in 1979 and implemented by the WTO.[57] Such concessions would need to go beyond the low-value goods, such as shoes and textiles, that are currently covered by the general system of preferences afforded to developing countries in order to include high-value goods and services that local firms employing refugees may produce. Although such waivers would have to address tricky issues like the categories of goods and services to be covered by such agreements, the level of concessions to be given to refugee-hosting states, rules of origin, and indeed how to define eligible categories of refugees and what constitutes a "refugee-hosting" state, the negotiating challenges are not insurmountable.

Innovative financing mechanisms that leverage the vast resources in the private sector and capital markets through instruments like refugee bonds (akin to green bonds in climate change) or special capital investment funds will also be critical means of going beyond traditional forms of direct humanitarian assistance and philanthropic support for refugees and their host communities by promoting investment and sustainable economic development in refugee-hosting states. Such instruments can complement the new, innovative instruments for concessional financing that the World Bank has developed to provide a combination of grants and low-interest loans to low- and medium-income refugee-hosting states. The International Monetary

Fund has an important role to play by allowing for greater flexibility in managing the public debt load of refugee-hosting states, especially if they are being subjected to austerity programs at the same time that they are experiencing a major influx of refugees, as was the case in Jordan in 2014.

LEADING BY EXAMPLE

For many years, Canada's Private Sponsorship of Refugees Program has provided other countries with a model of how to mobilize public and private support for the resettlement of refugees in local communities.[58] Under this program, "Canadian citizens and permanent residents can engage in the resettlement of refugees from abroad. As members of organizations, associations and groups, citizens and residents can sponsor refugees overseas as a Group of Five, a Community Sponsor or a Sponsorship Agreement Holder."[59] What is unique about the program is that it "does not rely on public resources, but rather taps the energy and funds of faith communities, ethnic groups, families and other benevolent associations. These groups and organizations typically raise funds or use their personal income to provide for and support the sponsored individual or family for their first year in Canada."[60]

A family or a group initiates the process by submitting an application to sponsor one or more refugees to Immigration, Refugees and Citizenship Canada. Once the application is approved, an individual or family to be sponsored is identified, and the commitment of support continues until the end of the sponsorship period, which normally runs for twelve months, beginning with the arrival of the sponsored individual or family in Canada.

The program was first developed when a total of some 76,000 Vietnamese refugees arrived in Canada by ship. The "boat people," as they were called, presented a major challenge because they had to be housed, fed, clothed, educated, and integrated into local communities. The Canadian government called on its citizens to help the countries latest newcomers by offering to match the contributions of those who agreed to sponsor the refugees. Thousands of Canadians joined the sponsorship program, setting a pattern of public-private refugee partnership that would play out in subsequent refugee crises, including the most recent influx of Syrian refugees under the Trudeau government.

Canada's refugee sponsorship program, where private citizens and the community are directly involved in the resettlement of refugees, is looked upon as a model by other countries around the world. The year 2019 marked the fortieth anniversary of the program's introduction with the arrival of the Vietnamese boat people, many of whom have gone on to become leaders in all walks of Canadian life, including business, medicine, law, academia, and politics. In all, more than 327,000 refugees have been beneficiaries of the sponsorship program, and more than 160 communities have welcomed privately sponsored refugees from more than 175 countries. Of the 62,000 Syrian refugees who have been resettled to Canada since 2015, more than half were privately sponsored.[61]

Other countries that have taken a keen interest in Canada's sponsorship program actually began to emulate it only in 2016 as they struggled with their own influx of refugees. Argentina, Ireland, New Zealand, the United Kingdom, Spain, and Germany have now all adopted variants of the Canadian sponsorship model. Much of the credit for "marketing" Canada's public-private sponsorship model goes to the Ottawa-based Global Refugee Sponsorship Initiative – a partnership between Canada, the United Nations Refugee Agency, Open Society Foundations, the Giustra Foundation, and the University of Ottawa – which aims to "increase and improve global refugee resettlement by engaging private citizens, communities, and businesses in resettlement efforts; strengthen local host communities that come together to welcome newcomers; and improve the narrative about refugees and other newcomers."[62]

The purpose of the Global Refugee Sponsorship Initiative is to "assist and inspire countries around the world to open new pathways for refugee protection ... by sharing Canada's history, experience, and leadership in private sponsorship and by supporting [through education and peer-to-peer mentorship] the creation of new programs that countries design to meet their unique needs."[63]

On the matter of upstream political accountability, another promising Canadian initiative is a new bill that would allow the Canadian government to confiscate and repurpose the seized assets of corrupt foreign leaders in order to help refugees and others who have suffered under their regimes. Bill S-259, An Act Respecting the Repurposing of Certain Seized, Frozen or Sequestrated Assets,[64] which was tabled by the Honourable Ratna Omidvar, a senator from Ontario and a member of the World Refugee Council, received its first reading on 21 March 2019. As Senator Omidvar explains, the "bill will make corrupt foreign leaders and dictators that perpetrate grave crimes against their people – including human rights abuses and mass forced displacement – pay for their crimes with their own ill-gotten gains."[65] Upon its second reading, on 30 May, the bill attracted considerable interest and support from all sides of the political aisle.

Under existing legislation, the federal government can freeze assets in Canada of foreign officials responsible for corruption or gross violations of human rights. However, Bill S-259 goes a step further by giving the government, in appropriate cases, the ability to use these assets to help refugees, internally displaced persons, and others who have been harmed as a result of violent, oppressive, or corrupt regimes.

A good example of how the legislation would operate is Myanmar. Canada has already frozen the assets of military generals in that country who have committed a genocide against the Rohingya and forced over 1 million people to flee to Bangladesh. Under Bill S-259, Canada, through its courts, could confiscate these assets and repurpose them to help the people who are struggling in refugee camps in Bangladesh.

Senator Omidvar's proposal draws on the work of the World Refugee Council and its report *A Call to Action: Transforming the Global Refugee System*. If Bill S-259 passes, Canada will become the second nation in the world to enact this type of legislation. Switzerland introduced similar legal tools under its Foreign Illicit Assets Act in 2015, which allows the Swiss government to exercise its administrative authority to seek a court order to confiscate frozen assets and restore them to the country of origin for the purposes of providing humanitarian aid and strengthening the rule of law.[66]

Canada also has a role to play in its own hemisphere to promote political change in Venezuela, where the policies of President Nicolás Maduro Moros have been directly responsible for a mass exodus of millions of Venezuelans into neighbouring countries. Canada's efforts in the Lima Group should be complemented by assistance to host countries in the Andean Region, which have been severely impacted by the large migration of Venezuelans into their countries. In June 2019 the UNHCR and the International Organization for Migration estimated that over 4 million Venezuelans – projected to be 5 million by the end of 2019 – had crossed into a variety of countries in Latin America and the Caribbean. The largest concentrations were in Colombia (1.3 million), Peru (768,000), Chile (288,000), Ecuador (263,000), Brazil (168,000), and Argentina (130,000).[67] These countries are struggling to provide adequate lodgings, food, healthcare, education, and water. The problem is further compounded by the wide dispersion of migrants into the main cities well beyond the borders of these countries. Other social issues are being exacerbated, such as crime, homelessness (including among many women and children), and challenges to local labour markets. Colombian authorities alone estimate that the cost to their government in basic support per every 1 million Venezuelan migrants exceeds US$2 billion per annum and is growing.[68]

There is also an important technological dimension to the refugee space, where Canadian tech firms also have an important role to play. New Internet-based technologies have been used in creative ways to support the delivery of services to refugees. For example, in the Middle East the UN World Food Programme successfully deployed one of the largest ever uses of the Ethereum blockchain. Thousands of Syrian refugees and internally displaced persons were given via their cell phones cryptocurrency-based vouchers that could be redeemed in participating markets.

Canada was a strong supporter of the intergovernmental process to adopt the United Nations' 2018 *Global Compact on Refugees*,[69] its 2018 *Global Compact for Safe, Orderly and Regular Migration*,[70] and its 2016 *Comprehensive Refugee Response Framework* to provide various forms of financial assistance to refugee-hosting states.[71] Both compacts were formally adopted by the UN General Assembly in December 2018 following a series of extensive consultations with civil society, governments, and various regional groupings. Although Conservative Opposition leader Andrew Scheer called on the government to oppose the migration compact, alleging it "would open the door to foreign bureaucrats directing [Canada's] immigration policy," he was called out by a former Conservative Cabinet minister, Christopher Alexander, who tweeted that the migration compact "is a political declaration, not a legally binding treaty. It has no impact on our sovereignty."[72] Canada can play a critical role in supporting the political spirit of both compacts, but there is clearly a need to go further than these hortatory declarations, which, like many consensus-based UN processes, fall to the lowest common denominator and fail to address the real political heart of the matter. As former high commissioner for refugees Sadako Ogata once pointedly remarked, "there are no humanitarian solutions to humanitarian problems."[73] The challenge is political.

"A SOBERING LESSON"

As the distinguished Georgetown University scholar Susan Martin reminds us, the Evian Conference of 1938 offers "a sobering lesson" for today's world: "The conference had a dual mission – to encourage countries to resettle refugees and to persuade Germany to establish an orderly emigration process. From the beginning, it was clear that not much would happen at the conference. In calling for it, US President Franklin Roosevelt made it clear that he was not asking any country, including the United States, to change its refugee policy. Subsequently, no government pledged to resettle significant numbers of refugees (except for the Dominican Republic's rather vague offer). Nor did the conference condemn the repressive policies that Germany had already taken against Jews, although individual delegations expressed sympathy for the victims." After the conference, in a speech to the Party Congress in Nuremberg in September 1938, Adolf Hitler pointed to the hypocrisy of the countries that condemned Germany's policies but would not admit Jewish refugees: "Lamentations have not led these democratic countries to substitute helpful activity at last for their hypocritical questions; on the contrary, these countries with icy coldness assured us that obviously there was no place for the Jews in their territory' ... This recognition that other countries would do little to save the Jews and other refugees paved the way for the Holocaust."[74]

Canadians must also work to help address the toxic political narrative around refugees. They are too often the easy scapegoats for racist, populist parties, whose leaders exploit the widespread erosion of confidence in globalization, free trade, and the multilateral system to argue for closing borders, building walls, and diminishing the role of international institutions and regional organizations. But as the World Refugee Council also makes clear, "*governments have a responsibility to protect their people, including through control of their borders.* Governments will be accorded social licence by their constituencies to resettle refugees only to the extent that the citizens are confident that their governments control the immigration process. Just as sheltering the dispossessed is integral to humanity, managing border entries is essential to stability. The two are not incompatible, as the highly successful rescue of the Vietnamese boat people demonstrated to an earlier generation."[75]

Being stateless through no fault of one's own is not a cardinal sin. Any kind of effective, global response begins with that basic understanding. But lofty rhetoric by Canada's leaders is not enough; it must be accompanied by concrete and effective action and proper follow-through at the national and global levels. The first priority for any government is to demonstrate to its citizens that it is able to control its borders and to enforce violations of its laws. The second equally important priority should be to hold to account those leaders who perpetrate the exodus of their own people.

10

Shaping Our Destiny

As America focuses more on its own self-interest in an increasingly precarious world and jockeys aggressively for pre-eminence over China, Canada will be obliged to take action and develop strategies that serve distinct national interests and strengthen its ability to control its own destiny. Canada will need economic policies that ensure a competitive advantage in North America, and it will need a commitment to disciplined and focused spending on national security assets, including for cyber security, commensurate with a realistic definition of its capabilities. Canada will also need a more focused approach to innovation, one that gives priority and support to made-in-Canada artificial intelligence and other technologies that will bolster its competitive advantages and enable it to take greater responsibility for its own security. Canada's ability to assert values on the world stage will depend ultimately on compelling examples of what it is able to achieve at home. It should also resist attempts to promote an ideologically driven agenda intended for domestic consumption as an instrument of foreign policy. This approach has backfired to the point where Canadian officials have been instructed not use the term "progressive" as part of the foreign policy mantra.[1]

The election of US president Donald Trump rattled conventional norms on relations within the Western alliance. The institutional glue that had delivered peace and prosperity for more than seven decades was shaken by his impulsive tweets and his abusive personal attacks against key members of the alliance, including Canada's prime minister in the wake of the 2018 G7 Summit in Charlevoix, Quebec.

Some suggest that Trump constitutes the main threat to the postwar era of peace and prosperity, for which his predecessors consistently served as guarantors. Compromise and nuance are never part of Trump's style. Unpredictable lunges at North Korea and Iran injected further uncertainty into attempts to comprehend America's role in the world. Trump's weaponization of tariffs against friends and foes alike has destabilized global commerce, which, for decades, had benefited from consistently constructive US leadership. These actions are outside the framework of international trade principles administered by the World Trade Organization (WTO) and, unless checked, threaten to break apart the global trading system

But Trump, the unfriendly Lone Ranger and a dangerous political maverick, is not one of a kind. He has kindred spirits in the leadership of China, Russia, Turkey, and other countries where populist pressures and nationalism are ascendant and manifesting themselves in different disruptive ways. There is, of course, no moral equivalency between the leaders of the world's democracies and the autocrats of Asia, Europe, and the Middle East. However, the confident power of these forces is destabilizing the international system, with profound consequences for democratic middle powers like Canada whose economic prosperity and global influence were intimately tied to the norms, rules, and principles of a liberal international order led by the world's leading democracy, the United States, which is now in decline. Regrettably, these autocracies also offer a more compelling model to developing countries looking for a rapid transition to prosperity.

As much as we might try or wish to do so, there is no turning the clock back to an older, more familiar, and more comfortable world of the era immediately after the Cold War. The "Canada is back"[2] refrain is a bit like driving while looking through the rear-view mirror rather than looking at the winding road ahead and the world Canada now confronts. Canadians have to realize that the era of a special or privileged relationship with their closest neighbour is now over. And even though Canada's relations with the emerging great powers of the international system – China, Russia, and India – have taken a steep nosedive in recent years, recalibration of these relations is clearly required to advance its vital economic and national interests. If anything, as Kelly McParland writes in the *National Post*, "far from inserting itself confidently into global events, seldom has

Canada felt so distant from the action, so utterly uninfluential, so relegated to the role of inconsequential observer as more potent players manoeuvre for position"[3] – in short, more spectator than player.

Canada can and should make a greater effort not just to promote its shared democratic values with its traditional alliance partners but also to step up to the plate by opening its wallet and deploying real military muscle to assert and defend those values. Canada's so-called "soft power" assets will resonate and be meaningful to others only if it can demonstrate that it is both strong and prepared to pay to play. Canadian leaders must follow through on tangible commitments to ensure effective diplomacy and defence. A new foreign policy and defence strategy will also require Canada to play on multiple chessboards. That too will require a modicum of dexterity and an understanding of how the game on one chessboard affects the games on the others.

RELATIONS WITH THE UNITED STATES

In the first instance, Canada needs a hard-headed blueprint of what will continue to be its vital relationship with the United States. This assessment should be predicated on a realistic understanding of the changing US approach to global affairs – one that will persist long after Trump – particularly as it affects alliance ties and commitments to multilateral institutions.

The immediate priority will be to lock in benefits from the United States–Mexico–Canada Agreement in order to give greater certainty to investors and exporters alike. Canada will also need to re-examine security links in North America and within NATO, giving greater attention to the Arctic and the threats of the twenty-first century, like cyber security. Specifically, it is time for Canada to assert its credentials as a country not simply of the Atlantic but also of the Pacific, recognizing that the Asia-Pacific region offers significant opportunities and risks related to global prospects and security.

The comfort and relative ease of Canada's relationship with the United States have lulled Canadians into an ingrained sense of complacency. Canada's first priority must be to move beyond the North American cocoon and establish strategies at home that will strengthen its competitiveness and enable it to strive for greater diversity on the global stage.

DIVERSIFICATION

A related priority is a trade and investment diversification strategy, one that moves beyond the rhythm of high-level junkets and lofty rhetoric to concentrate instead on pragmatic negotiations of new agreements that will provide new or greater market access within a stronger rule of law framework. Canada needs to start with a concerted effort, led by the prime minster, to ensure interprovincial free trade in Canada.

Prospects in Asia, especially in China, India, and Indonesia, should be at the core of a diversification strategy. The twin giants of Asia – China and India – offer distinct yet daunting prospects for closer economic partnerships with Canada. Neither has been addressed in a coherent or concentrated manner to date, but with careful analysis and steady political will, risks can be assessed and analyzed versus rewards. Nonengagement with the two fastest growing global economies is not a credible option. Canada could also use the leverage of dealing with each in order to advance interests with the other. It needs real, as opposed to aspirational, diversification.

In contemplating a major trade relationship with China, Canada has to be mindful of both the risk and the advantage that this relationship would offer to primordial relations with the United States. Deriving benefits from market openings stemming from the Comprehensive and Progressive Agreement for Trans-Pacific Partnership (CPTPP), or "mini TPP," notably in Japan, Vietnam, and Malaysia, should help to embolden actions by government and the private sector in tackling markets that will provide substantial growth opportunities. Canada is obliged to deal with what the world is becoming rather than bask in the aura of what the world once was.

COMPETITIVENESS

Closer to home, the topic most in need of recalibration is a plan for Canada to regain its "competitive edge" in North America. This had been a fundamental prerequisite of macroeconomic policy in Canada for decades but has been overshadowed in recent years by rhetorical policy choices aimed more at wealth redistribution and at the societal objectives of gender equity and diversity than at a foundation for the economic growth that is needed to sustain fundamental social programs like health, education, and pensions.

By diverging sharply from current US orthodoxy on tax, regulatory, and energy development policies, Canada has lost that competitive edge and, along with it, the investments and innovation required to spur economic growth, notably in knowledge-intensive industries. Bold policy action is needed. Equally, Canada's private sector should demonstrate less complacency and more entrepreneurial zeal about tackling markets beyond the North American continent. Canada can no longer be cossetted by its geographic proximity to, and almost exclusive reliance on, the US market.

The senior ranks of Canada's bureaucracy need a wake-up call as well. There should be less emphasis on process in the name of process, less genuflection to trendy societal norms, and more attention to delivering on real and substantive policy innovations and merit-based results with clear measures of accountability. Bureaucracy should be a springboard for fresh policy concepts, not a cushion or a sinecure of entitlement.

The private sector also needs a wake-up call to move it beyond the cautious, risk-averse manner that is deeply embedded in much of Canadian business. The heavy concentration in key industries and services in Canada is stifling competitiveness and constraining productivity and creativity.

NATIONAL SECURITY

Canada should also tailor its security capabilities more coherently to defending its sovereignty, notably in the Arctic. A sharper focus is also needed to meet the threats from cyber space, which many regard as the most serious emerging challenge in the decades ahead.

Trump's disdain for his NATO allies was not without merit. For too long, too many allies, including Canada, had wavered on NATO commitments to spend 2 per cent of GDP on defence on the assumption that the United States alone would fill the vacuum. Trump's reluctance to explicitly endorse article 5 of the North Atlantic Treaty, which guarantees that all will come to the rescue of any whose sovereignty is breached, poses an even graver threat to the alliance. NATO also needs to aggressively reposition itself on cyber threats with a refreshed mandate, and it should be at the forefront of taking action to prevent rogue regimes from abusing their own people. Canada has sustained its commitments to a shrinking NORAD, but by showing no inclination to share in anti-ballistic missile defence or to be little more than a cost-free straphanger in the challenges coming from cyber space, Canada's tangible contribution has become suspect, if not derisory.

The days of benign neglect from America or accepting without question US security guarantees may still have some nostalgic appeal, but Canada must begin to do more in defence of its own sovereignty, especially on its three coasts and in the Arctic. The attitudes, linkages, geographic proximity, and sense of neighbourliness that have served Canada well in terms of both prosperity and security can no longer be taken for granted.

Clear direction is needed on what priority defence spending should have and on how it can best be allotted, especially when it comes to the defence of North America in an era when the threats from cyber space are likely to be more serious than those from terrorists or nuclear proliferation, although these risks should not be discounted.

Warmed-over defence strategies from the past two decades are not the right foundation, nor are spasmodic attempts to patch or fill massive breaches in Canada's military equipment. The fact that Canada abandoned the purchase of F-35 fighter aircraft and instead ordered used F-18s from Australia speaks eloquently to the shallow approach taken to national security. This approach does little for defence and less for state-of-the-art innovation by Canadian industries.

The military threat and nuclear arsenal of Russia remain a problem for many of NATO's newest members. But as China's military muscle grows in proportion to its economic growth and as its territorial aspirations in the South and East China Seas intensify, the real security threat to global stability ultimately involves the United States and China. That is why the Pacific dimension of security merits a higher profile. In cyber space, as well, China, with its singular focus on artificial intelligence and other advanced technologies, poses a greater, more sophisticated challenge to the United States and the West than any other power.

Canada's security ties also need a broad rethinking. If Canada wants to strengthen its ties in North America, it needs to consider seriously joining the US anti-ballistic missile defence system. Unless Canada prefers to become more independent in North America, with all the attendant costs of providing more for its own defence, supporting this defence system would make it a more credible partner than it is today. NORAD is now a pale imitation of what it once was – designed for a different age and a different threat. Security for the continent that Canada shares with the United States and Mexico needs a fresh assessment.

Canada should, in any event, examine ways to move away from exclusive reliance on a Eurocentric NATO for global security and plan tangible commitments and linkages with allies in the Asia-Pacific region, namely Australia, New Zealand, Japan, Singapore, and Korea, presumably anchored by the United States. The evolving tussle has implications for Canada. With any claim to being a nation of the Asia-Pacific, Canada's involvement on questions of security in the region should amount to more than spasmodic naval visits.

CYBER SECURITY

Quite apart from the drift toward protectionism and customary flashpoints for hostilities, new threats to global stability from cyber space warrant special attention. Attacks and counterattacks could seriously cripple the Internet, financial systems like banking and credit cards, as well as power grids, ports, and transportation and communication systems. Canada is not adequately organized or equipped to meet this threat, yet there is little evidence to suggest that it has a structure or the technology required to help check or contain cyber attacks. Canada is too reliant on the resolve and technology of the United States to make up for shortfalls at home, a dependency that is no longer assured.

Because much of Canada's electricity and transportation infrastructure is shared with the United States, Canada tends to rely almost exclusively on the United States for surveillance and prevention. When it comes to developing new technologies, such as for quantum computing and for cryptography, Canada seems satisfied to be a fast follower of US technology and overly confident that the United States will share its advanced technology and its surveillance and prevention capabilities with alacrity even as economic competitiveness intensifies.

A more concerted effort by Canada to contribute to the safety and security of its own vital infrastructure should give greater emphasis to made-in-Canada technology. (Canada, after all, is a world leader in artificial intelligence and deep-learning systems.) It is a matter of political will and priority. Canada needs a strategy that induces more home-grown innovative technology, especially for cyber security. Canadians have to overcome their allergy to products with a Canadian label. Collaboration with Israel could be one option worth exploring on advanced technology more generally.

Canada also needs to make a substantial commitment independently or together with the United States to combat threats from cyber space in order to protect its shared infrastructure on energy transportation and telecommunications. Strong commitments on both anti-ballistic missile defence and cyber space would enhance Canada's ability to contribute tangibly to shared intelligence and security exchanges that serve distinct national interests.

THE ENERGY AND CLIMATE CHANGE NEXUS

Striking a balance to gain the social licence that would support both energy development and commitments to Paris Accord targets on climate change is proving to be illusory. Canada now has the worst of both worlds. It paid $4.5 billion for the Trans Mountain Pipeline, which still faces serious obstacles as costs escalate exponentially with every delay. Energy development and infrastructure have been stymied by policy gridlock, endless regulatory processes, and erratic judicial activists. Meanwhile, at the provincial level, resistance to tax or cap and trade measures to reduce carbon emissions is growing. Heavily carbon-emitting rail transport is rapidly filling the vacuum, with rail shipments of oil in 2018 doubling those of 2017. Canada's competitive position vis-à-vis the United States on energy has virtually disappeared, along with much-needed investment.

At the same time, the price for oil has dropped, and the discount price that Canada receives for shipments to the United States has risen sharply. A price of $13 per barrel means that all Canadian producers are losing money. Capital spending has stopped, layoffs are the order of the day, and sentiments supporting western Canada's separation from the rest of the country are gathering steam. The major problem is a lack of pipeline capacity or infrastructure to enable shipments east, west, and south of Canada's borders. Even if pipelines were approved expeditiously, they would provide a solution only two or three years down the road. What has customarily been a source of Canada's economic strength – energy – is rapidly becoming a liability swamped by gross government dysfunction, regulatory constipation, and a preference for consultation over decision making. The real victim is the national interest. More realistic and coherent strategies and clear political leadership are desperately needed to revive energy development and exports.

Canada's ability to export energy resources is essential to any notion of trade diversification. Its commitment to the Paris Accord goals, which the United States has abandoned, only compounds Canada's declining competitiveness. Not one of the G20 countries is actually meeting its Paris undertakings. A major recalibration or rebalancing of commitments is in order, preferably one in which the United States is re-engaged. Finding better solutions and a pragmatic balance between Canada's aspirations to exploit its energy resources and Canada's need to preserve its pristine environment begins with the recognition that what it is doing will not deliver either.

Canada needs to tailor its environmental aspirations so that they complement its need to continue developing fossil fuels in a manner consistent with, not contradictory to, that of its major trading partner. As well, Canada needs to work diplomatically to recalibrate global goals and policies on climate change that are effective and equitable among nations, not simply aspirational.

THE REFUGEE AND IMMIGRATION NEXUS

Canada prides itself on being open-minded, but it needs to put more emphasis on the values that unite Canadians than on measures aimed at individual elements that are divisive. A major influx of refugees from Syria, Nigeria, Haiti, and elsewhere beginning in 2017 is taxing Canada's bureaucratic capacities and the absorptive capacity of its social systems for health, education, and housing to an unprecedented degree as the federal government shifts the burdens of adjustment and integration to local municipalities without providing them with the requisite resources. This phenomenon is stimulating negative political attitudes similar to those experienced in America and Europe. The tougher stance adopted by the United States on migrant issues may give Canadians a better or more righteous sense of self emotionally, but blatant violations of the rules governing admissions to Canada are generating a predictable backlash and reinforcing unsavoury attitudes about race, religion, and multiculturalism, as well as about the benefits of diversity.

Although the openness of Canadian society is seen by many as a source of strength for Canada, it can just as easily become a source of weakness in the absence of respect for the rule of law and regulations. If the demands of citizenship are diluted or fragmented by loose standards of accommodation, the calibre of that citizenship will be the real loser. Canada needs to recalibrate policies and definitions on asylum seekers and refugees in order to prevent abuse and enrich selection processes that serve the national interest. Canada can better enforce access at its border while contributing tangibly to alleviating the greatest global refugee crisis since the end of the Second World War.

STRENGTHENING MULTILATERAL INSTITUTIONS

Canada should focus on strengthening and repositioning international institutions like NATO and the WTO that directly serve its national interests and values, enabling them to better meet the challenges of the twenty-first century. Similarly, it should scale back commitments to institutions and agencies whose shelf life and relevance have expired. In the case of the United Nations, some of its elements are replaceable, but others are not, such as the important work of its specialized agencies in the development and humanitarian sphere. Accordingly, the principle of selective versus indiscriminate multilateralism should be at the core of Canada's international focus.

SHAPING OUR DESTINY BEGINS AT HOME

Canada needs a new comprehensive strategy to address deficiencies in its domestic policy environment and a more selective approach to global affairs that reinforces Canadian interests and the fundamental values of freedom and human rights. In summary, Canada's priorities should be the following:

- implementing a major policy overhaul to address the decline and disappearance of Canada's competitive edge as its most serious domestic and international challenge
- acknowledging that relations with the United States are no longer special or privileged and present Canada's most serious global challenge, along with fractured relations with the two juggernauts of Asia: China and India
- relying more on Canada's own capabilities than on access or status in Washington to influence the world
- giving higher priority to national economic strengths – energy, agriculture, and knowledge industries – and determining whether Canada wishes to be "a landlord nation" or "a tenant nation in the new intangibles economy"[4]
- increasing diversity on trade, first at home with the removal of all interprovincial barriers
- repurposing defence strategy and planning a more coherent procurement program
- strengthening and redirecting key multilateral institutions that serve direct Canadian interests like the WTO and NATO and reducing commitments to those that are less relevant and ineffective
- a real, not theoretical, approach to balancing the energy and environmental policy nexus in Canada
- establishing a coherent strategy as well as streamlined surveillance and monitoring systems on cyber security
- bolstering made-in-Canada technologies
- no longer pandering with platitudes on immigration and refugee policy but instead preventing abuses, controlling the border, and penalizing those who perpetrate major refugee surges, like Bashar al-Assad
- implementing a foreign policy that is consistent with Canada's interests, fundamental values, and capacities, as well as with the realistic limitations on its scope for influence

Canada's place in the world should be accompanied by tangible commitments. It will have to focus on those areas where it has interests to advance or defend and relevant values to assert. And it should strive to occupy the mainstream, not the "progressive" slipstream, a tactic that in recent years has confined it to the periphery on many global issues.

Notes

PREFACE AND ACKNOWLEDGMENTS

1. See Stephen Harper, *Right Here, Right Now: Politics and Leadership in the Age of Disruption* (Toronto: Signal, 2018), 4.
2. David Sanger, *The Perfect Weapon: War, Sabotage, and Fear in the Cyber Age* (New York: Penguin Random House, 2018).
3. Canadian government official, confidential interview with authors, 2018.
4. Derek H. Burney and Fen Osler Hampson, *Brave New Canada: Meeting the Challenge of a Changing World* (Montreal and Kingston: McGill-Queen's University Press, 2014).

CHAPTER ONE

1. Derek H. Burney and Fen Osler Hampson, *Brave New Canada: Meeting the Challenge of a Changing World* (Montreal and Kingston: McGill-Queen's University Press, 2014).
2. Robert Kagan, *The Jungle Grows Back: America and Our Imperiled World* (New York: Penguin Random House, 2018), 163.
3. Bob Woodward, *Fear: Trump in the White House* (New York: Simon and Schuster, 2018), xxii.
4. See, for example, Josh Wingrove and Justin Sink, "Trump Threatens Canada 'Ruination' on Autos amid Nafta Talks," *Bloomberg*, 7 September 2018, https://www.bloomberg.com/news/articles/2018-09-07/trump-threatens-canada-s-ruination-on-autos-amid-nafta-talks.
5. Quoted in Meg Wagner and Brian Ries, "Trump Gives Remarks on US-Mexico-Canada Deal," *CNN Politics*, 1 October 2018, https://

edition.cnn.com/politics/live-news/trump-us-mexico-canada-remarks-oct-18/h_2c0a8c6bad4dc7a2f98acda7c57ea454.
6 Quoted in Jessica Vomiero, "Donald Trump Says NAFTA Has Been Replaced by U.S.-Mexico Trade Deal," *Global News*, 6 September 2018.
7 Stephen Harper, *Right Here, Right Now: Politics and Leadership in the Age of Disruption* (Toronto: Signal, 2018), ch. 4.
8 Francis Fukuyama, *Identity: The Demand for Dignity and the Politics of Resentment* (New York: Farrar, Straus and Giroux, 2018), 9.
9 Ibid.
10 Ibid., xi, citing Larry Diamond, "Facing Up to the Democratic Recession," *Journal of Democracy* 26, no. 1 (2015): 141–55.
11 World Bank Group and World Trade Organization, *The Role of Trade in Ending Poverty* (Geneva, Switzerland: World Trade Organization, 2015), 14, https://www.wto.org/english/res_e/booksp_e/worldbankandwto15_e.pdf.
12 Quoting Billie Holiday and Arthur Herzog Jr, "God Bless the Child" (1939), on the album *The Lady Sings* (Decca Records, 1956).
13 Rakesh Kochhar, "The American Middle Class Is Stable in Size, but Losing Ground Financially to Upper-Income Families," Pew Research Center, *Fact Tank: News in Numbers*, 6 September 2018, https://www.pewresearch.org/fact-tank/2018/09/06/the-american-middle-class-is-stable-in-size-but-losing-ground-financially-to-upper-income-families/.
14 Madeleine Albright, *Fascism: A Warning* (New York: Harper, 2018).
15 Fukuyama, *Identity*, 171.
16 Will Kymlicka, *Multicultural Citizenship: A Liberal Theory of Minority Rights* (Oxford: Oxford University Press, 1996).
17 Fukuyama, *Identity*, 119.
18 Hillary Clinton, quoted in Amy Chozick, "Hillary Clinton Calls Many Trump Backers 'Deplorables,' and G.O.P. Pounces," *New York Times*, 10 September 2016.
19 The National Center for Health Statistics reports that there were 47,590 deaths from opiates in 2017 and 31,897 deaths from synthetic opiates, for a total of 79,487.
20 Quoted in Christina Wilkie, "Trump to Manufacturers: 'The Era of Economic Surrender Is Over,'" 29 September 2017, *CNBC*, https://www.cnbc.com/2017/09/29/donald-trump-addresses-national-association-of-manufacturers.html.
21 Quoted in Matt Gurney, "This May Be How the West Might Be Lost," *National Post*, 29 March 2019.

22 Ibid.
23 Ibid.
24 Special Counsel's Office, US Department of Justice, *The Mueller Report: The Report of the Special Counsel on the Investigation into Russian Interference in the 2016 Presidential Election* (Washington, DC: US Department of Justice, 2019).
25 Quoted in Gurney, "This May Be How."
26 François Heisbourg, "War and Peace after the Age of Liberal Globalisation," *Survival* 60, no. 1 (2018): 211–28.
27 G. John Ikenberry, "The End of the Liberal International Order?" *International Affairs* 94, no. 1 (2018): 7–23; Daniel Deudney and G. John Ikenberry, "Liberal World: The Resilient Order," *Foreign Affairs*, July-August 2018.
28 Colum Lynch, "Trump's War on the World Order," *Foreign Policy*, 27 December 2018.
29 Quoted in Anne Perkins, "Donald Trump at G7: 'US Is Not a Piggy Bank to Be Robbed," *Guardian* (London), 9 June 2018.
30 Quoted in Angelique Chrisafis, "Macron Calls for 'Real' European Army at Start of War Centenary Tour," *Guardian* (London), 6 November 2018.
31 Quoted in Julian Borger, "Trump Says Macron's Call for European Army Is 'Insulting,'" *Guardian* (London), 9 November 2018.
32 Quoted in Graham Allison, "The Myth of the Liberal Order: From Historical Accident to Conventional Wisdom," *Foreign Affairs*, July-August 2018.
33 Allison, "Myth of the Liberal Order."
34 Francis Fukuyama, *The End of History and the Last Man* (New York: Free Press, 1992).
35 Allison, "Myth of the Liberal Order."
36 Quoted in ibid.
37 Allison, "Myth of the Liberal Order."
38 Ibid., quoting a 1963 speech by Kennedy at American University.
39 Ibid.
40 Globally, the number of people in extreme poverty dropped "from nearly 1.9 billion in 1990 to about 650 million in 2018." Max Roser and Esteban Ortiz-Ospina, "Global Extreme Poverty," *Our World in Data*, 27 March 2017, https://ourworldindata.org/extreme-poverty.
41 Infant mortality rates are derived from the UN Interagency Group for Child Mortality Estimates, as cited by the World Bank, UNICEF, and the World Health Organization, among others.

42 Walter Russell Mead, "Geopolitics Trumps the Markets," *Wall Street Journal*, 29 October 2018.

43 Lionel Barber and Henry Foy, "Vladimir Putin: Liberalism Has 'Outlived Its Purpose,'" *Financial Times*, 27 June 2019, quoting Putin.

44 Dan Sabbagh, "Method of Attack on Tankers Remains Key Evidence against Iran," *Guardian* (London), 18 June 2019; Romina McGuinness, "French Military 'Has Evidence' Iran Shot Down US Drone in International Airspace," *Express*, 27 June 2019, https://www.express.co.uk/news/world/1146326/Iran-news-us-drone-Donald-trump-usa-world-war-3.

45 Quoted in Sarah Jones, "Trump Wants to Prosecute Former Obama Sec. of State John Kerry," *PoliticusUSA*, 22 April 2019, https://www.politicususa.com/2019/04/22/trump-wants-to-prosecute-former-obama-sec-of-state-john-kerry.html.

46 See Akhilesh Pillalamarri, "Why Is Afghanistan the 'Graveyard of Empires'?" *The Diplomat*, 30 June 2017, https://thediplomat.com/2017/06/why-is-afghanistan-the-graveyard-of-empires/.

47 See Fen Osler Hampson, *Master of Persuasion: Brian Mulroney's Global Legacy* (Toronto: Signal, 2018).

48 See, for example, Roland Paris, *Can Middle Powers Save the Liberal World Order?* (London: Chatham House, 2019).

49 Richard Perle, "Democracies of the World, Unite," *The American Interest*, January-February 2007, https://www.the-american-interest.com/2007/01/01/democracies-of-the-world-unite/; G. John Ikenberry and Anne-Marie Slaughter, *Forging a World under Liberty and Law: U.S. National Security in the 21st Century* (Princeton, NJ: Woodrow Wilson School of International Affairs, Princeton University, 2006); Robert Kagan, "The Case for a League of Democracies," *Financial Times*, 13 May 2008; Daniele Archibugi, *The Global Commonwealth of Citizens: Toward Cosmopolitan Democracy* (Princeton, NJ: Princeton University Press, 2008).

CHAPTER TWO

1 Quoted in Meg Wagner and Brian Ries, "Trump Gives Remarks on US-Mexico-Canada Deal," CNN *Politics*, 1 October 2018, https://edition.cnn.com/politics/live-news/trump-us-mexico-canada-remarks-oct-18/h_2c0a8c6bad4dc7a2f98acda7c57ea454.

2 Quoted in Adrian Morrow, Barrie McKenna, and Stephanie Nolen, "From NAFTA to USMCA: Inside the Tense Negotiations That Saved North American Trade," *Globe and Mail*, 5 October 2018.
3 Livingston International, "From NAFTA to the USMCA: Free Trade in North America Today and Tomorrow," 2019, https://www.livingstonintl.com/nafta/.
4 Joan Bryden, "NAFTA Further Imperilled by U.S. Demand for Stringent American Auto Content," *National Newswatch*, 6 October 2017, https://www.nationalnewswatch.com/2017/10/06/nafta-further-imperilled-by-u-s-demand-for-stringent-american-auto-content-3/#.XYkTqShKjbo.
5 Maham Abedi, "Why U.S.-Mexico's NAFTA Agreement Could Be Good News for Canada's Auto Industry," *Global News*, 28 August 2018.
6 Barrie McKenna, "A Guide to Understanding the Dairy Dispute between the U.S. and Canada," *Globe and Mail*, 24 April 2017.
7 Quoted in "Here's Donald Trump's Rambling Explanation of What Happened at the G7 with Justin Trudeau – Transcript," *Maclean's*, 12 June 2018.
8 In her speech, Freeland said, "The 232 tariffs introduced by the United States are illegal under WTO and NAFTA rules. They are protectionism, pure and simple. They are not a response to unfair actions by other countries that put American industry at a disadvantage. They are a naked example of the United States putting its thumb on the scale, in violation of the very rules it helped to write. Canada has no choice but to retaliate – with a measured, perfectly reciprocal, dollar-for-dollar response – and we will do so. We act in close collaboration with our like-minded partners in the EU and Mexico. They too are your allies and they share our astonishment and our resolve. No one will benefit from this beggar thy neighbor dispute. The price will be paid, in part, by American consumers and by American businesses." Quoted in "As 'Angry Populism' Spreads, Freeland Calls for Facts, Open Trade and Rules-Based Order," *CTV News*, 13 June 2018.
9 Andres Rozental, "Mexico and Canada Must Stand Together on NAFTA," *Globe and Mail*, 29 August 2019.
10 Quoted in Katharine Starr, "EU Trade Chief Defends Freeland after Trump Trash-Talks 'Canada's Negotiator,'" *CBC News*, 27 September 2018.
11 Quoted in James McCarten, "Canada, U.S. Reach New NAFTA Deal; 'It's a Good Day for Canada,' Says Trudeau," *CityNews*, 30 September 2018,

https://toronto.citynews.ca/2018/09/30/canada-u-s-reach-new-nafta-deal-its-a-good-day-for-canada-says-trudeau/.
12 Jason Markusoff, "A New Poll on the USMCA Suggests Canadians Are Feeling Deal-Makers' Remorse," *Maclean's*, 23 October 2018.
13 C.D. Howe Institute, "CUSMA Generates Benefits for U.S. at Expense of Canada, Mexico," 25 July 2019, https://www.cdhowe.org/public-policy-research/cusma-generates-benefits-us-expense-canada-mexico-cd-howe-institute.
14 Quoted in Canadian Press, "A Chronology of Canada's Standoff with US over Steel, Aluminum Levies," *Toronto Star*, 18 May 2019.
15 Quoted in "Senators: Trump Called NAFTA Withdrawal Threat a 'Negotiating Tactic,' Urged Them to 'Trust Him,'" *Insidetrade.com*, 25 October 2017, https://insidetrade.com/daily-news/senators-trump-called-nafta-withdrawal-threat-%E2%80%98negotiating-tactic%E2%80%99-urged-them-%E2%80%98trust%E2%80%99-him.
16 Mulroney's comments were delivered at a Cabinet committee meeting in April 2017 that one of the authors attended.
17 "Brian Mulroney Testifies on NAFTA at the U.S. Senate," *Maclean's*, 30 January 2018.
18 Office of the Prime Minister of Canada, "Prime Minister Trudeau and Minister Freeland Speaking Notes for the United States–Mexico–Canada Agreement Press Conference," 1 October 2018, https://pm.gc.ca/en/news/speeches/2018/10/01/prime-minister-trudeau-and-minister-freeland-speaking-notes-united-states.
19 Gordon Mace and Gérard Hervouet, "Canada's Third Option: A Complete Failure?" *Canadian Public Policy/Analyse de Politiques* 15, no. 4 (1989): 387–404.
20 Anne Applebaum, "U.S. Isolationist Stance Could Outlast Trump," *National Post*, 6 August 2017.

CHAPTER THREE

1 Grant Bishop and Grant Sprague, *A Crisis of Our Own Making: Prospects for Major Natural Resource Projects in Canada* (Toronto: C.D. Howe Institute, 2019), 1.
2 Philip Cross, "Another Sprawling, Unfocused Budget, and So Little to Show for All the Red Ink," *Financial Post*, 19 March 2019.
3 Jack Mintz, "A Budget of Massive Spending and Not One Dollar Helping Competitiveness," *National Post*, 21 March 2019.

4 Olivier Blanchard, "Public Debt: Fiscal and Welfare Costs in a Time of Low Interest Rates," Peterson Institute for International Economics, February 2019, https://www.piie.com/system/files/documents/pb19-2.pdf.
5 See White House, "The Tax Cut and Jobs Act: The Most Significant Federal Tax Reform Enacted in the United States in Decades," February 2018, https://www.whitehouse.gov/wp-content/uploads/2018/02/WH_CuttingTaxesForAmericanWorkers_Feb2018.pdf.
6 Quoted in Steven Globerman and Joel Emes, *Innovation in Canada: An Assessment of Recent Experience* (Vancouver: Fraser Institute, 2019), 24. See also Business Council of Canada, *Competitiveness Scorecard*, 5 March 2019, https://thebusinesscouncil.ca/publications/competitiveness-scorecard/.
7 See, for example, Vincent Geloso, *Walled from Competition: Measuring Protected Industries in Canada* (Vancouver: Fraser Institute, 2019); Standing Senate Committee on Banking, Trade and Commerce, *Tear Down These Walls: Dismantling Canada's Internal Trade Barriers* (Ottawa: Senate of Canada, 2016); and C.D. Howe Institute, *International Competitiveness*, series of research reports, https://www.cdhowe.org/research-sub-categories/international-competitiveness.
8 Conrad Black, "Canada Must Start Competing, Assuming Trudeau and Morneau Let Us," *National Post*, 4 January 2019.
9 Cited in Globerman and Emes, *Innovation in Canada*, 27.
10 Cited in ibid., 28.
11 Andrew Willis, "Canadian CEOs Look Abroad for Investment as Confidence Sags in Leadership at Home," *Globe and Mail*, 24 March 2019.
12 Tegan Hill, Milagros Palacios, and Jason Clemens, "Federal Deficits Then and Now: Is Canada Repeating the Fiscal Mistakes of 1965 to 1995?" *Fraser Research Bulletin*, August 2019, 1, https://www.fraserinstitute.org/sites/default/files/federal-deficits-then-and-now.pdf.
13 Ian Burney, Canada's ambassador to Japan, communication with authors, August 2019.
14 Cited in Globerman and Emes, *Innovation in Canada*, 24-5.
15 Ronald Reagan Presidential Foundation and Institute, "Reagan Quotes and Speeches," 12 August 1986, https://www.reaganfoundation.org/ronald-reagan/reagan-quotes-speeches/news-conference-1/.
16 Brian Pallister, "Red Tape and Your Government: How Cutting Bureaucracy Boosted Manitoba's Growth," *Financial Post*, 21 January 2019.

17 Cited in Jesse Snyder, "'Regulatory Whack-a-Mole': Chamber of Commerce Casts Doubt on Liberal Efforts to Cut Red Tape as Investment Worries Mount," *National Post*, 8 August 2019.
18 Quoted in Ian McGugan, "Rising Rates, High Debt Could Lead to Financial Crisis in Canada," *Globe and Mail*, 12 December 2018.
19 Kevin Page and Randall Bartlett, "The Case for Strengthening Federal Fiscal Policy," *Globe and Mail*, 6 November 2018.
20 International Monetary Fund, "Canada: Staff Concluding Statement of the 2018 Article IV Mission," 4 June 2018, https://www.imf.org/en/News/Articles/2018/06/04/ms060418-canada-staff-concluding-statement-of-the-2018-article-iv-mission.
21 Cited in Black, "Canada Must Start Competing."
22 Bob Fay, "It Is Time to Reboot Canada's Tax and Benefit System," *Financial Post*, 20 February 2019.
23 International Monetary Fund, "Canada: Staff Concluding Statement of the 2019 Article IV Mission," 21 May 2019, https://www.imf.org/en/News/Articles/2019/05/20/mcs052119-canada-staff-concluding-statement-of-the-2019-article-iv-mission.
24 See, for example, Creig Lamb and Sarah Doyle, *Future-Proof: Preparing Young Canadians for the Future of Work* (Toronto: Brookfield Institute, 2017).
25 Globerman and Emes, *Innovation in Canada*, 23.
26 Ibid., 24.
27 Peter Nicholson, "Canada Must Encourage Business to Break Its Low-Innovation Streak," *Globe and Mail*, 23 October 2018.
28 Ibid.
29 Cited in Globerman and Emes, *Innovation in Canada*, 25.
30 Kevin Carmichael, "'Resistance Is Futile' in Slow March to Open Banking," *National Post*, 1 February 2019.
31 In point of fact, growing market concentration is not unique to the tech sector. See, for example, Jan De Loecker and Jan Eeckhout, *The Rise of Market Power and the Macroeconomic Implications* (Cambridge, MA: National Bureau of Economic Research, 2017), http://www.nber.org/papers/w23687. See also "Technology Firms Are Both the Friend and the Foe of Competition," *The Economist*, 15 November 2018.
32 Cited in John Lorinc, "Jim Balsillie Has Emerged from Retirement with a Mission to Save Canada's Tech Sector," *Maclean's*, 23 April 2019.

33 Quoted in James McLeod, "Intellectual Property May Be a State of Mind, but Canada's Mind Is Not on the Game," *Financial Post*, 19 December 2018.
34 Cited and quoted in Theophilos Argitis, "Canada Falling Behind in the 'Intangible' Economy as We Give Up Our Tech to Foreigners, Report Warns," *Financial Post*, 4 April 2019. See Robert Asselin and Sean Speer, *A New North Star: Canadian Competitiveness in an Intangibles Economy* (Ottawa: Public Policy Forum, 2019), https://ppforum.ca/wp-content/uploads/2019/04/PPF-NewNorthStar-EN4.pdf.
35 Asselin and Speer, *New North Star*, 43.
36 Innovation, Science and Economic Development Canada, "Canada's New Superclusters," 2019, https://www.ic.gc.ca/eic/site/093.nsf/eng/00008.html.
37 The intellectual property strategy "will amend key IP laws to ensure that we remove barriers to innovation, particularly any loopholes that allow those seeking to use IP in bad faith to stall innovation for their own gain," and it "will create an independent body to oversee patent and trademark agents, which will ensure that professional and ethical standards are maintained, and will support the provision of quality advice from IP professionals." Innovation, Science and Economic Development Canada, "Government of Canada Launches Intellectual Property Strategy," news release, 26 April 2018, https://www.canada.ca/en/innovation-science-economic-development/news/2018/04/government-of-canada-launches-intellectual-property-strategy.html.
38 Ivan Semeniuk, "Canada Struggling to Capitalize on Research and Development Sector," *Globe and Mail*, 10 April 2018.
39 Michael Wornow, "How Sports Teams Exploit City Budgets to Fund Stadiums," *Harvard Political Review*, (21 May 2018), https://harvardpolitics.com/united-states/how-sports-teams-exploit-city-budgets-to-fund-stadiums/.

CHAPTER FOUR

1 Parag Khanna, "The Future Is Asian," *Globe and Mail*, 2 February 2019.
2 Oliver Tonby, Jonathan Woetzel, Wonsik Choi, Jeongmin Seong, and Patti Wang, *Asia's Future Is Now* (New York: McKinsey Global Institute,

2019), https://www.mckinsey.com/featured-insights/asia-pacific/asias-future-is-now.
3 Clive Hamilton, *Silent Invasion: China's Influence in Australia*, Kindle edition (Melbourne, Australia: Hardie Grant, 2018), ch. 1.
4 Ibid.
5 Ibid., Preface.
6 Ibid., ch. 4.
7 Ibid.
8 Omid Ghoreishi, "Beijing Uses Confucius Institutes for Espionage, Says Canadian Intelligence Veteran," *Epoch Times*, 14 October 2014, https://www.theepochtimes.com/hosting-confucius-institute-a-bad-idea-says-intelligence-veteran_1018292.html.
9 Eric Rosenbaum, "1 in 5 Corporations Say China Has Stolen Their IP within the Last Year: CNBC CFO Survey," *CNBC*, 1 March 2019, https://www.cnbc.com/2019/02/28/1-in-5-companies-say-china-stole-their-ip-within-the-last-year-cnbc.html.
10 Mariama Sow, "Figures of the Week: Chinese Investment in Africa," Brookings Institution, 6 September 2018, https://www.brookings.edu/blog/africa-in-focus/2018/09/06/figures-of-the-week-chinese-investment-in-africa/.
11 President Xi Jinping, quoted in Anne-Marie Brady, "China's Undeclared Foreign Policy at the Poles," Lowy Institute, *The Interpreter*, 6 May 2017, emphasis in original, https://www.maritime-executive.com/editorials/chinas-undeclared-foreign-policy-at-the-poles.
12 Testimony of Professor Clive Hamilton to Parliamentary Joint Committee on Intelligence and Security, Parliament of Australia, 31 January 2018, https://parlinfo.aph.gov.au/parlInfo/search/display/display.w3p;query=Id%3A%22committees%2Fcommjnt%2F1e36c2f4-7e55-46ed-ab03-e9bd81f4cdb8%2F0004%22.
13 Nathan VanderKlippe, "China's Military Scientists Target Canadian Universities," *Globe and Mail*, 29 October 2018.
14 David Ljunggren, "Canada Should Ban Huawei from 5G Networks, Says Former Spy Chief," *Reuters*, 21 January 2019.
15 Tom Blackwell, "Tibetan-Canadian Student Politician, Uyghur Rights Activists Come under Attack by Chinese Students in Canada," *National Post*, 15 February 2019.
16 Ibid.
17 Department of Foreign Affairs and Trade, Government of Australia, "Australia's Composition of Trade 2008," media release, 17 June 2009,

https://dfat.gov.au/news/media/Pages/australia-s-composition-of-trade-2008.aspx.
18 Government of Canada, "Canadian Total Exports, Top 10 Countries, 2008," *Report – Trade Data Online*, https://www.ic.gc.ca/app/scr/tdst/tdo/crtr.html?&productType=HS6&lang=eng.
19 Department of Foreign Affairs and Trade, Government of Australia, "Australia's Top 10 Two-Way Trading Partners," 2019, https://dfat.gov.au/TRADE/RESOURCES/TRADE-AT-A-GLANCE/Pages/default.aspx.
20 Government of Canada, "Canadian Total Exports, Top 10 Countries, 2017," *Report – Trade Data Online*, https://www.ic.gc.ca/app/scr/tdst/tdo/crtr.html?&productType=HS6&lang=eng.
21 Hamilton, *Silent Invasion*, ch. 10.
22 Michael Pillsbury, *The Hundred-Year Marathon: China's Secret Strategy to Replace America as the Global Superpower* (New York: Henry Holt, 2015).
23 Fareed Zakaria, "Pillsbury: What U.S. Can Learn from China," interview, *CNN Videos*, 6 January 2019, https://edition.cnn.com/videos/tv/2019/01/06/exp-gps-0106-pillsbury-china.cnn.
24 Ibid.
25 Pillsbury, *The Hundred-Year Marathon*, 39.
26 "The East Is Grey," *The Economist*, 10 August 2013.
27 Thomas C. Frohlich and Liz Blossom, "These Countries Produce the Most CO_2 Emissions," *USA Today*, 14 July 2019, https://www.usatoday.com/story/money/2019/07/14/china-us-countries-that-produce-the-most-co-2-emissions/39548763/.
28 Pillsbury, *The Hundred-Year Marathon*, 99.
29 Ibid., 28.
30 Elizabeth C. Economy, "The Great Firewall of China: Xi Jinping's Internet Shutdown," *Guardian* (London), 29 June 2018. See also Elizabeth C. Economy, *The Third Revolution: Xi Jinping and the New Chinese State* (New York: Oxford University Press, 2018).
31 Pillsbury, *The Hundred-Year Marathon*, 200.
32 Ibid., 230.
33 Ibid., passim.
34 Howard W. French, *Everything under the Heavens: How the Past Helps Shape China's Push for Global Power* (New York: Alfred A. Knopf, 2017).
35 Ibid., 10.
36 Ibid., 242, 247.

37 Graham Allison, *Destined for War: Can America and China Escape Thucydides's Trap?* (Boston: Houghton Mifflin Harcourt, 2017), xvii.
38 Quoted in ibid., 138.
39 Robert Kaplan, "A New Cold War Has Begun," *Foreign Policy*, 7 January 2019.
40 Ibid.
41 Ibid.
42 See John Ibbitson, *The Big Break* (Waterloo, ON: Centre for International Governance Innovation, 2014); and Duane Bratt, "Implementing the Reform Party Agenda: The Roots of Stephen Harper's Foreign Policy," paper presented at the Annual Meeting of the Canadian Political Science Association, University of Calgary, 31 May to 2 June 2016.
43 Keith Brasher, "China's Economic Growth Hits 27-Year Low as Trade War Stings," *New York Times*, 24 July 2019.
44 Jonathan Manthorpe, *Claws of the Panda: Beijing's Campaign of Influence and Intimidation in Canada*, Kindle edition (Toronto: Cormorant Books, 2019), Introduction.
45 Jonathan Manthorpe, "Trudeau Blew It in Beijing. That's the Good News," *iPolitics*, 5 December 2017, https://ipolitics.ca/2017/12/05/trudeau-blew-beijing-thats-good-news/.
46 Ibid.
47 Public Policy Forum, *Diversification Not Dependence: A Made-in-Canada China Strategy* (Ottawa: Public Policy Forum, 2018), 9, https://ppforum.ca/wp-content/uploads/2018/10/DiversificationNotDependence-PPF-OCT2018-EN.pdf.
48 Michael Hart, with Bill Dymond and Colin Robertson, *Decision at Midnight: Inside the Canada-US Free-Trade Negotiations* (Vancouver: UBC Press, 1994), 61–2.
49 Manthorpe, *Claws of the Panda*, ch. 11.
50 International Monetary Fund, "World Economic Outlook Update, January 2019: A Weakening Global Expansion," January 2019, https://www.imf.org/en/Publications/WEO/Issues/2019/01/11/weo-update-january-2019.
51 Zhang Hui, "China Readies Its Counterattack against Canada," *Global Times*, 14 December 2018, http://www.globaltimes.cn/content/1131951.shtml.
52 Mike Blanchfield and Andy Blatchford, "John McCallum Says He 'Misspoke' about Huawei Executive Meng Wanzhou's Case," *HuffPost*,

24 January 2019, https://www.huffingtonpost.ca/2019/01/24/john-mccallum-says-he-misspoke-about-huawei-executive-meng-wanzhous-case_a_23652103/.
53 Ibid.
54 Rod Nickel and David Ljunggren, "First Canola, Now Pigs: China Blocks Imports from Two Canadian Pork Producers amid Diplomatic Row," *Financial Post*, 2 May 2019.
55 Martin Wolf, "The Future Might Not Belong to China," *Financial Times*, 1 January 2019.
56 Ibid.
57 Ibid.
58 Quoted in Aakanksha Tangri, "Trudeau Believes Indian Government 'Factions' Wrecked His Diplomatic Visit," *Vice*, 2 March 2018, https://www.vice.com/en_ca/article/wj4y7m/trudeau-believes-indian-government-factions-wrecked-his-diplomatic-visit-jaspal-atwal-daniel-jean-international-sikh-youth-federation-raveesh-kumar.
59 Alex Lockie, "Canadian PM Trudeau Roundly Mocked for Political, Fashion Blunders during Disastrous Trip to India," *Business Insider*, 23 February 2018, https://www.businessinsider.com/canadian-pm-trudeau-mocked-for-political-fashion-blunders-in-india-2018-2.
60 John Ivison, *Trudeau: The Education of a Prime Minister* (Toronto: Signal, 2019), 226–7.
61 Elizabeth Thompson, "Trudeau's India Trip Cost More Than the Government First Disclosed," CBC *News*, 18 September 2018.
62 Candice Malcolm, "Why Justin Trudeau's India Tour Turned Out to Be a Diplomatic Disaster," *Economic Times*, 25 February 2018, https://economictimes.indiatimes.com/news/politics-and-nation/why-justin-trudeaus-india-tour-turned-out-to-be-a-diplomatic-disaster/articleshow/63059621.cms?from=mdr.
63 Gurprit S. Kindra, "Trudeau's Trip to India Both Misinformed and Myopic," *Ottawa Citizen*, 26 February 2018.
64 Joe Chidley, "India's Deepening Economic Ties with Canada Show Modi Evolution Is Making Progress, Even If It Isn't Perfect," *Financial Post*, 4 July 2019.
65 Ibid.
66 Arvind Subramian, quoted in Martin Wolf, "India Will Rise, Regardless of Its Politics," *Financial Times*, 5 February 2019.
67 Ajai Shukla, "India's Dispute with Pakistan over Jammu & Kashmir Has a Loser – New Delhi's Cherished Secularism," *This Week in Asia*,

5 August 2019, https://www.scmp.com/week-asia/opinion/article/3021525/indias-dispute-pakistan-over-jammu-kashmir-has-loser-new-delhi.
68 Wolf, "India Will Rise."
69 Khanna, "Future Is Asian."

CHAPTER FIVE

1 See, for example, Forest Reinhardt, "Stop Thinking of Climate Change as a Religious or Political Issue," Harvard Business School, *Working Knowledge: Business Research for Business Leaders*, 24 September 2014, https://hbswk.hbs.edu/item/stop-thinking-of-climate-change-as-a-religious-or-political-issue; and Willis Jenkins, Evan Berry, and Luke Beck Kreider, "Religion and Climate Change," *Annual Review of Environment and Resources* 43 (2018): 85–108.
2 Earle Gray, *The Great Canadian Oil Patch: The Petroleum Era from Birth to Peak* (Toronto: Maclean Hunter, 1970), 180.
3 Quoted in Fen Osler Hampson, "Fraught with Risk: The Political Economy of Petroleum Policies in Canada and Mexico" (PhD diss., Harvard University, 1982), 618. See also François Bregha, *Bob Blair's Pipeline: The Business and Politics of Northern Energy Development Projects* (Toronto: James Lorimer, 1979).
4 Thomas R. Berger, *Northern Frontier, Northern Homeland: The Report of the Mackenzie Valley Pipeline Inquiry*, vol. 1 (Ottawa: Minister of Supply and Services Canada, 1977).
5 Hampson, "Fraught with Risk," 598–608.
6 Aaron Wherry, "Rachel Notley Helped Strike a Grand Bargain on Oil and Climate, Can Trudeau Save It?" *CBC News*, 18 April 2019.
7 John Dillon, "Huge Challenges for Canada after the Paris Climate Conference," KAIROS: Canadian Ecumenical Justice Initiatives, January 2016, http://www.climatefast.ca/sites/default/files/files/Paris%20Research%20Paper.pdf.
8 Quoted in Canadian Press, "'Canada Is Back,' Says Trudeau in Paris. 'We're Here to Help,'" *Toronto Star*, 30 November 2015.
9 Interview with authors, Ottawa, 23 May 2019.
10 Quoted in Canadian Press, "Trudeau Signs Paris Climate Treaty at UN, Says 'Canada's Efforts Will Not Cease,'" *Global News*, 22 April 2016.

11 Environment and Climate Change Canada, *Technical Paper on the Federal Carbon Pricing Backstop* (2017), https://www.fin.gc.ca/activty/consult/fcpb-fsftc-eng.pdf.
12 Mia Rabson, "Ottawa to Return 90% of Money It Collects from Carbon Tax to the Canadians Who Pay It," *Financial Post*, 23 October 2018.
13 Shawn McCarthy and Jeff Lewis, "Court Overturns Ottawa's Approval of Northern Gateway Pipeline," *Globe and Mail*, 30 June 2016.
14 National Energy Board, Government of Canada, "Energy East and Eastern Mainline Projects," 2019, https://www.cer-rec.gc.ca/pplctnflng/mjrpp/nrgyst/index-eng.html?=undefined&wbdisable=true.
15 Kalina Lafromboise and Kamila Hickson, "Quebec Politicians, Environmentalists Hail Demise of Controversial Energy East Pipeline," CBC *News*, 5 October 2017.
16 Bruce Cheadle, "Justin Trudeau Halts Northern Gateway, Approves Kinder Morgan Expansion, Line 3," *Global News*, 29 November 2016.
17 Ibid.
18 "More British Columbians Now Support the Trans Mountain Pipeline Project: Poll," CBC *News*, 18 April 2018.
19 Cited in "'It's What's in the Pipeline': Green Party Outlines Plan to Only Use Canadian Crude," CBC *News*, 28 May 2019.
20 Department of Finance Canada, "Agreement Reached to Create and Protect Jobs, Build Trans Mountain Expansion Project," 29 May 2018, https://www.fin.gc.ca/news-nouvelles/speeches-discours/2018/2018-05-29-eng.asp.
21 Shawn McCarthy, Justine Hunter, and James Keller, "NEB Says Trans Mountain Pipeline Expansion in Public Interest Despite 'Adverse' Impact on Whale Population," *Globe and Mail*, 22 February 2019.
22 Mike Hager, Justine Hunter, Shawn McCarthy, and James Keller, "B.C. Court of Appeal Says Province Can't Restrict Oil Shipments within Its Borders," *Globe and Mail*, 25 May 2019.
23 House of Commons of Canada, 1st Session, 42nd Parliament, 21 June 2019, Bill C-48, An Act Respecting the Regulation of Vessels That Transport Crude Oil or Persistent Oil to or from Ports or Marine Installations Located along British Columbia's North Coast, https://www.parl.ca/LegisInfo/BillDetails.aspx?Language=E&billId=8936657&View=0.

24 House of Commons of Canada, 1st Session, 42nd Parliament, 21 June 2019, Bill C-69, An Act to Enact the Impact Assessment Act and the Canadian Energy Regulator Act, to Amend the Navigation Protection Act and to Make Consequential Amendments to Other Acts, https://www.parl.ca/legisinfo/BillDetails.aspx?Language=E&billId=9630600.
25 Diane Francis, "This Goofy Clause in Bill C-69 Will Ensure Resource Development in Canada Stops Cold," *Financial Post*, 13 May 2019.
26 Marla Orenstein, "Bill C-69 and the Intersection of Identity and Pipelines," *Globe and Mail*, 19 February 2019.
27 Kenneth B. Green and Taylor Jackson, *Safety First: Intermodal Safety for Oil and Gas Transportation* (Vancouver: Fraser Institute, 2017).
28 Elmira Aliakbari and Ashley Stedman, "Senate Committee Rejects Oil Tanker Ban," *Fraser Forum*, 21 May 2019, https://www.fraserinstitute.org/blogs/senate-committee-rejects-oil-tanker-ban.
29 Ibid.
30 Brad Wall, "Want a Unity Crisis? Pass C-69 and C-48 into Law," *National Post*, 30 May 2019.
31 Ibid.
32 Greenhouse Gas Pollution Pricing Act, SC 2018, c. 12, s. 186, 21 June 2018, https://laws-lois.justice.gc.ca/eng/acts/G-11.55/.
33 Quoted in John Paul Tasker, "'A Stampede of Stupid': Rachel Notley Urges Senate to Block Oil Tanker Ban Bill," *CBC News*, 9 April 2019.
34 Quoted in Josh Dehaas, "As Alberta Cuts Oil Production, Notley Has List of Demands for Trudeau," *CTV News*, 3 December 2018.
35 Rachel Alello, "PM's 'Grand Bargain' on Energy Died on Alberta Election Day: Kenny," *CTV News*, 21 April 2019.
36 David Ljunggren, "Provinces Vow to Resist after New Federal Carbon Tax Takes Effect," *Reuters*, 1 April 2019.
37 Justin Giovanetti and James Keller, "Kenney to Launch Fresh Court Challenge to Federal Carbon Tax," *Globe and Mail*, 23 May 2019.
38 Climate Action Tracker, https://climateactiontracker.org.
39 Robert P. Murphy, "William Nordhaus versus the United Nations on Climate Change Economics," *Econlib*, 5 November 2018, https://www.econlib.org/library/Columns/y2018/MurphyNordhaus.html.
40 David Bailey and Greg Bertelsen, "Analysis of the Baker-Shultz Plan vs. Other Policy Pathways through 2025," in Climate Leadership Council, *Exceeding Paris: How The Baker-Shultz Carbon Dividends Plan Would Significantly Exceed the U.S. Paris Commitment & Achieve 50% CO2*

Reduction by 2035, 4–9 (London: Climate Leadership Council, 2018), https://www.clcouncil.org/media/Exceeding-Paris.pdf; Marc Hafstead, "Analysis of Alternative Carbon Tax Price Paths for the Climate Leadership Council (CLC) Carbon Dividends Plan," *Resources for the Future*, 20 June 2018, https://www.rff.org/publications/issue-briefs/analysis-of-alternative-carbon-tax-price-paths-for-the-climate-leadership-council-clc-carbon-dividends-plan/.

41 Cited in Nelson Bennett, "Canada Lost $100B in Energy Projects in Two Years: Report," *JWN: Trusted Energy Intelligence*, 13 March 2019, https://www.jwnenergy.com/article/2019/3/canada-just-lost-100b-cancelled-stalled-oil-and-gas-projects-report/.

42 Cited in Geoff Zochodne, "'We're Squandering an Opportunity': CEOs of RBC and Enbridge Urge Action on Energy Strategy," *Financial Post*, 21 February 2019.

43 Andrew Coyne, "Carbon Tax Smackdown, Part 2: Andrew Coyne Asks What Is This Argument Really About?" *National Post*, 25 May 2019.

44 Dave Sawyer and Seton Stiebert, "The True Measure of BC's Carbon Tax," *Policy Options*, 2 May 2019, https://policyoptions.irpp.org/magazines/may-2019/true-measure-bcs-carbon-tax/.

45 Charles Lammam and Taylor Jackson, *Examining the Revenue Neutrality of British Columbia's Carbon Tax* (Vancouver: Fraser Institute, 2017), ii.

46 Quoted in Nick Murray, "Nunavut Gov't Unveils First Part of Carbon Tax Mitigation Measures," *CBC News*, 30 May 2019.

47 Philip Cross, "The Problem with the Carbon Tax," *The Hill Times* (Ottawa), 11 March 2019, https://www.hilltimes.com/2019/03/11/191557/191557.

48 See Terence Corcoran, "Carbon Tax Smackdown, Part 1: Terence Corcoran Says Higher Prices at the Pump Don't Mean Fewer Emissions," *National Post*, 25 May 2019.

49 David Muller, "Light Trucks Are Now a Record 69 Percent of the U.S. Market," *Autoweek*, 7 January 2019, https://autoweek.com/article/car-news/light-trucks-take-record-69-us-market.

50 Éric Grenier, "Canadians Are Worried about Climate Change, but Many Don't Want to Pay Taxes to Fight It: Poll," *CBC News*, 18 June 2019.

51 William Watson, "Even a Nobel-Winning Carbon-Tax Economist Admits Carbon Taxes Have Problems," *Financial Post*, 16 October 2018.

52 Ibid.

53 Inayat Singh, Andrew Culbert, and Connie Walker, "Confronting Carbon: How Does Canada Meet Its Climate Targets?" *CBC News*, 18 June 2019.
54 Cited and quoted in "Mark Jaccard: Carbon Taxes Are 'Good Policy, Bad Politics' When Regulations Do Most of the Work," *The Energy Mix*, 19 December 2019, https://theenergymix.com/2018/12/19/jaccard-carbon-taxes-are-good-policy-bad-politics-when-regulations-do-most-of-the-work/. See also Mark Jaccard, "Divisive Carbon Prices Are Much Ado about Nothing," *Globe and Mail*, 14 December 2018.
55 Geoffrey Morgan, "Innovation Energy: Oil Sands Step Up to Take on Clean Tech Challenge," *Financial Post*, 4 July 2019.
56 Ibid.
57 Justin Gillis, "To Make Headway on Climate Change, Let's Change the Subject," *New York Times*, 30 May 2019.
58 North Carolina, Department of Environmental Quality, *Energy Policy Council Biennial Report*, May 2018, 21–2, https://deq.nc.gov/about/divisions/energy-mineral-land-resources/energy-policy-council.
59 Cited in Jack Mintz, "Only One Country Is Contemplating Destroying Its Own Resource Sector: Canada," *Financial Post*, 13 June 2019. See Mark P. Mills, *The "New Energy Economy": An Exercise in Magical Thinking* (New York: Manhattan Institute, 2019), https://media4.manhattan-institute.org/sites/default/files/R-0319-MM.pdf.
60 Bret Stephens, "France's Combustible Climate Politics: Climate Policy Should Be about Solving Problems, Not Salving Consciences," *New York Times*, 6 December 2018.
61 Ibid.
62 Juliette Jowit, "Bjørn Lomborg: $100bn a Year Needed to Fight Climate Change," *Guardian* (London), 30 August 2010. See also Bjørn Lomborg, ed., *Smart Solutions to Climate Change: Comparing Costs and Benefits* (Cambridge, UK: Cambridge University Press, 2010), 292–359.
63 Emma Foehringer Merchant, "With 43 Carbon-Capture Projects Lined Up Worldwide, Supporters Cheer Industry Momentum," *Greentechmedia.com*, 11 December 2018, https://www.greentechmedia.com/articles/read/carbon-capture-gains-momentum.
64 Jan Christoph Minx and Gregory Nemet, "The Inconvenient Truth about Carbon Capture," *Washington Post*, 31 May 2018.
65 Rio Tinto, "Rio Tinto and Alcoa Announce World's First Carbon-Free Aluminum Smelting Process," *Cision PR Newswire*, 10 May 2018, https://www.prnewswire.com/news-releases/rio-tinto-and-alcoa-

announce-worlds-first-carbon-free-aluminium-smelting-process-300646602.html.

66 Mac Van Wielingen, "Canada's Energy Policy, and Its Increasingly Fact-Free Discourse, Demands a Rethink," *Globe and Mail*, 17 May 2019.

67 Shell, "What Is Shell's Net Carbon Footprint Ambition?" https://www.shell.com/energy-and-innovation/the-energy-future/what-is-shells-net-carbon-footprint-ambition.html. See also Olivia Pulsinelli, "Royal Dutch Shell to Set More Climate Targets, Plans to Link Them to Executive Compensation," *Houston Business Journal*, 3 December 2018, https://www.bizjournals.com/houston/news/2018/12/03/royal-dutch-shell-to-set-more-climate-targets.html.

68 Governor of the Bank of England Mark Carney, Governor of Banque de France François Villeroy de Galhau, and Chair of the Network for Greening the Financial Services Frank Elderson, "Open Letter on Climate-Related Financial Risks," Bank of England, 17 April 2019, https://www.bankofengland.co.uk/news/2019/april/open-letter-on-climate-related-financial-risks.

69 Cited in Chris Flood, "BlackRock Issues Climate Change Warning," *Financial Times*, 6 September 2016. See BlackRock Investment Institute, *Adapting Portfolios to Climate Change: Implications and Strategies for All Investors*, September 2016, https://www.blackrock.com/us/individual/literature/whitepaper/bii-climate-change-2016-us.pdf.

70 Global Commission on the Economy and Climate, *Unlocking the Inclusive Growth Story of the 21st Century: Accelerating Climate Action in Urgent Times* (Washington, DC: World Resources Institute, 2018), 9, https://newclimateeconomy.report/2018/wp-content/uploads/sites/6/2018/09/NCE_2018_FULL-REPORT.pdf.

71 Edward Waitzer, "Data Gap," *Corporate Knights*, 2 May 2018, https://www.corporateknights.com/channels/responsible-investing/data-gap-15252372/.

72 Quoted in Elizabeth McSheffrey, "Europe's Biggest Bank Retreats from the Oilsands," *Canada's National Observer*, 20 April 2018, https://www.nationalobserver.com/2018/04/20/news/europes-biggest-bank-retreats-oilsands. See also Jennifer Thompson, "BlackRock and HSBC Launch Saudi Investment Funds," *Financial Times*, 4 May 2019.

73 Citigroup, *Energy Darwinism II: Why a Low Carbon Future Doesn't Have to Cost the Earth* (New York: Citi GPS: Global Perspectives & Solutions, 2015), 8, https://www.longfinance.net/media/documents/

Citi_2015_-_Energy_Darwinism_II_-_Why_a_Low_Carbon_Future_Doesnt_Have_to_Cost_ZcXVxiq.pdf.

74 Simon Zadek, "The Critical Frontier: Reducing Emissions from China's Belt and Road," Brookings Institution, 25 April 2019, https://www.brookings.edu/blog/future-development/2019/04/25/the-critical-frontier-reducing-emissions-from-chinas-belt-and-road/.

75 Jonathan Watts, "Belt and Road Summit Puts Spotlight on Chinese Coal Funding," *Guardian* (London), 25 April 2019.

76 Gwyn Morgan, "Here Are a Few Climate Change Head Scratchers," *National Post*, 30 July 2019.

77 Dennis Normille, "Bucking Global Trends, Japan again Embraces Coal Power," *Science*, 2 May 2018, https://www.sciencemag.org/news/2018/05/bucking-global-trends-japan-again-embraces-coal-power.

78 "Japan to Rule Out Coal-Fired Plants as International Criticism Rises," *The Asahi Shimbun*, 28 March 2019, http://www.asahi.com/ajw/articles/AJ201903280066.html.

79 Lawrence Solomon, "Trudeau Stands Alone as Canada – and the World – Abandons Green Energy," *Financial Post*, 28 September 2018.

80 Quoted in Nelson Bennett, "Canadian Fossil Fuels Could Lower China's GHGs: Resource Works," *JWN: Trusted Energy Intelligence*, 26 September 2018, https://www.jwnenergy.com/article/2018/9/canadian-fossil-fuels-could-lower-chinas-ghgs-resource-works/.

81 Josha MacNab, "Will B.C. LNG Exports Reduce Global Carbon Pollution?" Pembina Institute, 27 April 2017, https://www.pembina.org/blog/lng-global-emissions.

82 Cited in Ian Bickis, "Study Casts Doubts about Canada's Liquefied Natural Gas Exports," *Global News*, 24 August 2016.

83 Conrad Black, "How Trump Stood Up to the Environmentalist Left," *National Review*, 14 November 2018, https://www.nationalreview.com/2018/11/donald-trump-stood-up-to-environmentalist-left-climate-change/.

84 Mintz, "Only One Country."

85 Stephens, "France's Combustible Climate Politics."

86 Fiona Harvey, "What Was Agreed at COP24 in Poland and Why Did It Take So Long?" *Guardian* (London), 16 December 2018.

87 On the history of these negotiations, see Fen Osler Hampson, *Master of Persuasion: Brian Mulroney's Global Legacy* (Toronto: Signal, 2018), 117–44.

CHAPTER SIX

1 See, for example, Alex Inkeles and David E. Smith, *Becoming Modern* (Cambridge, MA: Harvard University Press, 1971); Ramesh Mishra, "Convergence Theory and Social Change: The Development of Welfare in Britain and the Soviet Union," *Comparative Studies in Society and History* 18, no. 1 (1976): 28–56; Talcott Parsons, *Societies: Evolutionary and Comparative Perspectives* (Englewood Cliffs, NJ: Prentice Hall, 1966); Walt Rostow, *The Stages of Economic Growth: A Non-Communist Manifesto* (Cambridge, UK: Cambridge University Press, 1960); and Pitirim A. Sorokin, "Mutual Convergence of the United States and the U.S.S.R. to the Mixed Sociocultural Type," *International Journal of Comparative Sociology* 1, no. 2 (1960): 143–76.
2 See, for example, G. John Ikenberry, "The Future of Liberal Internationalism," *Foreign Affairs*, May-June 2011; and Thomas J. Wright, *All Measures Short of War: The Contest for the Twenty-First Century and the Future of American Power* (New Haven, CT: Yale University Press, 2017).
3 See Erika Simpson, "The Principles of Liberal Internationalism According to Lester Pearson," *Journal of Canadian Studies* 34, no. 1 (1999): 75–92. Some analysts were critical of the policies of Stephen Harper's government for deviating from this approach. See, for example, Paul Heinbecker, *Getting Back in the Game: A Foreign Policy Playbook for Canada* (Toronto: Key Porter Books, 2010); and Roland Paris, "Are Canadians Still Liberal Internationalists? Foreign Policy and Public Opinion in the Harper Era," *International Journal* 69, no. 3 (2014): 274–307.
4 See, for example, John English, *Ice and Water: Politics, Peoples and the Arctic Council* (Toronto: Allen Lane, 2013).
5 Speech by the Honourable Noel Kinsella, Speaker of the Senate of Canada, delivered on the 65th Anniversary of Canada-Russia Bilateral Relations, Diplomatic Academy of the Ministry of Foreign Affairs of the Russian Federation, 7 November 2007, https://sencanada.ca/media/169955/canadarussia65-e.pdf.
6 Ibid.
7 Quoted in Bob Plamondon, "The Kremlin's Interpreter," *National Post*, 21 June 2013.

8   John J. Kirton and Ella Kokotsis, "The G7/8 Contribution at Kananaskis and Beyond," in Michele Fratianni, Paolo Savona, and John Kirton, eds, *Sustaining Global Growth and Development: G7 and IMF Governance*, 207–28 (London: Routledge, 2003).
9   Embassy of the Russian Federation in Canada, "Bilateral Relations," https://canada.mid.ru/web/canada-en/bilateral-relations.
10 Quoted in Canadian Press, "Justin Trudeau Would Tell Off 'Bully' Vladimir Putin 'Directly to His Face' If He Becomes Prime Minister," *National Post*, 13 October 2015.
11 Marie-Danielle Smith, "New Book Reveals Trudeau's Frosty Relationship with Stéphane Dion," *National Post*, 12 April 2018.
12 Quoted in Evan Dyer, "Trudeau Government Signals Thaw in Relations with Russia," *CBC News*, 29 March 2016.
13 Ragnhild Grønning, "Canada Signals Shift in Arctic Policy – Towards Engagement with Russia," *High North News*, 10 October 2016, https://www.highnorthnews.com/en/canada-signals-shift-arctic-policy-towards-engagement-russia.
14 "Canada's Foreign Minister Stéphane Dion 'It's Important to Be an Interlocutor for Peace,'" *Diplomat Magazine*, 4 October 2016, http://diplomatonline.com/mag/2016/10/canadas-foreign-minister-stephane-dion-its-important-to-be-an-interlocutor-for-peace/.
15 Christopher Westdal, "Planning Next Steps for Canada-Russia Relations," *OpenCanada.org*, 11 April 2016, https://www.opencanada.org/features/planning-next-steps-canada-russia-relations/.
16 Alex Boutilier, "Officials Considered One-on-One Meeting between Trudeau and Putin, Documents Say," *Toronto Star*, 7 July 2017.
17 See Bill Browder, *Red Notice: A True Story of High Finance, Murder, and One Man's Fight for Justice* (New York: Simon and Schuster, 2014).
18 Amy Minsky, "Why Is Canada's Top Diplomat, Chrystia Freeland, Banned from Russia?" *Global News*, 12 January 2017.
19 Margaret Vice, "Publics Worldwide Unfavorable toward Putin, Russia" Pew Research Center, *Global Attitudes and Trends*, 16 August 2017, https://www.pewresearch.org/global/2017/08/16/publics-worldwide-unfavorable-toward-putin-russia/.
20 Samuel P. Huntington, *The Third Wave: Democratization in the Late Twentieth Century* (Norman: University of Oklahoma Press, 1993), 16.
21 Freedom House, "Freedom in the World 2018: Democracy in Crisis," 2018, https://freedomhouse.org/report/freedom-world/freedom-world-2018.

22 Special Counsel's Office, US Department of Justice, *The Mueller Report: The Report of the Special Counsel on the Investigation into Russian Interference in the 2016 Presidential Election* (Washington, DC: US Department of Justice, 2019).

23 Bert Ely, "Russia Is an Economic Pipsqueak; Trump's Putin infatuation Is baffling," *The Hill* (Washington, DC), 13 July 2018, https://thehill.com/opinion/international/396877-russia-is-an-economic-pipsqueak-trumps-infatuation-is-baffling.

24 Cited in Quora and Bruce Jones, "As An American, Why Should I Care about the Russians Taking Back Crimea?" *Forbes*, 31 March 2014.

25 Ely, "Russia Is an Economic Pipsqueak."

26 Ibid.

27 Leonid Ragozin, "Putin's Star Is Fading," *Politico*, 11 September 2019, https://www.politico.eu/article/putins-star-is-fading/.

28 Arms Control Association, "Nuclear Weapons: Who Has What at a Glance," *Fact Sheet and Briefs*, July 2019, https://www.armscontrol.org/factsheets/Nuclearweaponswhohaswhat.

29 Jeremy Bender, "Ranked: The World's 20 Strongest Militaries," *Business Insider*, 3 October 2015, https://www.businessinsider.com/these-are-the-worlds-20-strongest-militaries-ranked-2015-9.

30 Idrees Ali, "With an Eye on Russia, U.S. to Increase Nuclear Capabilities," *Reuters*, 2 February 2018.

31 Neil MacFarquhar and David E. Sanger, "Putin's 'Invincible' Missile Is Aimed at U.S. Vulnerabilities," *New York Times*, 1 March 2018.

32 Mikhail Troitskiy, "Negotiating Russia's Status in Post-Soviet Eurasia," in Fen Osler Hampson and Mikhail Troitskiy, eds, *Tug of War: Negotiating Security in Eurasia* (Waterloo, ON: Centre for International Governance Innovation, 2017), 31.

33 North Atlantic Treaty Organization, "NATO-Russia Relations: A New Quality," 28 May 2002, https://www.nato.int/cps/en/natohq/official_texts_19572.htm.

34 Troitskiy, "Negotiating Russia's Status," 24.

35 Michael McFaul, "Russia as It Is: A Grand Strategy for Confronting Putin," *Foreign Affairs*, July-August 2018.

36 Ibid.

37 Stephen Collinson, "Discord over Trump's Helsinki Humiliation Hands Putin Another Win," CNN *Politics*, 18 July 2018, https://edition.cnn.com/2018/07/18/politics/donald-trump-vladimir-putin-finland-summit-fallout/index.html.

38 These are some of the conclusions of a major joint study conducted by the Atlantic Council and the Centre for International Governance Innovation. See Ash Jain, Damon Wilson, Fen Osler Hampson, Simon Palamar, and Camille Grand, with Go Myong-Hyun, James Nixey, Michal Makocki, and Nathalie Tocci, *Strategy of "Constrainment": Countering Russia's Challenge to the Democratic Order* (Waterloo, ON: Centre for International Governance Innovation, 2017).

39 Michael Krepon, "The New Age of Nuclear Confrontation Will Not End Well," *New York Times*, 3 March 2019.

40 J. Robert Oppenheimer, "Atomic Weapons and American Policy," *Bulletin of the Atomic Scientists* 9, no. 6 (1953): 203.

41 Quoted in Justin Huggler and Matthew Day, "Merkel Pledges German Support to Deploy Thousands of NATO Troops to Deter Russian Aggression," *Telegraph* (London), 7 July 2016.

42 Quoted in Teresa Wright, "Trump Sends Letter to Trudeau Calling for Increase in NATO Defence Spending," CBC *News*, 22 June 2018.

43 Matt Gurney, "Canada's Back? We're Barely Here at All," *National Post*, 2 August 2019.

44 Richard Wike, "6 Charts on How Germans and Americans View One Another," Pew Research Center, *Fact Tank: News in Numbers*, 26 April 2018, https://www.pewresearch.org/fact-tank/2018/04/26/6-charts-on-how-germans-and-americans-view-one-another/.

45 Robert E. Litan and Roger Noll, "As Trump Twists NATO's Arm, Let's Run the Math on Defense Spending," Brookings Institution, 12 July 2018, https://www.brookings.edu/blog/up-front/2018/07/12/as-trump-twists-natos-arm-lets-run-the-math-on-defense-spending/.

46 Fen Osler Hampson, *Master of Persuasion: Brian Mulroney's Global Legacy* (Toronto: Signal, 2018), 202–3.

47 Editorial, "Why Increase Canadian Military Spending? One Word: Trump," *Globe and Mail*, 7 June 2017.

48 Ibid.

49 James Stavridis, "Russia and NATO Show War Games Aren't Just Games," *The Morning Call*, 14 September 2018, https://www.mcall.com/opinion/mc-opi-nato-russia-war-games-20180914-story.html.

50 "The Kerch Strait Incident," *International Institute of Strategic Studies* 24 (December 2018), https://www.iiss.org/publications/strategic-comments/2018/the-kerch-strait-incident.

51 Viktors Domburs, "No One Will Deter Russia in the Baltic Region – OpEd," *Eurasia Review*, 18 December 2018, https://www.eurasiareview.com/18122018-no-one-will-deter-russia-in-the-baltic-region-oped/.
52 Editorial, "The Liberals Promised New Fighter Jets. They Delivered Utter Lunacy Instead," *National Post*, 23 November 2018.
53 Ibid.
54 Office of the Auditor General of Canada, *Report 3 – Canada's Fighter Force – National Defence* (2018), http://www.oag-bvg.gc.ca/internet/English/parl_oag_201811_03_e_43201.html.
55 John Robson, "Canada Must Get Real about Defence," *National Post*, 10 October 2018.
56 David J. Bercuson, "NATO Has Problems," *National Post*, 4 September 2018.
57 Jean-Francois Revel, "The Myths of Eurocommunism," *Foreign Affairs*, January 1978.

CHAPTER SEVEN

1 Quoted in "Massachusetts Bay – 'The City upon a Hill,'" *U.S. History*, 2019, http://www.ushistory.org/us/3c.asp.
2 Quoted in Canadian Press, "'Canada Is Back,' Says Trudeau in Paris. 'We're Here to Help,'" *Toronto Star*, 30 November 2015.
3 See, for example, Roland Paris, "The Promise and Perils of Justin Trudeau's Foreign Policy," in Norman Hillmer and Philippe Lagassé, eds, *Justin Trudeau and Canadian Foreign Policy*, 17–29 (Cham, Switzerland: Palgrave Macmillan, 2018).
4 Editorial, "The Mystery of Canada's 'Values' Foreign Policy," *Globe and Mail*, 7 February 2014.
5 See, for example, Andrew F. Cooper, *Canadian Foreign Policy: Old Habits and New Directions* (Scarborough, ON: Prentice Hall Allyn and Bacon Canada, 1997); and Jennifer Welsh, *At Home in the World: Canada's Global Vision for the 21st Century* (Toronto: HarperCollins, 2004).
6 Gareth Evans, *Values and Interests in Foreign Policy Making* (Vancouver: School for International Studies, Simon Fraser University, 2016), 6, http://www.gevans.org/opeds/SimonsWorkingPaper53ValuesInterests.pdf.
7 Ibid., emphasis in original.

8 Ibid.
9 Sigal Samuel, "The Two Words That Made Saudi Arabia Furious at Canada," *The Atlantic*, 6 August 2018.
10 Ibid., quoting Ali Shihabi, founder of the Arabia Foundation.
11 Canadian Press, "'A Brave New Canadian': Freeland Welcomes Saudi Teen Granted Asylum after Fleeing Family," *National Post*, 13 January 2019.
12 "Canada Is 'Complicit' in Saudi Mass Execution, Say Relatives of Victims," *Middle East Monitor*, 2 May 2019, https://www.middleeastmonitor.com/20190502-canada-is-complicit-in-saudi-mass-execution-say-relatives-of-victims/.
13 Les Perreaux and Steven Chase, "Dion Chose Jobs over Human Rights When Approving Saudi Arms Deal, Lawyers Argue," *Globe and Mail*, 19 December 2016.
14 Marc Montgomery, "Canadians Divided over Arms Sales to Saudi Arabia," *Radio Canada International*, 6 November 2018, https://www.rcinet.ca/en/2018/11/06/canadians-divided-over-arms-sales-to-saudi-arabia/.
15 Quoted in Editorial, "Mystery of Canada's 'Values.'"
16 John Noble, "Has Canada Become a Diplomatic Scold?" *iPolitics*, 15 November 2013, https://ipolitics.ca/2013/11/15/has-canada-become-a-diplomatic-scold/.
17 Lina Dib, "UN Agency Slams Harper's Maternal Health Policy," *iPolitics*, 9 March 2016, https://ipolitics.ca/2016/03/09/un-agency-slams-canadas-maternal-health-policy/.
18 This discussion is drawn from Derek H. Burney and Fen Osler Hampson, "Baird: A 'Pragmatic Internationalist,'" *Diplomat Magazine*, 4 April 2015, http://diplomatonline.com/mag/2015/04/john-baird-a-pragmatic-internationalist/.
19 Quoted in "In Wake of Iran Protests, Should Canada Reopen Embassy in Tehran?" CBC *Radio*, 8 January 2018.
20 Konrad Yakabuski, "On Israel, Trudeau Is Harper's Pupil," *Globe and Mail*, 10 May 2018, quoting Dalhousie University professor Steven Seligman.
21 See, for example, Emanuel Adler, "Imagined (Security) Communities: Cognitive Regions in International Relations," *Millennium: Journal of International Studies* 26, no. 2 (1997): 249–77; Emanuel Adler, *Communitarian International Relations: The Epistemic Foundations of International Relations* (London: Routledge, 2004); G. John Ikenberry, "Liberal Internationalism 3.0: America and the Dilemmas of Liberal World Order," *Perspectives on Politics* 7, no. 1 (2009): 71–87; Joseph S.

Nye Jr, "Will the Liberal Order Survive? The History of an Idea," *Foreign Affairs*, January-February 2017; and Oliver Richmond, *A Post-Liberal Peace* (London: Routledge, 2012).

22 See, for example, Peter McLaverty, "Civil Society and Democracy," *Contemporary Politics* 8, no. 4 (2002): 303–18. For a skeptical view, see David Brooks, "Building Democracy out of What?" *The Atlantic*, 1 June 2003.

23 Michael Bell, Michael Molloy, David Sultan, and Sallama Shaker, "Practitioners' Perspectives on Canada-Middle East Relations," in Paul Heinbecker and Bessma Momani, eds, *Canada and the Middle East: In Theory and Practice* (Waterloo, ON: Wilfred Laurier University Press, 2007), 8.

24 Ibid., 9.
25 Ibid., 9–10.
26 Ibid., 11, 12.
27 Ibid., 12.
28 Ibid., 13.
29 Ibid., 14.
30 Bessma Momani and Agata Antkiewicz, "Canada's Economic Interests in the Middle East," in Paul Heinbecker and Bessma Momani, eds, *Canada and the Middle East: In Theory and Practice*, 161–84 (Waterloo, ON: Wilfred Laurier University Press, 2007).
31 David Barette, Managing Director, CAE-Emirates, personal communication with one of the authors, 2012.
32 Michael Bonner, "What Role for Canada in the Arab Spring?" NATO Association of Canada, 24 September 2012, http://natoassociation.ca/what-role-for-canada-in-the-arab-spring/.
33 Alex J. Bellamy and Paul D. Williams, "The New Politics of Protection? Côte d'Ivoire, Libya and the Responsibility to Protect," *International Affairs* 87, no. 4 (2011): 825–50.
34 Shadi Hamid, "Problems of State: Security and Insecurity in a Changing Middle East," in Chester A. Crocker, Fen Osler Hampson, and Pamela Aall, eds, *Is Peace and Conflict Diplomacy Broken? Global Peacemaking in an Era of Diminished Capacity/Resources and Growing Political Constraints* (Waterloo, ON: Centre for International Governance Innovation, forthcoming).
35 Ibid.
36 Patrick Wintour, "Why Does Syria Still Have Chemical Weapons?" *Guardian* (London), 18 April 2018.

37 Jeffrey Goldberg, "The Obama Doctrine, R.I.P.," *The Atlantic*, 7 April 2016.
38 Jack Thompson, "Trump's Middle East Policy," CSS *Analyses in Security Policy*, no. 233 (October 2018), 1, https://www.research-collection.ethz.ch/handle/20.500.11850/292962.
39 Ibid.
40 Liz Sly, "In the Middle East, Russia Is Back," *Washington Post*, 5 December 2018.
41 Lara Seligman and Robbie Gramer, "U.S. and Turkey Escalate Feud over Russian Missile System," *Foreign Policy*, 2 April 2019.
42 Sly, "In the Middle East."
43 James Osborne, "US Predicts That Crude Production Will Rise to 13.1M Barrels a Day in 2020," *Houston Chronicle*, 7 May 2019.
44 See, for example, Kamaran M.K. Mondal, "Canada's Role in the Arab-Israeli Peace Process through the United Nations and Beyond," IUP *Journal of International Relations* 12, no. 3 (2018): 36–43.
45 Government of Canada, "Country Profile: Israel," 12 September 2019, https://www.international.gc.ca/trade-commerce/trade-agreements-accords-commerciaux/agr-acc/israel/country_profile-israel-profil_pays.aspx?lang=eng.
46 Sam Hamad, "'Reforms' in Saudi Arabia Exist Only as a Tool to Appease Western Allies," TRT *World*, 19 April 2019, https://www.trtworld.com/opinion/reforms-in-saudi-arabia-exist-only-as-a-tool-to-appease-western-allies-26006.
47 Royal Canadian Air Force, "Canada's Air Task Force-Iraq Flies First Missions," 3 November 2014, http://www.rcaf-arc.forces.gc.ca/en/article-template-standard.page?doc=canada-s-air-task-force-iraq-flies-first-missions/i1pgn9hq.
48 Canadian Press, "Sajjan Pledges Support for Iraq War against ISIS, Will Not Extend Canada's Military Mission," *Global News*, 6 December 2018.
49 Murray Brewster, "Canada Extending Military Missions in Ukraine, Iraq," CBC *News*, 18 March 2019.
50 Tom Fletcher, *The Naked Diplomat: Understanding Power and Politics in the Digital Age* (London: Williams Collins, 2017), 10.
51 David Ljunggren, Aziz El Yaakoubi, and Katie Pau, "A Canadian Tweet in a Saudi King's Court Crosses a Red Line," *Reuters*, 10 August 2018.

52 Jacques Marcoux and Caroline Barghout, "How Events Unfolded after Foreign Affairs Minister Sent Tweet Rebuking Saudi Arabia," CBC News, 6 December 2018.
53 Amnesty International, "Saudi Arabia: Two More Women Human Rights Activists Arrested in Unrelenting Crackdown," 1 August 2018, https://www.amnesty.org/en/latest/news/2018/08/saudi-arabia-two-more-women-human-rights-activists-arrested-in-unrelenting-crackdown/.
54 Quoted in Marcoux and Barghout, "How Events Unfolded."
55 Quoted in Kathleen Harris, "Ottawa Engaged in 'Delicate' Talks to Protect Pakistani Woman Released from Blasphemy Death Sentence," CBC News, 5 November 2018.
56 "Saudi to Free 850 Indian Prisoners from Its Jails: India Government," Reuters, 20 February 2019.
57 Ben Farmer, "Saudi Arabia to Release 2,000 Pakistani Prisoners as Part of Lavish Diplomatic Visit," Telegraph (London), 18 February 2019.
58 Nathan C. Funk, "Applying Canadian Principles to Peace and Conflict Resolution in the Middle East," in Paul Heinbecker and Bessma Momani, eds, Canada and the Middle East: In Theory and Practice (Waterloo, ON: Wilfred Laurier University Press, 2007), 28.
59 Amy Minsky, "Explained: So What If Saudi Arabia Is Using Canadian-Made Arms to Fight Citizens?" Global News, 8 August 2017.
60 Quoted in Jeffrey Simpson, "Truculent Moralizing for a Domestic Audience," Globe and Mail, 4 February 2012.

CHAPTER EIGHT

1 Melissa Hathaway, interview with one of the authors, 28 May 2019.
2 Fen Osler Hampson and Eric Jardine, Look Who's Watching: Surveillance, Treachery and Trust Online (Waterloo, ON: Centre for International Governance Innovation, 2016), 55.
3 Quoted in ibid., 191.
4 Yamri Taddese, "Law Firms Targeted in Top 10 Worst Cyber Attacks," Canadian Lawyer Magazine, 19 April 2013, https://www.canadianlawyermag.com/news/general/law-firms-targeted-in-top-10-worst-cyber-attacks/271945.
5 "Toronto Policy Website Shut Down in String of Cyber Attacks across Canada," National Post, 24 November 2014.

6 "Ottawa Police Website Overwhelmed in Denial of Service Attack," *CBC News*, 24 November 2014.
7 Canadian Press, "Ottawa Hospital Targeted by Cyberattack," *CBC News*, 13 March 2016.
8 Howard Solomon, "Top Canadian Cyber Security Stories of 2017," *IT World Canada*, 22 December 2017, https://www.itworldcanada.com/article/top-canadian-cyber-security-stories-of-2017/400255.
9 Howard Solomon, "Cyber Security Today: Personal Information Accessed at Canada Revenue, Facebook's War on Terrorists and New Banking Malware Found," *IT World Canada*, 18 June 2018, https://www.itworldcanada.com/article/cyber-security-today-personal-information-accessed-at-canada-revenue-facebooks-war-on-terrorists-and-new-banking-malware-found/406382.
10 James McLeod, "Data Breach Laws Lack Teeth," *National Post*, 1 August 2019.
11 Carleton University, "Tech Corner: Strengthening Student Security in an Era of Online Attacks," 18 June 2018, https://carleton.ca/cuol/2018/tech-corner-strengthening-student-security-in-an-era-of-online-attacks/.
12 Timothy B. Lee, "The WannaCry Ransomware Attack Was Temporarily Halted. But It's Not Over Yet," *Vox*, 15 May 2017, https://www.vox.com/new-money/2017/5/15/15641196/wannacry-ransomware-windows-xp.
13 Howard Solomon, "Canada Third Most Exposed Country to Possible Cyber Attacks, Says Vendor Study," *IT World Canada*, 7 June 2018, https://www.itworldcanada.com/article/canada-third-most-exposed-country-to-possible-cyber-attacks-says-vendor-study/406044.
14 "Port of San Diego Hit by Cyber Attack," *World Maritime News*, 28 September 2018, https://worldmaritimenews.com/archives/261525/port-of-san-diego-hit-by-cyber-attack/.
15 Cited in Dan Healing, "Cyberattacks Pose Serious Threat to Canada's Automated Resource Firms," *Globe and Mail*, 27 November 2017.
16 Ethan Lou, "Risk of Cyber, Bomb Attacks Grows for Canada's Energy Security, CSIS Says," *Global News*, 17 January 2017.
17 Canadian Internet Registration Authority, *2018 Cybersecurity Survey Report* (2018), https://cira.ca/resources/cybersecurity/report/2018-cybersecurity-survey-report.
18 Canadian Chamber of Commerce, "Small & Medium-Sized Businesses," 2019, http://www.chamber.ca/advocacy/issues/small-and-medium-sized-businesses/.

19 Canadian Internet Registration Authority, *2018 Cybersecurity Survey Report*.
20 Ibid.
21 Jonathan Montpetit, "Personal Data of 2.7 Million People Leaked from Desjardins," CBC *News*, 20 June 2019.
22 Global Security and Politics Program, *Report to Public Safety on ISPs* (Waterloo, ON: Centre for International Governance Innovation, forthcoming).
23 Ibid.
24 Public Safety Canada, *National Cyber Security Strategy: Canada's Vision for Security and Prosperity in the Digital Age* (2018), https://www.publicsafety.gc.ca/cnt/rsrcs/pblctns/ntnl-cbr-scrt-strtg/ntnl-cbr-scrt-strtg-en.pdf.
25 McKinsey & Company, "Defense of the Cyberrealm: How Organizations Can Thwart Cyberattacks," podcast, January 2019, https://www.mckinsey.com/business-functions/risk/our-insights/defense-of-the-cyberrealm-how-organizations-can-thwart-cyberattacks.
26 Steven Chase, "Canada Joins U.S., U.K., in Calling Out China for State-Sponsored Hacking Campaign," *Globe and Mail*, 20 December 2018.
27 Quoted in Joseph Marks, "The Cybersecurity 202: U.S. Officials: It's China Hacking That Keeps Us Up at Night," *Washington Post*, 6 March 2019.
28 Melissa Hathaway, interview with one of the authors, 28 May 2019.
29 House of Commons of Canada, 42nd Parliament, 1st Session, 21 June 2019, Bill C-59, An Act Respecting National Security Matters, https://www.parl.ca/legisinfo/BillDetails.aspx?billId=9057418&Language=E.
30 Warren Frey, "Budget Addresses Digital Expansion and Cyber Threats to Infrastructure," *Daily Commercial News*, 19 March 2019, https://canada.constructconnect.com/dcn/news/technology/2019/03/budget-addresses-digital-expansion-cyberthreats-infrastructure.
31 Melissa Hathaway, interview with one of the authors, 28 May 2019.
32 Quoted in Jim Heintz, "Bolton Says Russia Hurt Itself by Meddling in US Vote," *Daily Herald* (Chicago), 23 October 2018.
33 US Department of Homeland Security, "Joint Statement from the Department of Homeland Security and Office of the Director of National Intelligence on Election Security," 7 October 2016, https://www.dhs.gov/news/2016/10/07/joint-statement-department-homeland-security-and-office-director-national.

34 Special Counsel's Office, US Department of Justice, *The Mueller Report: The Report of the Special Counsel on the Investigation into Russian Interference in the 2016 Presidential Election* (Washington, DC: US Department of Justice, 2019).
35 John Ibbitson, "Liberal and Conservative Worldview So Close That Election Isn't Worth Hacking," *Globe and Mail*, 3 February 2019.
36 Cited in Michael MacDonald, "Russian Aggression and Cyberwarfare Key Issues for Canada to Confront: Sajjan," *CTV News*, 16 November 2018.
37 Communications Security Establishment, *Cyber Threats to Canada's Democratic Process* (2017), https://cyber.gc.ca/sites/default/files/publications/cse-cyber-threat-assessment-e.pdf. See also Canadian Centre for Cyber Security, *National Cyber Threat Assessment 2018* (Ottawa: Communications Security Establishment, 2018), https://cyber.gc.ca/sites/default/files/publications/national-cyber-threat-assessment-2018-e_1.pdf.
38 Allan Rock, "Canada's Perspective on Election Interference," paper presented at the conference "The Past, Present and Future of Election Interference," Hudson Institute, Washington, DC, 30 November 2018.
39 Ibid.
40 Quoted in Sharon Gaudin, "Facebook CEO Zuckerberg Causes Stir over Privacy," *Computerworld*, 11 January 2010, https://www.computerworld.com/article/2522445/facebook-ceo-zuckerberg-causes-stir-over-privacy.html.
41 "Transcript of Mark Zuckerberg's Senate Hearing," *Washington Post*, 10 April 2018; Thomson Reuters, "Canadian MPs Criticize Facebook's Zuckerberg for U.K. Parliament No-Show," *CBC News*, 27 November 2018.
42 Quoted in Dakin Andone, "Bella Thorne Shares Nude Photos on Twitter after a Hacker Threatened to Release Them," *CNN Entertainment*, 16 June 2019, https://edition.cnn.com/2019/06/15/entertainment/bella-thorne-nude-photos-hack/index.html.
43 Maya Kosoff, "The 6 Fakest Fake-News Stories of 2017," *Vanity Fair*, 17 January 2018.
44 Frank Bruni, "The Internet Will Be the Death of Us," *New York Times*, 30 October 2018.
45 Brent Kendall, "Justice Department to Open Broad, New Antitrust Review of Big Tech Companies," *Wall Street Journal*, 23 July 2019.
46 Mike Isaac, "How Facebook Is Changing to Deal with Scrutiny of Its Power," *New York Times*, 12 August 2019.

47 Dirk Helbing, Bruno S. Frey, Gerd Gigerenzer, Ernst Hafen, Michael Hagner, Yvonne Hofstetter, Jeroen van den Hoven, Roberto V. Zicari, and Andrej Zwitter, "Will Democracy Survive Big Data and Artificial Intelligence?" *Scientific American*, 25 February 2017, emphasis in original, https://www.scientificamerican.com/article/will-democracy-survive-big-data-and-artificial-intelligence/.
48 Ibid.
49 Alexandra Ma, "China Is Building a Vast Civilian Surveillance Network – Here Are 10 Ways It Could Be Feeding Its Creepy 'Social Credit System,'" *Business Insider*, 29 April 2018, https://www.businessinsider.com/how-china-is-watching-its-citizens-in-a-modern-surveillance-state-2018-4.
50 Centre for International Governance Innovation and Ipsos, "2018 CIGI-Ipsos Global Survey on Internet Security and Trust," 2018, https://www.cigionline.org/internet-survey-2018.
51 Bill Curry, "More Than Six in 10 Canadians Say Facebook Will Have a Negative Impact on Fall Election: Survey," *Globe and Mail*, 11 February 2019.
52 Allan Rock, *Election Risk Monitor: Canada* (Waterloo, ON: Centre for International Governance Innovation, 2019), 16.
53 Eileen Donahoe and Fen Osler Hampson, eds, *Governance Innovation for a Connected World: Protecting Free Expression, Diversity and Civic Engagement in the Digital Ecosystem: Special Report* (Waterloo, ON: Centre for International Governance Innovation, 2018), https://www.cigionline.org/sites/default/files/documents/Stanford%20Special%20Report%20web.pdf.
54 Bill Graham, *Governance Innovation for a Connected World: Protecting Free Expression, Diversity and Civic Engagement in the Digital Ecosystem: International Working Meeting* (Waterloo, ON: Centre for International Governance Innovation, 2018), 5, https://issuu.com/cigi/docs/2018__stanford_californiaweb.
55 Ibid.
56 Government of Canada, Democratic Institutions, "Combatting Foreign Interference," 2019, https: www.canada. ca/en/democratic-institutions/news/2019/01/ combatting-foreign-interference.html.
57 Government of Canada, Democratic Institutions, "G7 Rapid Response Mechanism," 2019, https://www.canada.ca/en/democratic-institutions/news/2019/01/g7-rapid-response-mechanism.html.

58 German Bundestag, Network Enforcement Act, *German Law Archive*, 1 September 2017, https://germanlawarchive.iuscomp.org/?p=1245.
59 Eva Sweet, "The New EU General Data Protection Regulation – Benefits and First Steps to Meeting Compliance," *ISACA Journal* 6 (2016), https://www.isaca.org/Journal/archives/2016/volume-6/Pages/the-new-eu-general-data-protection-regulation.aspx.
60 Edward Greenspon and Taylor Owen, *Democracy Divided: Countering Disinformation and Hate in the Digital Public Sphere* (Ottawa: Public Policy Forum, 2018), https://ppforum.ca/wp-content/uploads/2018/08/DemocracyDivided-PPF-AUG2018-EN.pdf.
61 Ibid., 1.
62 Quoted in Joshua Tauberer, "Sunlight as a Disinfectant," in *Open Government Data: The Book*, 2nd ed. (2014), https://opengovdata.io/2014/sunlight-as-disinfectant/.
63 Jim Balsillie, "'Data Is Not the New Oil – It's the New Plutonium,'" *Financial Post*, 28 May 2019.
64 Ibid.
65 Ibid.
66 Ibid.

CHAPTER NINE

1 Peter Nicholson, *Facing the Facts: Reconsidering Business Innovation Policy in Canada* (Montreal: Institute for Research on Public Policy, 2018), https://irpp.org/wp-content/uploads/2018/10/Facing-the-Facts-Reconsidering-Business-Innovation-Policy-in-Canada.pdf.
2 World Population Review, 2019, http://worldpopulationreview.com/countries/life-expectancy-by-country/.
3 Jason Clemens and Sasha Parvani, "Canada Must Prepare for Our Aging Population," Fraser Institute, 26 November 2017, https://www.fraserinstitute.org/article/canada-must-prepare-for-our-aging-population.
4 See, for example, Daniel Tencer, "Canada's Labour Shortage Intensifies, with Nearly 400,000 Vacant Jobs," *HuffPost*, 13 March 2018, https://www.huffingtonpost.ca/2018/03/13/labour-shortage-canada-job-vacancies_a_23384818/; and Dan Kelly, "Immigrants Are the Solution to Canada's Labor Shortage," Canadian Federation of Independent Business,2019,https://www.cfib-fcei.ca/en/immigrants-are-solution-canadas-labour-shortage.
5 Clemens and Parvani, "Canada Must Prepare."

6 See Irvin Studin, "Review: Doug Saunders's Maximum Canada Argues the More the Merrier," *Globe and Mail*, 6 October 2017.
7 Kareem El-Assal and Daniel Fields, *Canada 2040: No Immigration versus More Immigration* (Ottawa: Conference Board of Canada, 2018), iii.
8 Cited in Stephen Smith and Eman Katem, "Canada Extends Immigration Targets into 2021 with Prominent Roles for Express Entry, PNPs," *CIC News*, 1 November 2018, https://www.cicnews.com/2018/11/canada-extends-immigration-targets-into-2021-with-prominent-roles-for-express-entry-pnps-1111368.html#gs.1dcwj6.
9 Ibid.
10 Darrell Bricker, *Populism, Immigration, and Canada* (Paris: Ipsos, 2019), 16, https://www.conferenceboard.ca/docs/default-source/conf-pres-public/19-0049_p2_bricker.pdf?sfvrsn=e2e74d13_2.
11 Ibid., 17.
12 Ibid., 18.
13 Ibid., 20.
14 Amnesty International Canada (English Branch), British Columbia Civil Liberties Association, Canadian Association of Refugee Lawyers, Canadian Civil Liberties Association, and Canadian Council for Refugees, "Letter to Prime Minister Regarding Refugee Measures in Budget Bill," Canadian Council for Refugees, 11 April 2019, https://ccrweb.ca/en/letter-prime-minister-regarding-refugee-measures-budget-bill.
15 Ibid.
16 Andrew Coyne, "An Inhumane Betrayal on Immigration," *National Post*, 13 April 2019.
17 John Ibbitson, "Liberals' Immigration Plan Is Sound Policy Delivered Poorly," *Global and Mail*, 10 April 2019.
18 Cited in Michelle Zilio and Adrian Morrow, "Canada, U.S. Move to Redraft Border Treaty to Cut Flow of Asylum Seekers," *Globe and Mail*, 1 April 2019.
19 Douglas Quan, "Alleged Human-Smuggling Operation May Have Brought Hundreds of Chinese Migrants across B.C. Border," *National Post*, 20 June 2019.
20 Quoted in Agence France-Presse, "Justin Trudeau Shows up at Airport to Welcome Canada's First Syrian Refugees," *Public Radio International*, 11 December 2015, https://www.pri.org/stories/2015-12-11/justin-trudeau-shows-airport-welcome-canadas-first-syrian-refugees.

21 Nicholas Kristof, "Thank God for Canada! Our Boring Neighbor Is a Moral Leader of the Free World," *New York Times*, 6 February 2019.
22 Nayla Rush, "Refugee Resettlement Admissions in FY 2018," Center for Immigration Studies, 1 October 2018, https://cis.org/Rush/Refugee-Resettlement-Admissions-FY-2018.
23 Diane Francis, "Trudeau's Holier-Than-Thou Tweet Causes Migrant Crisis – Now He Needs to Fix What He Started," *Financial Post*, 13 July 2018.
24 Bill Curry and Sean Fine, "Trudeau Defends Tougher Stand on Border," *Globe and Mail*, 11 April 2019.
25 Quoted in Teresa Wright, "Refugee Advocates 'Shocked and Dismayed' over Asylum Changes in Ottawa's Budget Bill," *Globe and Mail*, 9 April 2019.
26 Quoted in Zilio and Morrow, "Canada, U.S. Move to Redraft."
27 Cited in "How Are Canadian Attitudes towards Immigration Changing?" CBC *Radio*, 23 September 2018.
28 Teresa Wright, "Canadians Supportive of Immigration but Concerned about Asylum Seekers: Survey," *Globe and Mail*, 17 August 2018.
29 Office of the Auditor General of Canada, *Report 2 – Processing of Asylum Claims* (2019), http://www.oag-bvg.gc.ca/internet/English/parl_oag_201905_02_e_43339.html.
30 Ibid.
31 Garnett Picot, Yan Zhang, and Feng Hou, *Labour Market Outcomes among Refugees to Canada* (Ottawa: Statistics Canada, 2019), 6, http://publications.gc.ca/collections/collection_2019/statcan/11f0019m/11f0019m2019007-eng.pdf.
32 Ibid., 5.
33 Teresa Wright, "Growing Number of Newcomers, Refugees, Ending up Homeless in Canada, Studies Say," *Globe and Mail*, 9 August 2019.
34 René Houle, *Results from the 2016 Census: Syrian Refugees Who Resettled in Canada in 2015 and 2016* (Ottawa: Statistics Canada, 2019), https://www150.statcan.gc.ca/n1/en/pub/75-006-x/2019001/article/00001-eng.pdf?st=A742Gjxk.
35 Statistics Canada, "Study: Syrian Refugees Who Resettled in Canada in 2015 and 2016," *The Daily*, 12 February 2019, https://www150.statcan.gc.ca/n1/daily-quotidien/190212/dq190212a-eng.htm.
36 Ibid.
37 UNHCR, "Figures at a Glance," 2019, https://www.unhcr.org/figures-at-a-glance.html.
38 UNHCR, "Refugees," 2019, https://www.unhcr.org/refugees.html.

39 UNHCR, *Global Trends: Forced Displacement in 2018* (2019), 18, https://www.unhcr.org/5d08d7ee7.pdf.
40 Gil Loescher and James Milner, "Understanding the Challenge," *Forced Migration Review*, no. 33 (September 2009), 9, https://www.fmreview.org/sites/fmr/files/FMRdownloads/en/FMRpdfs/FMR33/FMR33.pdf.
41 Baher Kamal, "Climate Migrants Might Reach One Billion by 2050," Inter Press Service News Agency, 21 August 2017, http://www.ipsnews.net/2017/08climate-migrants-might-reach-one-billion-by-2050/?utm_source=rss&utm_medium=rss&utm_campaign=climate-migrants-might-reach-one-billion-by-2050.
42 UNHCR, "Uganda," *Global Focus: UNHCR Operations Worldwide*, http://reporting.unhcr.org/uganda.
43 Amnesty International, "Amnesty International Report 2017/18 – Uganda," 22 February 2018, https://www.refworld.org/docid/5a993842a.html.
44 Adam Rasmi, "The Caveats behind Canada's Feel-Good Refugee Numbers," *Quartz Daily*, 31 January 2019, https://qz.com/1536578/canadas-refugee-policy-in-context/. How do these figures stack up to Canada's historical intake of resettled refugees? The biggest wave of resettled refugees came after the Second World War. In the period 1947–52, Canada resettled roughly 250,000 displaced by the war and the Soviet occupation of eastern and central Europe. In 1956 and 1968, 37,000 Hungarians and 11,000 Czechoslovaks respectively resettled in Canada to escape persecution following the Soviet-led intervention in both countries. Canada opened its arms to 60,000 Vietnamese "boat people" after South Vietnam fell to the Vietcong in 1979–80. Government of Canada, "A History of Refuge," https://www.canada.ca/en/immigration-refugees-citizenship/services/refugees/canada-role/timeline.html.
45 "Country Comparison Uganda vs Canada," CountryEconomy.com, https://countryeconomy.com/countries/compare/uganda/canada.
46 UNHCR, "South Sudan Regional Refugee Response Plan Revised: January-December 2017 (May 2017)," Relief Web, 15 May 2017, https://reliefweb.int/report/uganda/south-sudan-regional-refugee-response-plan-revised-january-december-2017-may-2017.
47 UNHCR, "Uganda," *Operational Update*, January 2019, 1, http://reporting.unhcr.org/sites/default/files/unhcr%20Uganda%20Operational%20Update%20-%20January%202019.pdf.

48 Farha Bhoyroo, "Funding Shortfall Leaves South Sudanese Refugees at Risk," United Nations High Commissioner for Refugees, 18 December 2018, https://www.unhcr.org/news/stories/2018/12/5c191fcc4/funding-shortfall-leaves-south-sudanese-refugees-risk.html.

49 Martin Chulov, "Thousands of Refugees and Militants Return to Syria from Lebanon," *Guardian* (London), 14 August 2019.

50 UNHCR, *Update on Budgets and Funding for 2017 and 2018* (2018), https://www.unhcr.org/5a9fd8b12.pdf.

51 World Refugee Council, *A Call to Action: Transforming the Global Refugee System* (Waterloo, ON: Centre for International Governance Innovation, 2019), 7.

52 Beth McKernan, "Alan Kurdi's Father Condemns Politicians for Failing to Act: 'People Are Still Dying and Nobody Is Doing Anything about It,'" *The Independent*, 1 September 2016, https://www.independent.co.uk/news/world/middle-east/alan-kurdi-anniversary-abdullah-syria-war-kobani-aylan-a7220481.html.

53 Worldometers, https://www.worldometers.info/world-population/.

54 World Refugee Council, *A Call to Action*, 61.

55 The Magnitsky Act is named after Russian lawyer Sergei Magnitsky, who was imprisoned on fabricated charges while investigating corrupt business practices and fraud by Russian officials and who died in custody under mysterious circumstances. See Bill Browder, *Red Notice: A True Story of High Finance, Murder, and One Man's Fight for Justice* (New York: Simon and Schuster, 2014). Both the United States and Canada introduced legislation targeting the assets of corrupt officials globally who have committed gross violations of internationally recognized human rights. In Canada, the law is known as the Justice for Victims of Corrupt Foreign Officials Act and was passed in 2017. Equivalent US legislation, known as the Magnitsky Rule of Law Accountability Act, was adopted in 2012.

56 World Trade Organization, *Aid for Trade Global Review 2017: Promoting Trade, Inclusiveness and Connectivity for Sustainable Development* (2017), https://www.wto.org/english/tratop_e/devel_e/a4t_e/gr17_e/glossy_summary_report_e.pdf.

57 Lawrence L. Herman, *Harnessing Trade Law to Support Refugees and Host Countries* (Waterloo, ON: Centre for International Governance Innovation, 2018).

58 Government of Canada, *Guide to the Private Sponsorship of Refugees Program* (2019), https://www.canada.ca/en/immigration-refugees-

citizenship/corporate/publications-manuals/guide-private-sponsorship-refugees-program/section-2.html.
59 Refugee Sponsorship Training Program, "The Private Sponsorship of Refugees (PSR) Program," 2019, http://www.rstp.ca/en/refugee-sponsorship/the-private-sponsorship-of-refugees-program/.
60 Ibid.
61 Immigration, Refugees and Citizenship Canada, "By the Numbers – 40 Years of Canada's Private Sponsorship of Refugees Program," 9 April 2019, https://www.canada.ca/en/immigration-refugees-citizenship/news/2019/04/by-the-numbers-40-years-of-canadas-private-sponsorship-of-refugees-program.html.
62 Global Refugee Sponsorship Initiative, "About GRSI," http://refugeesponsorship.org/who-we-are.
63 Ibid.
64 Senate of Canada, 1st Session, 42nd Parliament, 21 March 2019, Bill S-259, An Act Respecting the Repurposing of Certain Seized, Frozen or Sequestrated Assets, https://www.parl.ca/LegisInfo/BillDetails.aspx?Language=E&billId=10382249.
65 Quoted in World Refugee Council, *News*, 21 March 2019, https://www.worldrefugeecouncil.org/article/world-refugee-council-report-spurs-canadian-legislation-would-use-frozen-assets-dictators. For further details on Bill S-259, see Ratna Omidvar, "Bill S-259, Frozen Assets Repurposing Act," 2019, http://www.ratnaomidvar.ca/senate-business/in-the-chamber/frozen-assets-bill/.
66 Federal Department of Foreign Affairs, Government of Switzerland, *No Dirty Money: The Swiss Experience in Returning Illicit Assets* (2016), https://www.eda.admin.ch/dam/eda/en/documents/aussenpolitik/voelkerrecht/edas-broschuere-no-dirty-money_EN.pdf.
67 UNHCR, "Refugees and Migrants from Venezuela Top 4 Million: UNHCR and IOM," 7 June 2019, https://www.unhcr.org/news/press/2019/6/5cfa2a4a4/refugees-migrants-venezuela-top-4-million-unhcr-iom.html.
68 Michael J. Camilleri and Fen Osler Hampson, *No Strangers at the Gate: Collective Responsibility and a Region's Response to the Venezuelan Refugee and Migration Crisis* (Washington, DC: Inter-American Dialogue; Waterloo, ON: Centre for International Governance Innovation, 2018), 19n64.
69 UNHCR, *Global Compact on Refugees* (2018), https://www.unhcr.org/gcr/GCR_English.pdf.

70 United Nations, *Global Compact for Safe, Orderly and Regular Migration* (2018), https://refugeesmigrants.un.org/sites/default/files/180713_agreed_outcome_global_compact_for_migration.pdf.
71 UNHCR, *Comprehensive Refugee Response Framework: From the New York Declaration to a Global Compact on Refugees* (2016), https://www.unhcr.org/584687b57.pdf.
72 Peter Zimonjic, "Ex-Harper Immigration Minister Calls Out Scheer over 'Factually Incorrect' Statements on UN Migration Pact," CBC *News*, 4 December 2018.
73 Sadako Ogata, *The Turbulent Decade: Confronting the Refugee Crises of the 1990s* (New York: Norton, 2005), 25. See also Vivian Tan, "Ogata Calls for Stronger Political Will to Solve Refugee Crises," United Nations High Commissioner for Refugees, 27 May 2005, https://www.unhcr.org/news/latest/2005/5/4297406a2/ogata-calls-stronger-political-solve-refugee-crises.html.
74 Susan Martin, "A Sobering Lesson," in World Refugee Council, *A Call to Action*, 2.
75 World Refugee Council, *A Call to Action*, 2, emphasis added.

CHAPTER TEN

1 Marie-Danielle Smith, "Canadian Officials Instructed to Stop Using 'Progressive' to Describe Trade Deals, Documents Show," *National Post*, 4 July 2019.
2 Justin Trudeau, quoted in Canadian Press, "'Canada Is Back,' Says Trudeau in Paris. 'We're Here to Help,'" *Toronto Star*, 30 November 2015.
3 Kelly McParland, "If Canada's Back, Why Are We Getting So Little Done?" *National Post*, 31 July 2019.
4 Robert Asselin and Sean Speer, *A New North Star: Canadian Competitiveness in an Intangibles Economy* (Ottawa: Public Policy Forum, 2019), 43, https://ppforum.ca/wp-content/uploads/2019/04/PPF-NewNorthStar-EN4.pdf.

Index

5G infrastructure, 65, 67, 144, 200
9/11 terrorist attacks, 17

Aall, Pamela, 217
Abe, Shinzō, 11
Abedi, Maham, 195
Acheson, Dean, 136
Adler, Emanuel, 216
Aecon, 63
Afghanistan, 10, 13, 17, 116, 167, 194
Agence France-Presse, 225
Aid for Trade Global Review 2017, 173, 228. *See also* World Trade Organization (WTO)
Akita Drilling Ltd, 85
al-Assad, Bashar, 16–17, 108–9, 126–30, 172–3, 190–1
al-Jubeir, Adel, 134
al-Sadah, Nassima, 134
Alberta, 73–4, 76–9, 82–3, 85–6, 95, 100, 129, 165, 206
Albright, Madeleine, 192
Alello, Rachel, 206
Alex J. Bellamy, 217
Alexander, Christopher, 177

Ali, Idrees, 213
Aliakbari, Elmira, 206
Allison, Graham, 12, 57, 193, 202
Alqunun, Rahaf Mohammed, 120, 164
Amazon, 150
Ambrose, Rona, 79
"America First," vii, 3, 9, 14, 17, 30, 56
Amnesty International, 219, 227
Amnesty International Canada, 163, 225
Andone, Dakin, 222
Angus Reid Institute, 82, 121, 165
Antarctica, 51
anti-ballistic missile defence, 61, 185–7. *See also* Anti-Ballistic Missile Treaty
Anti-Ballistic Missile Treaty, 110
Antkiewicz, Agata, 217
Apple, 45, 55, 91–2
Applebaum, Anne, 10, 33, 196
Arab League, 126
Arab Spring, 126, 131, 217. *See also* Egypt; Libya; Syria
Arctic, 74–5, 93, 98–9, 101–3, 108, 130, 182, 184–5, 211–12

Arctic Council, 102–3, 211
Argentina, 28, 175, 177
Argitis, Theophilos, 199
Arms Control Association, 213
artificial intelligence (AI), 41–2, 44–6, 67, 151–2, 180, 185, 187, 223
Asahi Shimbun, The, 210
Asia-Pacific Economic Cooperation Forum, 101
Asia-Pacific region, 48, 101, 130, 182, 186, 200. See also Asia-Pacific Economic Cooperation Forum; China; Indonesia; Korea (North); Korea (South); Trans-Pacific Partnership (TPP); Vietnam
Asian Infrastructure Investment Bank, 15, 58
Assange, Julian, 146
Asselin, Robert, 46, 199, 230
asylum seekers, ix-x, 121–2, 134–5, 159–72, 189–90, 216, 225–6
asylum shopping, 165. See also asylum seekers
Atlantic, The (magazine), 120, 182, 214, 216–18
Atwal, Jaspal, 69
auditor general of Canada, 115, 166, 215, 226
Australia, 21, 37, 62, 72, 94, 113–14, 143–4, 160, 185–6, 200–1; Department of Foreign Affairs and Trade, 200–1; free trade agreement, 53; relations with China, 49–52
Australian F-18s, 115, 185

Badawi, Samar, 133–4
Bahrain, 122
Bailey, David, 206
Baird, John, 101, 121
Baker-Shultz Carbon Dividends Plan, 84, 206
Balsillie, Jim, x, 45, 157, 198, 224
Baltic States, 111–12, 114, 148
Bangladesh, 93, 176
Bank of Canada, 40, 44, 85
Bank of England, 92, 209
Banque de France, 92, 209
Barber, Lionel, 194
Barette, David, 217
Barghout, Caroline, 219
Bartlett, Randall, 40, 198
Beck, Luke, 204
Bell, Michael, 124–5, 217
Bell Canada, 65, 140
Bender, Jeremy, 213
Bennett, Nelson, 207, 210
Bercuson, David J., 116–17, 215–16
Berry, Evan, 204
Bertelsen, Greg, 206
Bethune, Norman, 59
Bhoyroo, Farha, 228
BHP Billiton, 139
Bibi, Asia, 134
Bickis, Ian, 210
Bieber, Justin, 150
big data, ix, 44, 46, 150–1, 157, 223
Big Six, 44
Bill C-59, 145, 221
Bill C-76, 154
Bill C-97, 162–3. See also asylum seekers; Canadian Department of Immigration, Refugees and Citizenship: unofficial border crossings
Bill S-259, 175–6, 229. See also Omidvar, Ratna

Bills C-48 and C-69, 81–3, 205–6;
  Canada West Foundation, 82;
  Diane Francis, 82, 206;
  Fraser Institute, 82, 206;
  opposition, 82
bin Salman, Mohammad, 120, 135
Bishop, Grant, 196
Bitcoin, 140–1
Black, Conrad, 37, 96, 197, 210
BlackRock Investment Institute, 92–3, 209
Blackwell, Tom, 200
Blair, Bill, 163
Blanchard, Olivier, 35, 197
Blanchfield, Mike, 202
Blatchford, Andy, 202
Blossom, Liz, 201
Boeing, 54
Bolton, John, 146
Bombardier Inc., 46
Bonner, Michael, 217
Borger, Julian, 193
Bouchard, Charles, 132
Boutilier, Alex, 212
Brady, Anne-Marie, 200
Brandeis, Louis, 157
Brasher, Keith, 202
Bratt, Duane, 202
Brazil, 64, 99, 177
Bregha, François, 204
Bretton Woods institutions, viii, 58, 98. *See also* General Agreement on Tariffs and Trade; International Monetary Fund (IMF); World Bank; World Trade Organization (WTO)
Brewster, Murray, 218
Bricker, Darrell, 162, 225

British Columbia, 69, 74, 76, 78–9, 83, 86–7, 156, 163–4, 205, 207, 225;
  Court of Appeals, 81;
  Environmental Management Act, 81
Brookings, 127, 200, 210, 214
Brooks, David, 217
Browder, Bill, 212, 228
Bruni, Frank, 150, 222
Bryden, Joan, 195
Burney, Derek H., ii-iii, 191, 216
Burney, Ian, 197
Burney, Jeff, x
Burney, Joan, x
Burundi, 169, 171
Bush, George H.W., 31
Bush, George W., 128, 137
Business Development Bank of Canada, 44
Business Insider, 151, 203, 213, 223
Butts, Gerry, 25, 28

CAE Inc., 125
Call to Action, A: Transforming The Global Refugee System, 172, 176, 228. *See also* World Refugee Council
Cambodia, 112
Cambridge Analytica, 149, 152
Camilleri, Michael J., 229
Canada Border Services Agency, 167
"Canada is back," 19, 77, 118, 181, 204, 215, 230
Canada's Business Council, 36
Canada-US Auto Pact, 62
Canadian Association of Refugee Lawyers, 163, 225
Canadian Centre for Cyber Security, 144–5, 147, 154, 222

Canadian Chamber of Commerce, 40, 142, 198, 220
Canadian Charter of Rights and Freedoms, 156
Canadian Council for Refugees, 163, 225
Canadian Criminal Code, 156
Canadian Department of Employment and Social Development, 168
Canadian Department of Environment and Climate Change, 205
Canadian Department of Finance, 205
Canadian Department of Global Affairs, 25, 133, 136
Canadian Department of Immigration, Refugees and Citizenship, 161; Private Sponsorship of Refugees Program, 167, 174–5, 229; refugee hearings, 163, 166; Safe Third Country Agreement, 163; Syrian refugees, 164, 168, 175, 177, 225–6; unofficial border crossings, 165–6; Vietnamese "boat people," 174–5, 179, 227
Canadian Department of Innovation, Science and Economic Development, 199
Canadian Department of National Defence, 40, 112, 115, 145, 215
Canadian Department of Public Safety and Energy Preparedness, 221
Canadian Energy Regulator, 81, 206
Canadian Federal Court of Appeal, 78
Canadian Government, 91, 199, 201, 205, 218, 223, 227–8
Canadian House of Commons, 205–6, 221; Standing Committee on Access to Information, Privacy and Ethics, 152; Standing Committee on National Security, 148
Canadian Internet Registration Authority, 142, 220–1
Canadian National Energy Board (NEB), 74–5, 80–1, 205
Canadian Natural Resources, 85
Canadian Parliament, 139
Canadian Press, 196, 204, 212, 215–16, 218, 220, 230
Canadian Senate, 147, 197, 211, 229
Canadian Security Intelligence Service (CSIS), 50, 52, 61, 142, 147–8, 220
Canadian Supreme Court, 81, 139
Canadian Treasury Board, 154
Cannon, Lawrence, 100–1
Canoe Canada, 140
cap-and-trade schemes, 83, 91, 187
Capital One, 140
carbon-capture projects, 91, 208
carbon emissions, 55, 76, 83, 86, 89–92, 94, 187
carbon footprint, 92, 94–5, 209
carbon tax, 35, 41, 73, 76, 78, 83–8, 205–8
carbon-pricing regime, 78, 82
Caribbean, 177
Carleton University, 102, 140, 220
Carmichael, Kevin, 44–5, 198–9
Carney, Mark, 92, 209
Carr, Bob, 49–50
Carson, Bruce, x

CBC *News*, 77, 88, 134, 195, 203–8, 212, 214, 218–22, 230
C.D. Howe Institute, 28, 34, 36, 85, 95, 196–7
Central America, 112
Centre for International Governance Innovation (CIGI), 143, 202, 213–14, 217, 219, 221, 228–9; *Governance Innovation for a Connected World: Protecting Free Expression, Diversity and Civic Engagement in the Digital Ecosystem*, 153, 223. *See also* Digital Policy Incubator (Stanford University)
Cercone, Philip, x
CF-18 fighter jets, 114–15, 132
Chase, Steven, 216, 221
Cheadle, Bruce, 205
Chidley, Joe, 71, 203
Chile, 177
China, vii, ix, 4, 13–14, 19–20, 22, 30, 38, 41, 48–9, 51–2, 71–2, 84, 98, 105, 107, 109–10, 113–14, 126, 135, 139, 141, 144, 147–8, 151, 167, 172, 180–1, 183, 185, 190, 200, 202–3, 210, 221, 223; Belt and Road Initiative, 12, 15, 50, 94; Chinese Uyghur minority, 52–3, 61–2, 200–1; Communist Party, 50, 57, 61, 116; Energy and Environment Forum, 95; environmental footprint, 95–6 (*see also* Jiang, Wenran; King, Blair); Extradition Treaty, 64; free trade agreement, 53; global rise, 54–6; "Great Firewall of China," 55, 201; Huawei case, 64–7; McCallum,
John, 64, 202–3; relations with Australia, 49–52; relations with Canada, 57–69; relations with United States, 17–18, 56–7; Sinochem Group, 139; South and East China Sea, 66 (*see also* East China Sea; South China Sea); Wanzhou, Meng, 18–19, 64–6, 202–3
Choi, Wonsik, 199
Chozick, Amy, 192
Chrétien, Jean, 100, 123
Chrisafis, Angelique, 193
Chulov, Martin, 228
CIGI-Ipsos Global Survey (2018), 152, 223
Citigroup, 40, 93, 209
Clark, Christy, 79
Claws of the Panda, 59, 202
Clemens, Jason, 197, 224
Climate Action Tracker, 206
climate change, viii, x, 22, 35, 37, 55, 73, 76–9, 82–4, 86, 88–9, 92–7, 120, 173, 187–8, 204–10
Clinton, Hillary Rodham, 24, 31, 146, 150, 192
Clinton, William Jefferson, 100, 123
cloud whitening, 91
Clow, Brian, 25
coal-powered electricity, 27, 55–6, 76–7, 89–91, 93–6, 210–11
Coca-Cola, 150
Coderre, Denis, 78–9
Cold War, ix, 13, 57, 98–9, 106–9, 111, 113, 116, 154, 181, 202
Collinson, Stephen, 110, 213
Colombia, 167, 170, 177
Columbia Pipeline Group, 79

Communications Security Establishment (CSE), 144–5, 147–8, 222
Comprehensive and Progressive Agreement for Trans-Pacific Partnership (CPTPP), 39, 48, 67, 72, 183
Comprehensive Economic and Trade Agreement, 38
Conference Board of Canada, 161, 225
Confucius, 50, 57, 200
Confucius Institutes, 50, 200
Congo, Democratic Republic of, 169
"constructive engagement," 123–4, 126
Cooper, Andrew F., 215
Copenhagen Consensus Center, 91
Corcoran, Terence, 207
Corporate Knights, 93, 209
counterterrorism, 108, 122, 132
CountryEconomy.com, 227
Coyne, Andrew, 86, 163, 207, 225
CP-140 long-range patrol aircraft, 132
Crimea, 101–2, 108, 213
Crocker, Chester A., 217
Cross, Philip, 87, 196, 207
CTV News, 195, 206, 222
Culbert, Andrew, 208
currency manipulation, 54, 61
Curry, Bill, 223, 226
cyber attacks, 110, 137–45, 147, 158, 186, 219–20
cyber security, viii–ix, 22, 42, 66, 140, 142–5, 147, 154, 180, 182, 186–7, 190, 220–2
cyber space, viii, 17, 21, 67, 110, 150, 154, 184–7

CyberGreen, 143
Czechoslovakia, 159

Dalai Lama, 49
Daniel, Jean, 69
data footprints, 137
Day, Matthew, 214
DCLeaks.com, 146
De Loecker, Jan, 198
decarbonization efforts, 89–91
"deep fakes," 139
Dehaas, Josh, 206
Democracy Divided: Countering Democratic Institutions, viii, 110, 147–8, 153–4, 158, 223
Democratic National Convention (DNC), 146
Desjardins Group, 143, 221
Devon Energy Corp, 85
Diamond, Larry, 7, 192
Dib, Lina, 216
Digital Policy Incubator (Stanford University), 153
digital world, 147, 149, 151, 153
Dillon, John, 204
Dion, Stéphane, 101–4, 136, 212, 216
Diplomat Magazine, 102, 212, 216
Disinformation and Hate in the Digital Public Sphere, 156, 224
displacement, 169, 172, 176, 227
dispute resolution, 5, 12, 23, 26, 29
distributed denial-of-service attacks (DDOS), 138–9, 143
Domburs, Viktors, 215
Dominican Republic, 178
Donahoe, Eileen, 223
Dong, Falun, 49
Dosanjh, Ujjal, 69

"downstream," 168, 171–2
Doyle, Sarah, 198
Dyer, Evan, 212
Dynamic Integrated Model of Climate Change and the Economy, 84

e-commerce, ix, 46
East China Sea, 49, 51, 185
East Timor, 112
economic growth, 4, 12, 14–15, 34, 37, 42, 50, 59, 80, 86, 123, 159, 184–5, 202, 211
economic protectionism, 20
Economic Times of India, 70
Economist, The (magazine), 198, 201
Economy, Elizabeth C., 201
Ecuador, 177
Eeckhout, Jan, 198
Egypt, 99, 122, 124–5, 127, 129, 131
El-Assal, Kareem, 225
El Yaakoubi, Aziz, 218
Elcock, Ward, 63
Elderson, Frank, 92, 209
Ely, Bert, 213
Emes, Joel, 197
Enbridge Inc., 78–9, 207
Encana, 85
"end of history," 13, 193
Energy East, 78–9, 205
Energy Mix, The, 208
English, John, 211
environmental protection, v, 36–7, 73, 75, 77, 79, 81, 83, 85, 87, 89, 91, 93, 95, 97
Equifax, 140–1
Estonia, 114

Europe, vii, ix, 9–10, 15–16, 27, 63, 74, 87, 90, 93, 98–9, 101, 110, 129, 135, 147, 155, 159, 166, 181, 189, 209, 227
European Union (EU), vii, 8, 19, 26, 30, 38, 56, 72, 108, 159, 173, 195, 213; General Data Protection Regulation, 155, 224
Evans, Gareth, 119, 215
Evian Conference, 178

F-35 fighter jets, 115, 129, 185
Facebook, 55, 137, 148–50, 152, 220, 222–3
Fadden, Richard, 52, 63
failed state, 17
fake news, 8, 139, 147–9, 156–7
Farmer, Ben, 219
Fay, Bob, x, 41, 198
Fear: Trump in the White House, 3, 191
Fields, Daniel, 225
Financial Post, 35, 78, 82, 88, 164, 196–9, 203, 205–8, 210, 224, 226
Financial Times, 67, 104, 194, 203, 209
Fine, Sean, 226
Finland, 104, 213
First Ministers' Meetings, 41–2
Five Eyes, 52, 65
Fletcher, Tom, 133, 218
Flood, Chris, 209
Foehringer Merchant, Emma, 208
Ford, Doug, 83
Foreign Policy (magazine), 26, 57, 193, 202, 218
Forum on China-Africa Cooperation, 51

fossil fuels, 78, 90–1, 188, 210
Foy, Henry, 194
France, 65, 87, 92, 106, 112, 116, 141, 172, 208–10, 225
Francis, Diane, 164, 226
Franco, Francisco, 116
Fraser Institute, 36, 38, 41–2, 82, 207, 224; *Innovation in Canada (2019)*, 42, 197–8
Freedom House, 105, 212
Freeland, Chrystia, 20, 23, 25–6, 28, 101, 104, 113, 120, 133, 164, 212
French, Howard W., 201
Frey, Bruno S., 223
Frey, Warren, 221
Frohlich, Thomas C., 201
Fukushima, 94
Fukuyama, Francis, 7, 13, 192–3
Funk, Nathan C., 135, 219

G7/8, 19, 21, 26, 38, 98, 100–1, 105, 122, 154, 180, 193, 195, 212, 223; Global Partnership Program Against the Spread of Nuclear Weapons and Materials of Mass Destruction (G8 2002), 110
G20, 19, 28, 64, 84, 101, 103, 188
Gambia, 84
Gaudin, Sharon, 222
GDP, viii, 8, 13, 28, 35, 38, 40, 42, 49, 74, 85, 93–4, 106–7, 112–13, 115, 142, 169, 184
Geloso, Vincent, 197
General Agreement on Tariffs and Trade, 173
General Dynamics Land Systems–Canada, 121, 136
General Motors, 29, 46

Georgia, 108
Germany, ix, 11, 45, 57, 65, 90, 106, 112, 134, 141, 159, 175, 178; Bundestag, 224; NetzDG, 155
Ghana, 99
Ghoreishi, Omid, 200
Gigerenzer, Gerd, 223
"gilets jaunes" protests, 87–8
Gillis, Justin, 208
Giovanetti, Justin, 206
Giustra Foundation, 175. *See also* Global Refugee Sponsorship Initiative
Global Commission on the Economy and Climate, 92, 209
Global News, 79, 104, 136, 192, 195, 204–5, 210, 212, 218–20
Global Refugee Sponsorship Initiative, 175, 229
global refugee system, 171–2, 176, 228; camps, 169; global crisis, ix-x, 159, 164, 168, 171, 174, 189, 230; Global Refugee Sponsorship Initiative, 175, 229; internally displaced persons (IDPs), 169–70, 176–7; refugee-hosting state, 173–4, 177; Refugee Working Group, 124, 130 (*see also* Bell, Michael)
global supply chains, 14, 139, 142, 144
globalization, 9, 138, 178
Globe and Mail, 27, 113, 118, 121, 152, 163, 195, 197–200, 205–6, 208–9, 214–16, 219–23, 225–6
Globerman, Steven, 197
Goldberg, Jeffrey, 128, 218
Goldman Sachs, 54

Goldsmith-Jones, Pamela, 102
"good governance," 131
Google, 150
Gorbachev, Mikhail, 100–1
Graham, Bill, 153, 223
Gramer, Robbie, 218
Grand, Camille, 214
Gray, Earle, 74, 204
Great Recession, 13
Greece, 116, 159
Green, Kenneth B., 206
Green Revolution, 122
greenhouse gas (GHG) emissions, 77, 82, 84, 86, 89, 92, 95, 206, 210
Greenhouse Gas Pollution Pricing Act (Canada), 82, 206
Greenspon, Edward, 156, 224
Grenier, Éric, 207
Gromyko, Andrei, 99
Grønning, Ragnhild, 212
Guaranteed Income Supplement, 160–1
Guccifer 2.0, 146
Gulf Cooperation Council, 122, 126
Gulf of Oman, 16
Gulf War, 124, 132
Gurney, Matt, 192, 214

Hafen, Ernst, 223
Hafstead, Marc, 207
Hager, Mike, 205
Hagner, Michael, 223
Haiti, 188
Halifax Security Conference, 147
Hamad, Sam, 218
Hamid, Shadi, 127, 217
Hamilton, Clive, 49–55, 59–60, 200–2

Hampson, Fen Osler, ii–iii, 191, 194, 204, 210, 213–14, 216–17, 219, 223, 229
Hampson, Philip, x
Hannigan, Robert, 144
hard power, 131
Harper, Stephen, vii, 7, 19, 52, 70, 76, 123, 161, 191–2, 202, 211; policy stances toward China, Russia, Middle East, 58, 100–1, 121
Harris, Kathleen, 219
Hart, Michael, 202
Harvey, Fiona, 210
hate speech, 150, 155–6
Hathaway, Melissa, x, 137, 145, 219, 221
Healing, Dan, 220
Heinbecker, Paul, x, 211, 217, 219
Heintz, Jim, 221
Heisbourg, François, 193
Helbing, Dirk, 223
"helpful fixer," 118–19
Herman, Lawrence L., 173, 228
Hervouet, Gérard, 196
Herzog, Arthur, Jr, 192
Hezbollah, 170
Hickes, George, 87
Hickson, Kamila, 205
Hill, Tegan, 197
Hill, The, 106, 207, 213
Hindu, 69
Hiroshima, 111
Hitler, Adolf, 156, 178
Hofstetter, Yvonne, 223
Holiday, Billie, 192
honest broker, 118–19
Horgan, John, 79–81
Hou, Feng, 226

Houle, René, 226
Howard, John, 57
Huawei Technologies, 18, 144, 200
Huggler, Justin, 214
Hui, Zhang, 202
human equality, 8
human rights, viii-ix, 20, 77, 110, 120–2, 126, 132, 168–9, 171–2, 176, 189, 216, 219, 228; in China, 49, 60–2, 66–8; in Saudi Arabia, 132, 134–6, 163–4
humanitarian assistance, 21, 123, 172–3
Humphrey, John Peters, 67
Hundred-Year Marathon, The, 54, 201
Hungary, 8, 10, 116, 159
Hunter, Justine, 205
Huntington, Samuel P., 57, 105, 212

Ibbitson, John, 147, 163, 202, 222, 225
identity politics, 7–8
IHS Markit, 92
Ikenberry, G. John, 193–4, 211, 216
illegal immigration, 24, 164
immigrants, 39, 159–62, 224
India, vii, ix, 20–2, 41, 48, 62, 67–9, 84, 94–6, 181, 183, 190, 203–4, 219; relations with Canada, 69–72
Indigenous peoples of Canada, 73, 78–80, 97
Indo-Pacific region, vii, ix, 21. *See also* Australia; Bangladesh; Cambodia; East Timor; India; Indonesia; Japan; Laos; Malaysia; Myanmar; New Zealand; Philippines; Singapore; Taiwan; Vietnam
Indonesia, vii, 51, 64, 93, 183
Industrial Revolution, 41, 55
Inkeles, Alex, 211
Institute of Fiscal Studies and Democracy, 40
intellectual property (IP) rights, 15, 23–4, 26, 45–6, 50, 54, 61, 63, 137, 144, 199–200
Intergovernmental Panel on Climate Change, 84
interlocuteur valable, 32
Intermediate-Range Nuclear Forces Treaty, 110
International Criminal Court, 172
International Energy Agency, 91
International Grand Committee on Big Data, Privacy and Democracy, 157
International Institute of Strategic Studies, 214
international institutions, vii-ix, 5, 18–19, 94, 98, 126, 178, 189
International Monetary Fund (IMF), 40–2, 63, 198, 202, 212
International Organization for Migration (IOM), 176
International Support Group for Syria, 103
Internet, 10, 55, 137–8, 141–4, 150–4, 156–7, 177, 186, 201, 215, 220–3, 226
Internet service providers (ISPs), 143, 221
invented mercantilism, 54
Ipsos, 152, 161–2, 223, 225

Iran, 6, 14, 16–18, 54, 99, 108, 122–3, 128–9, 135, 181, 194, 216
Iraq, 10, 13, 16, 113, 127–8, 131–3, 218
Isaac, Mike, 222
Islam, 127; Sharia law, 132; Shia, 134–5; Sunni, 132, 135; "*Wali* and *Namus* practices," 132
Islamic State of Iraq and Syria (ISIS), 113, 127, 132, 218
Israel, 16, 45, 69, 129, 187, 216, 218; Canada's policy stance toward, 121–5, free trade agreement, 131
Israeli-Palestinian conflict, 130. *See also* Israel; Palestine
Italy, 106, 112, 116, 143, 159
ITF Technologies, 63
Ivison, John, 203

Jaccard, Mark, 89, 208
Jackson, Taylor, 87, 206–7
Jain, Ash, 214
Japan, 11, 15–16, 19, 39, 48, 51, 56, 62, 66–8, 72, 94–5, 141, 183, 186, 197, 210
Jardine, Eric, 219
Jaruzelski, Wojciech, 99
Jean, Michaëlle, 100
Jenkins, Willis, 204
Jiang, Wenran, 95
Jinping, Xi, 15, 51, 54, 57, 60, 200–1
Joint Comprehensive Plan of Action (JCPOA), 128
Jones, Bruce, 213
Jones, Sarah, 194
Jong-un, Kim, 3, 16, 26

Jordan, 122–5, 127, 173–4
Jowit, Juliette, 208

Kagan, Robert, 3, 191, 194
Kamal, Baher, 227
Kaplan, Robert, 57, 202
Kashmir, 71, 203–4
Katem, Eman, 225
Keating, Paul, 49
Keller, James, 205–6
Kelly, Dan, 224
Kendall, Brent, 222
Kennan, George, 13
Kennedy, John F., 13, 118
Kenney, Jason, 73, 83
Kequiang, Li, 59
Kerry, John, 17, 194
Keystone Pipeline, 76
Khalistan, 70
Khan, Imran, 135
Khanna, Parag, 72, 199
Khashoggi, Jamal, 17, 93, 120, 135
Kinder Morgan, 79–80, 205
Kindra, Gurprit S., 203
King, Blair, 95
Kinsella, Noel, 99, 211
Kirton, John J., 212
Kochhar, Rakesh, 192
Kokotsis, Ella, 212
Korea (North), 3–4, 6, 16, 54, 94, 141, 181
Korea (South), 3–4, 6, 15–16, 19, 21, 38, 45, 48, 51, 54, 56, 61–2, 66, 72, 94, 141, 143, 181, 186; free trade agreement with Canada, 38, 48
Kosoff, Maya, 222

Kosovo, 116
Krebs, Chris, 144. See also United States of America: Department of Homeland Security
Krepon, Michael, 111, 214
Kristof, Nicholas, 164, 226
Kuan Yew, Lee, 55–6, 220
Kuibyshev (Samara), 99
Kurdi, Alan, 171, 228
Kurdish Peshmerga, 132
Kymlicka, Will, 192
Kyoto Accord, 88

labour-force participation rate, 160
Lafromboise, Kalina, 205
Lagassé, Philippe, 215
Lammam, Charles, 87, 207
landlord nation, 46, 190
Laos, 102
Latin America, 4, 94, 177
Latvia, 114, 148, 152
Lavrov, Sergey, 101–2
"law of the jungle," 15, 18, 30
Lawrence, Jennifer, 149
Lebanon, 123, 170, 228
Lee, Timothy B., 220
Lenin, Vladimir, 51–2
Leningrad, 99
Les Perreaux, 216
Leslie, Andrew, 134
Lewis, David, 75
Lewis, Jeff, 205
Lhamo, Chemi, 52
liberal internationalism, viii, 11–12, 18, 124, 126, 181, 193, 211, 216
Libya, 13, 108, 116, 126–7, 129, 171, 217

light armoured vehicles (LAVs), 136. See also Saudi Arabia: Canada–Saudi Arabia arms deal
Lightizer, Robert, 4, 24
Lima Group, 176
Litan, Robert E., 214
Lithuania, 114
Livingston International, 195
Ljunggren, David, 133, 200, 203, 206, 218
Loblaws, 140
Lockheed Martin F-35, 115
Lockie, Alex, 203
Loescher, Gil, 227
Lomborg, Bjørn, 91, 208
Lorinc, John, 198
Lotte Corporation, 61
Lou, Ethan, 220
Lynch, Colum, 193

Ma, Alexandra, 223
MacDonald, Michael, 222
Mace, Gordon, 196
MacEwan University, 140
MacFarquhar, Neil, 213
Mackenzie Valley Pipeline, 74–5, 204; Berger Commission, 75, 204
Maclean's, 195–6, 198
MacNab, Josha, 210
Macron, Emmanuel, 11–12
Madrid Conference, 124, 130
Maduro Moros, Nicolás, 176
Magnitsky, Sergei, 104, 228
Magnitsky Act, 120, 148, 172, 228
"Make America Great Again," 9. See also "America First"
Makocki, Michal, 214

Malaysia, 19, 48, 72, 183
Malcolm, Candice, 70, 203
malware, 138, 140, 144, 220
Manitoba, 39, 78, 83, 197
Manthorpe, Jonathan, 59, 61, 202
Marcoux, Jacques, 219
market liberalization, 71
Marks, Joseph, 221
Markusoff, Jason, 196
Martin, Paul, 123
Martin, Susan, 178, 230
Marx, Karl, 106
May, Elizabeth, 80
McCain, John, 106
McCarten, James, 195
McCarthy, Shawn, 205
McFaul, Michael, 109–10, 213–14
McGugan, Ian, 198
McKay, David, 85
McKenna, Barrie, 195
McKenna, Catherine, 77
McKernan, Beth, 228
McKinsey & Company, 221
McLaverty, Peter, 217
McLeod, James, 199, 220
McParland, Kelly, 181, 230
McSheffrey, Elizabeth, 209
Mead, Walter Russell, 14, 194
Melle, John, 25
Merkel, Angela, 11, 111
Mexico, 5, 24–9, 34, 38, 58, 141, 160, 182, 186, 191–2, 194–6, 204. *See also* United States–Mexico–Canada Agreement (USMCA)
Microsoft, 45, 141
"Middle America," 7, 9, 11
Middle East Monitor, 121, 216

middle power, 21, 119, 181, 194
military capabilities, 13, 107–8, 114, 127
Military Council of National Salvation, 99
Mills, Mark P., 90–1, 208–9
Milner, James, 227
Minsky, Amy, 212, 219
Mintz, Jack, 35, 96, 196, 208
Minx, Jan Christoph, 91, 208
Mishal, Khalid, 125
Mishra, Ramesh, 211
Modi, Narendra, 69–73, 135–6, 203–4
Molloy, Michael, 125, 217
Molotov, Vyacheslav, 99
Momani, Bessma, 217, 219
Mondal, Kamaran M.K., 218
Montgomery, Marc, 216
Montpetit, Jonathan, 221
Morgan, Geoffrey, 208
Morgan, Gwyn, 94, 210
Morgan Stanley, 54
Morneau, Bill, 80
Morocco, 84, 127
Morrow, Adrian, 195, 225
Mueller, Robert, 10, 105, 147
Muller, David, 207
Mulroney, Brian, ii–iii, 19–20, 31–2, 76–7, 100–1, 112–13, 194–7, 210–11, 214–15
multiculturalism, 8, 189
Murmansk, 99
Murphy, Robert P., 206
Murray, Nick, 207
Muslim Brotherhood, 122, 127
Muslim travel ban, 128, 164

Myanmar, 171, 176
Myong-Hyun, Go, 214

Nagasaki, 111
Namibia, 112
Nanchang, 151
Nanos, 152
National Center for Health Statistics, 192
National Energy Program (NEP), 76, 82
national identity, 8–9, 99
National Post, 114–15, 163, 181, 192, 196–8, 200, 206–7, 210–12, 214–16, 219–20, 225, 230
National Public Radio, 150
natural gas, 37, 63, 74–6, 78–9, 89–90, 94–5, 107, 129, 210
natural resources, 42–3, 45, 62, 85
Navarro, Peter, 4
Navius Research, 88–9
Nemet, Gregory, 91, 208
Netanyahu, Benjamin, 128
Netflix, 150
Netherlands, 112, 141
Network for Greening the Financial Services, 92, 209
New York Times, viii, 90, 96, 150, 164, 192, 202, 208, 213–14, 222, 226
New Zealand, 50–2, 175, 186
Nicholson, Peter, 43–4, 198–9, 224–5
Nickel, Rod, 203
Nigeria, 130, 188
Nixey, James, 214
Noble, John, 216
Nolen, Stephanie, 195
Noll, Roger, 214

nongovernmental organizations, 163
Nordhaus, William, 84, 206
Norilsk, 99
Norman, Mark, 59–60, 99, 115–16, 212–13, 215–16
Normille, Dennis, 210
Norsat, 63
North American Aerospace Defense Command (NORAD), 115, 119, 185–6
North American Free Trade Agreement (NAFTA), vii, 5, 19, 23–5, 29–31, 35, 191–2, 195–6
North American Treaty Alliance (NATO), v–vi, viii–ix, 10, 12, 18, 21–2, 26, 30, 98–9, 109–17, 119, 126, 129, 132, 156, 182, 184–6, 189–90, 214–15, 217; Founding Act on Mutual Relations, Cooperation and Security between NATO and Russia, 108; NATO Battle Group, 148; NATO-Russia Council, 103; "NATO-Russia Relations: A New Quality," 108, 213
North Carolina, 89–90, 95, 208
Northern Gateway Pipeline, 78–9, 205
Notley, Rachel, 76, 79, 83, 204, 206
Nunavut, 87, 207
Nuremberg, 178
Nye, Joseph S., Jr, 216–17

Obama, Barack, 7, 58, 76, 127, 137, 164
O'Blenis, Cara, x
October Crisis, 100
Ogata, Sadako, 178, 230

oil and natural gas, 37, 76, 107
Old Age Security, 160–1
Oman, 16
Omidvar, Ratna, 176, 229
Ontario, 29, 74, 78, 83, 89, 122, 136, 176
OPEC, 130
Open Society Foundations, 175. *See also* Global Refugee Sponsorship Initiative
Operation Desert Storm, 132
Operation Impact, 132
Oppenheimer, J. Robert, 111, 214
Orenstein, Marla, 206
Organisation for Economic Co-operation and Development (OECD), 39, 45, 47, 161
Organization for Security and Co-operation in Europe (OSCE), 98, 103; Conference on Security and Cooperation in Europe, 98
Organization of Islamic Cooperation, 126
Ortiz-Ospina, Esteban, 193
Orwell, George, 151
Osborne, James, 218
Ottawa Civic Hospital, 140
Ottawa Police, 139, 220
Owen, Taylor, 156, 224

Page, Kevin, 40, 198
Pakistan, 54, 71, 134–5, 167, 203–4
Palacios, Milagros, 197
Palamar, Simon, 214
Palestine, 121–5, 128–9, 131–2
Pallister, Brian, 39–40, 83–4, 197–8
Pan-Canadian Framework on Climate Change, 78; *Technical Paper on the Federal Carbon Pricing Backstop*, 78, 205
Paris, Roland, 102, 194, 211, 215
Paris Accord, 35, 73, 77, 84, 88, 91, 94–6, 187–8
Parsons, Talcott, 211
Party Congress, 178
Parvani, Sasha, 224
Pau, Katie, 218
PayPal, 140
peacekeeping missions, 112–13, 119–20, 172–3
Pearson, Lester B., 99, 118, 130, 211
Pembina Institute, 95, 210
Perfect Weapon, The, viii, 191
Perkins, Anne, 193
Perle, Richard, 194
Persian Gulf, 116, 129
Peru, 177
Peterson Institute for International Economics, 35, 197
Pew Foundation, 112, 192, 212, 214; Global Attitudes Project (2017), 104
Philippines, vii, 8, 51, 66, 94
phishing email, 143
Picot, Garnett, 226
Pillalamarri, Akhilesh, 194
Pillsbury, Michael, 54–7, 201–2
Plamondon, Bob, 211
Podesta, John, 146
Poland, 8, 10, 96, 99, 111–12, 116, 159, 167, 210
polarization, 4
populism, v, vii–viii, x, 3, 5, 7–11, 13, 15, 17–21, 68, 168, 195, 225; left-wing, 7; right-wing, ix
Portugal, 116

Potash Corporation, 139
power vacuum, 130
Precision Drilling Corporation, 85
Prime Minister's Office, 25, 65, 102–3
privacy breaches, 140
progressive trade, 59, 61
protectionism, v, 3, 5, 7, 9, 11, 13, 15, 17–21, 26, 186, 195
prudent internationalism, 17, 20
Public Policy Forum, 46, 62, 156, 199, 202, 224, 230
Putin, Vladimir, ix–x, 3–4, 16–17, 100–12, 129–30, 146–8, 194–5, 212–14

Qatar, 129
Quan, Douglas, 225
Quebec, 26, 63, 78, 82–3, 91, 143, 154, 161, 165, 180, 205
"quiet diplomacy," 134
Quora, 213

Rabson, Mia, 205
Ragozin, Leonid, 213
RAND Corporation, 114
ransomware, 140–1, 220
Rapid7, 141; National Exposure Index, 141
Rapid Response Mechanism, 154, 223
Rasmi, Adam, 227
Reagan, Ronald, 31, 39, 118, 197
Reed, Walter, 128
Refugee Board of Canada, 167
Refugee Sponsorship Training Program, 229
Regional Economic Partnership, 67

Reinhardt, Forest, 204
renewable energy/resource generation, 89–90, 93–6
research and development, 43, 45–7, 70, 91, 199
Research in Motion, 45
"responsible stakeholder," 15, 60
Reuters, 133, 200, 206, 213, 218–19, 222
Revel, Jean-Francois, 215
Revenue Canada, 140, 145
Rhodes, Ben, 135
Ries, Brian, 191, 194
Rio Tinto, 91–2, 208
Robb, Andrew, 49
Roberts, Pat, 30
Robertson, Norman A., 99
Robson, John, 115, 215
Rock, Allan, x, 148, 152, 222–3
Rogers, Michael, 139
rogue states, 18
Rohingya, 171, 176
Romania, 106, 116
Ronald Reagan Presidential Foundation and Institute, 197
Rongji, Zhu, 68
Roosevelt, Franklin, 178
Rosenbaum, Eric, 200
Roser, Max, 193
Ross, Wilbur, 4
Rostow, Walt, 211
Royal Bank of Canada (RBC), 85
Royal Canadian Air Force, 218
Royal Canadian Mounted Police (RCMP), 144–5, 165; National Cybercrime Coordination Unit, 144
Rozental, Andres, 27, 195

rule of law, 8, 10, 61, 105, 124, 126, 131–2, 172, 176, 183, 189, 228
Runnalls, David, x
Rush, Nayla, 226
Russian Federation, v, 3–4, 10, 12–14, 16, 18, 20, 22, 98, 117, 126, 135, 143–4, 172, 181, 185, 211–15, 218, 221 (*see also* North American Treaty Alliance (NATO): Founding Act on Mutual Relations, Cooperation and Security between NATO and Russia); actions in the Middle East, 129; electoral interference and cyber threat, 146–8; Embassy of the Russian Federation in Canada, 212; Helsinki Summit, 110; Intergovernmental Economic Commission, 101; relations with Canada, 99–104, 111–16; relations with the United States, 105–6; Russian Television (RT), 148; strategies for a West-Russia relationship, 110–11
Ryan, Paul, 26

S-400 surface-to-air missiles, 129
Sabbagh, Dan, 194
Sajjan, Harjit, 113, 147
Samuel, Sigal, 216
Sanders, Bernie, 24
Sanger, David E., viii, 191, 213
Sarai, Randeep, 69
Sarbanes-Oxley, 158
Saskatchewan, 76, 78, 82–3
Saudi Arabia, viii, 16–17, 20, 64, 93, 122–3, 130, 132–4, 136, 218–19; Canada–Saudi Arabia arms deal, 120–1, 135, 216; relations with United States, 128–9; Saudi Aramco, 93
Sawyer, Dave, 86, 207
Sayoc, Cesar, 150
Scheer, Andrew, 58, 69, 165, 177
Scientific American, 151, 223
Seligman, Lara, 218
Semeniuk, Ivan, 199
Seong, Jeongmin, 199
Serbia, 116
Shaker, Sallama, 217
Shekhawat, Gajendra Singh, 69
Shell, 88, 92, 209
Shihabi, Ali, 216
Shoppers Drug Mart, 140
Shukla, Ajai, 203
Siberia, 74
Sikh, 69–70, 203
Silent Invasion, 49, 200–1
Simpson, Erika, 211
Simpson, Jeffrey, 219
Singapore, 26, 51, 72, 186
Singh, Inayat, 208
Sink, Justin, 191
Slaughter, Anne-Marie, 194
Sly, Liz, 218
small and medium-sized enterprises (SMEs), 43–4, 142
Smith, Craig Damian, 165
Smith, Marie-Danielle, 212, 230
Smith, Stephen, 225
Smith, David E., 211
smog levels, 86
Snowden, Edward, 138
Snyder, Jesse, 198
social media, 8, 10, 23, 52, 133, 148–9, 152, 154–7
soft power, 127–8, 130–1, 182

solar energy, 89–92, 94–6
Solomon, Howard, 220
Solomon, Lawrence, 210
Somalia, 112, 167, 169
Sorokin, Pitirim A., 211
South Africa, 64, 94
South China Sea, 56
South Sudan, 169–71, 227
Soviet Union, 13, 16, 54, 60, 98–100, 119, 124, 211; *glasnost* and *perestroika*, 100; Treaty on Concord and Cooperation, 100
Sow, Mariama, 200
Spain, 112, 116, 175
Spectra Energy Corp, 78
Speer, Sean, 46, 199, 230
Sprague, Grant, 196
Stalin, Joseph, 154
Starr, Katharine, 195
Statistics Canada, 167, 226
Stavridis, James, 113–14, 214–15
Stedman, Ashley, 206
Steinmeier, Frank-Walter, 111
Stephens, Bret, 90–1, 96–7, 208–11
Stiebert, Seton, 86, 207
Studin, Irvin, 225
Subramian, Arvind, 203
Suez Canal, 129–30
Suez Crisis, 118, 130
Sultan, David, 217
Sweden, ix, 134, 171
Sweet, Eva, 224
Switzerland, 36, 39, 45, 176, 192, 215, 229; Federal Department of Foreign Affairs, 229; Foreign Illicit Assets Act, 176

Syria, ix, 16, 102–3, 108, 113, 122–3, 126–9, 131, 159, 171–2, 188, 217, 228

Taddese, Yamri, 219
Taiwan, 49, 52, 95, 143
Tangri, Aakanksha, 203
Target stores, 142
tariffs on softwood lumber, 29, 41
tariffs on steel and aluminum, 32, 41
Task Force on Climate-Related Financial Disclosures, 93
Tasker, John Paul, 206
Tauberer, Joshua, 224
Telford, Katie, 25
Telus, 65
"tenant nation," 46, 190
Tencer, Daniel, 224
"Third Option," 32, 196
Thompson, Andrew, x
Thompson, Elizabeth, 203
Thompson, Jack, 128, 218
Thompson, Jennifer, 209
Tiananmen Square, 54
Tibet, 49, 52, 61, 200
Tocci, Nathalie, 214
Tonby, Oliver, 199
Toronto Star, 103, 196, 204, 212, 215, 230
trade diversification, 41, 86, 188
trade liberalization, 4, 71
TransAtlantic Commission on Electoral Integrity, 148
TransCanada Pipelines, 74, 78–9
Trans-Mountain Pipeline, 73, 79–81, 83, 187, 205

Trans-Pacific Partnership (TPP), 5, 19, 39, 48, 72, 183
Treaty on the Non-Proliferation of Nuclear Weapons, 103
Troitskiy, Mikhail, 108, 213
Trudeau, Justin, x, 11, 34, 52, 73, 76–7, 101, 103, 111, 118, 120–1, 143, 159, 162, 195, 203, 205, 212, 215, 225, 230
Trudeau, Pierre Elliott, 32, 75, 99
Trump, Donald, viii–x, 3–20, 23–37, 41–2, 50–2, 60–1, 64–5, 76–7, 84–5, 104–14, 119–20, 123–4, 127–9, 132–4, 147–8, 161–2, 164–5, 180–5, 191–7, 210–11, 213–15, 218–19; Trumpism, vii, 30
TSX SmallCap, 44
TSX Venture Composite, 44
Turkey, 8, 103, 106, 112, 116, 120, 129, 159, 181, 218
Twitter/tweets, 4, 20, 23, 28, 31, 104, 120, 133–4, 137, 148, 150, 180, 222
Twitter diplomacy, 133

Uber, 137, 140–1
Uganda, 169–70, 227
Ukraine, ix, 101–3, 105, 108, 114, 132, 139, 218
United Arab Emirates, 69, 122, 127
United Kingdom, viii, 52, 57, 59, 65–6, 112, 129, 134, 141, 144, 172, 175, 194, 208–9, 211, 228; Boris Johnson and Theresa May, 11; Brexit, vii, 8, 11, 162
United Nations (UN), viii, 3, 12, 15, 26–7, 56, 67, 77, 84, 98, 102–3, 118, 168, 173, 178, 189, 193, 204, 206, 216, 218; Charter, 126; Climate Change Conference (2018), 96; Comprehensive Refugee Response Framework (2016), 177, 230; Economic and Social Council, 21; General Assembly, 27, 121, 123, 134; Global Compact for Safe, Orderly and Regular Migration (2018), 177, 230; Global Compact on Refugees (2018), 177, 229; High Commissioner for Refugees (UNHCR), 170–2, 176, 226–8; Law of the Sea, 56 (*see also* South China Sea); Refugee Agency, 175 (*see also* Global Refugee Sponsorship Initiative); Refugee Convention (1951), 170–2; Security Council, 19, 108, 126; World Food Programme, 177
United States of America, vii–x, 5–9, 11–12, 14, 16–18, 20, 22, 25, 32, 34, 36–9, 41, 49–53, 55–9, 61–3, 65–7, 69, 76, 79, 81, 84–9, 91, 95–6, 99, 106–7, 109–10, 112–13, 124, 127, 130–2, 141, 143, 159–60, 162, 164, 172, 181–90, 195–6, 211, 228; Comprehensive National Cybersecurity Initiative, 137; Congress, 15, 23–4, 26–8, 30–1, 111, 147, 149–50, 178; Cyberspace Policy Review, 137 (*see also* Hathaway, Melissa); Department of Homeland Security, 144, 146, 221; Department of Justice, 150, 193, 213, 222; Energy

Information Administration (EIA), 129; Federal Bureau of Investigation (FBI), 146–7; Intelligence Community (USIC), 146; National Security Agency, 138–9; National Security Strategy (2017), 13; Office of National Intelligence on Election Issues, 146; Tax Cuts and Job Act, 35; Standing Senate Committee on Banking, Trade and Commerce, 197; White House, 3–4, 24–7, 33, 51, 119, 135, 191, 197
United States–Mexico–Canada Agreement (USMCA), 5, 29, 34, 58, 62, 67, 182, 195–6
University of Calgary, 140, 202
University of Ottawa, 102, 175
"upstream," 168, 171, 175
U.S. History, 215
"useful idiots," 154

"values-based framework," 119
van den Hoven, Jeroen, 223
Van Wielingen, Mac, 92, 209
VanderKlippe, Nathan, 200
Vanity Fair, 149, 222
Venezuela, 170–1, 176, 229
Verheul, Steve, 25
Vice, Margaret, 212
Vietnam, vii, 17, 19, 48, 93, 183, 227
Villarreal, Ildefonso Guajardo, 25
Villeroy de Galhau, François, 92, 209
virtue signalling, 20, 68
Vomiero, Jessica, 192

Wagner, Meg, 191, 194
Waitzer, Edward, 93, 209

Walker, Connie, 208
Wall, Brad, 82, 206
Wall Street, 7, 194, 222
Wang, Patti, 199
WannaCry, 141, 220
Washington Post, 129, 208, 218, 221–2
Wasserman Schultz, Debbie, 146
Watson, William, 43, 88, 207
Watts, Jonathan, 210
Weather Channel, 137
#WelcomeToCanada, 164
Wells, Orson, 156
Welsh, Jennifer, 215
Westdal, Christopher, 103, 212
WestJet, 140
WhatsApp, 137
Wherry, Aaron, 204
Wike, Richard, 214
WikiLeaks, 146
Wilgress, Dana, 99
Wilkie, Christina, 192
Williams, Paul D., 217
Willis, Andrew, 197
Wilson, Damon, 214
wind energy, 89–91, 95
Wingrove, Josh, 191
Wintour, Patrick, 217
Woetzel, Jonathan, 199
Wolf, Martin, 46, 67–9, 71–2, 203–5
Woodward, Bob, 3, 191
World Bank, 15, 54, 58, 71, 94, 173, 192–3
World Economic Forum, 39, 94; Global Competitiveness Index, 37; *Global Competitiveness Report (2017–18)*, 36
World Maritime News, 220

World Population Review, 224
World Refugee Council, 172–3, 176, 178, 228–30
World Trade Organization (WTO), viii, 12, 18, 21, 30, 54, 56, 60, 62, 98, 173, 181, 189–90, 192, 195, 228
Worldometers, 228
Wornow, Michael, 199
Wright, Teresa, 214, 226
Wright, Thomas J., 211
Wylie, Christopher, 149

xenophobia, ix, 20

Yakabuski, Konrad, 216
"yellow vest" protests, 87–8
Yeltsin, Boris, 100
Yemen, 127–8, 131, 135
YourNewsWire, 150
Yugoslavia, 167; Yugoslav Wars, 116

Zadek, Simon, 210
Zakaria, Fareed, 201
Zedong, Mao, 15, 54, 60
Zhang, Yan, 226
Zicari, Roberto V., 223
Zilio, Michelle, 225
Zimonjic, Peter, 230
Zochodne, Geoff, 207
Zubkov, Victor, 100
Zuckerberg, Mark, 149, 222
Zwitter, Andrej, 223